PENGUIN  CLASSICS

SELECTED LETTERS

MARCUS TULLIUS CICERO (106–43 B.C.), Roman orator and states-man, was born at Arpinum of a wealthy local family. He was taken to Rome for his education with the idea of a public career, and by 70 B.C. he had established himself as the leading barrister in Rome. In the meantime his political career was well under way and he was elected praetor for the year 66. His ambitious nature enabled him to obtain those honours which would normally only have been con-ferred upon members of the Roman artistocracy, and he was duly elected consul for 63. One of the most permanent features of his political life was his attachment to Pompey. As a politician his notable quality was his consistent refusal to compromise; as a states-man his ideals were more honourable and unselfish than those of his contemporaries. Cicero was the greatest of the Roman orators, pos-sessing a wide range of technique and an exceptional command of the Latin tongue. He followed the common practice of publishing his speeches, but he also produced a large number of works on the theory and practice of rhetoric, on religion, and on moral and political philosophy. He played a leading part in the development of the Latin hexameter. Perhaps the most interesting of all his works is the collection of 900 letters published posthumously. These not only contain a first-hand account of social and political life in the upper classes at Rome, but also reflect the changing personal feelings of an emotional and sensitive man.

D. R. SHACKLETON BAILEY was born in 1917 and educated at Lancaster Royal Grammar School and at Gonville and Caius College, Cambridge, where he was a Fellow from 1944 to 1955 and again, as Deputy and Senior Bursar, from 1964 to 1968. From 1948 to 1968 he was University Lecturer in Tibetan and from 1955 to 1964 Fellow and Director of Studies in Classics at Jesus College, Cambridge. From 1968 to 1974 he was Professor of Latin at the University of Michigan and from 1975 to 1982 Professor of Greek and Latin at Harvard University. From 1982 to 1988 he was Pope Professor of the Latin Language and Literature at Harvard. Since 1989 he has been

Emeritus Professor at the University of Michigan. He is a Doctor of Letters (Cambridge, 1957), a Fellow of the British Academy (1958), and a member of the American Philosophical Society (1977). Among his classical publications are *Propertiana* (1956), *Towards a Text of Cicero ad Atticum* (1960), *Cicerónis Epistulae II.ii* (1961), *Cicero's Letters to Atticus* (1965–1970), *Cicero* (1971), *Two Studies in Roman Nomenclature* (1976), *Cicero: Epistulae ad Familiares* (1977), *Cicero: Epistulae ad Q. Fratrem et M. Brutum* (1981), *Profile of Horace* (1982), *Anthologia Latina II* (1982), *Horatius* (1985), *Quintilianus: Declamationes minores* (1989), *Martialis* (1990) and *Back from Exile* (1991).

CICERO
SELECTED LETTERS

Translated with an Introduction by
D. R. Shackleton Bailey

Penguin Books

PENGUIN BOOKS

Published by the Penguin Group
Penguin Books Ltd, 27 Wrights Lane, London W8 5TZ, England
Penguin Books USA Inc., 375 Hudson Street, New York, New York 10014, USA
Penguin Books Australia Ltd, Ringwood, Victoria, Australia
Penguin Books Canada Ltd, 10 Alcorn Avenue, Toronto, Ontario, Canada M4V 3B2
Penguin Books (NZ) Ltd, 182–190 Wairau Road, Auckland 10, New Zealand

Penguin Books Ltd, Registered Offices: Harmondsworth, Middlesex, England

First published 1986
5 7 9 10 8 6

Printed in England by Clays Ltd, St Ives plc
Set in Monophoto Photina

CONTENTS

PREFACE

THIS volume reproduces, with some appropriate modifications, parts of the complete translation of Cicero's correspondence published in the same series in 1978 and now out of print. I have chosen the letters mainly for their intrinsic interest or the glimpses they give of Cicero's personality. Some of them are important historically, but I have not tried to present a conspectus of historical source-material. The translations follow the text of my Cambridge edition (see Bibliographical Note).

August, 1982

INTRODUCTION

CICERO's letters only come fully to life against a historical and biographical background, though a bare outline is all that can be attempted here.

Marcus Tullius Cicero was born on 3 January 106 B.C.[1] at his family home near the hill town of Arpinum (still Arpino) about seventy miles to the east of Rome. For nearly a century the Arpinates had been citizens of Rome, a status attained by most of Italy south of the Po only after the bloody 'Social War' of 90–88. The family was old and well-to-do, and like many locally prominent Italian families, had good Roman connections; but from the standpoint of a Roman aristocrat he was a nobody, a 'new man', a fact of lasting practical and psychological importance.

About ten years after Cicero's birth his father took up residence in a fashionable part of Rome. Cicero and his younger brother received the best education money could buy and he is said to have easily outshone his socially superior classmates. On coming of age at sixteen or seventeen he served for a short time in the Roman army against the insurgent Italian allies. He lived in stormy times. Roman political institutions were turning out to be inadequate for the government of an already large empire. The authority of the Senate, the only permanent governing body, had been seriously shaken in the last three decades of the second century. The career of the great general Marius, also a native of Arpinum and a family connection of the Ciceros, had pointed the way to future army commanders who were to build positions of personal power on the loyalty of their troops.

The 'Social War' was followed by the terrible internal struggles of the eighties. In 88 the Consul Sulla, a brilliant general from an impoverished noble family who combined conservative sympathies with a contempt for constitutional forms, set a fateful precedent by marching his army on the capital in rebuttal of a personal injustice. His chief opponents were killed or, like Marius, escaped into exile. But Sulla had business elsewhere. Later in the year he left for the East to deal with a foreign enemy, the redoubtable

---

1. Henceforward all dates are to be understood as B.C. unless otherwise specified.

Mithridates of Pontus. Turmoil ensued. Rome stood a siege before being captured again by the forces of the anti-Sullan Consul Cinna and old Marius, emerging from banishment like an avenging ghost. The resulting massacre was the bloodiest of its kind so far known in Roman history. Marius died a few months later, but Rome and Italy remained under the control of Cinna and his associates for the next four years.

In 83 Sulla brought his victorious legions home. Fighting followed up and down the peninsula, and Rome had another Marian blood-bath before Sulla came out master of the situation. His ruthless reprisals left a grim memory, but to people of traditional outlook he was the restorer of the Republic. As Dictator he produced a new constitution guaranteeing control of affairs to an enlarged Senate, and, this task completed, he retired voluntarily into private life (79). His work was not wholly undone for thirty years.

Despite close Marian connections Cicero seems to have disliked and despised Cinna's régime and only began his public career, as an advocate, after Sulla's victory. He scored a sensational triumph with his defence of a certain Roscius, the victim of persecution by an influential freedman of the Dictator's, and his services in court became much in demand. But in 79 his voice was suffering from overstrain and for this and perhaps other reasons he left Rome for three years of travel in Greece and Asia Minor. After a fresh start in 76 his star rose rapidly and steadily. The next twelve years brought him the two great objects of his ambition, primacy at the Roman bar and a political career culminating in the Consulship. Without one setback he climbed the official ladder, elected Quaestor, Plebeian Aedile, and Praetor by handsome majorities and at the earliest age allowed by law. The Consulship at this period was almost a preserve of the nobility, consisting of descendants of previous Consuls, though now and again a man of praetorian family was let in. For more than a generation before Cicero's candidature in 64 'new men' had been excluded. Nevertheless he easily topped the poll.

His year of office would not have been particularly memorable but for a timely attempt at a *coup d'état* by his unsuccessful fellow-candidate Catiline, a patrician champion of the bankrupt and the disinherited. The plot was discovered and suppressed by Cicero. Catiline had left Rome to join his armed followers, and had to be defeated and killed next year, but five of his chief associates were arrested and brought before the Senate. After a memorable debate they were executed under Cicero's supervision. In and out of the Senate he was hailed as the saviour of Rome, but the legality of the action was disputed, and it brought him lasting un-popularity with the have-nots.

Cicero's prestige had reached a peak (from which it gradually declined), but the principal figure of the Roman world was not in Rome. Gnaeus Pompeius Magnus (Pompey the Great) rose early to fame by his brilliant military exploits against the adversaries of Sulla. His reputation was consolidated by years of finally successful warfare against the Marian leader Sertorius in Spain and the suppression of Spartacus' slave revolt in Italy. In 70 he became Consul in defiance of legal qualifications as to age and previous offices. Three years later, against the opposition of the senatorial leaders, he received an extraordinary commission to clear the Mediterranean of piracy. Prompt and complete success was followed by something even bigger – an overall command in the East, where Mithridates and his ally the King of Armenia were still defying the empire. Pompey's campaigns established Roman control over a vast area of western Asia, which he reorganized as he saw fit. In 62 he returned to Italy and, to the relief of the home authorities, at once disbanded his army.

Pompey had two demands, both reasonable: ratification of his arrange-ments in the East and land for his veteran soldiers. But the senatorial conservatives, now tending to revolve around a strong-minded young nobleman called M. Porcius Cato, distrusted his intentions and resented a career so conspicuously out of conformity with oligarchical norms. Several, in particular his predecessor in the eastern command, L. Lucullus and a Metellus (Creticus) who had fallen foul of him in Crete, nursed bitter personal grudges. Their unwisely stubborn obstructiveness resulted in a coalition between Pompey and two prominent politicians, both out of sympathy with the post-Sullan establishment: C. Julius Caesar and M. Licinius Crassus. The former, son of a Marian Praetor and former son-in-law of Cinna, was a favourite with the city populace, none the less so because he came of one of Rome's most ancient families; the latter, also a nobleman and Pompey's colleague in 70, was, next to Pompey himself, the richest man in Rome. This alliance, often called the First Triumvirate though it had no official status, dominated the scene for years to come. Cicero could have made a fourth, but although much dissatisfied with the 'optimates', who were apt to remember his origins rather than the public services of which he so often reminded them, his principles would not let him take part in a conspiracy against the constitution.

In 59 Caesar became Consul. Almost literally over the dead body of his 'optimate' colleague Bibulus, in defiance of senatorial opposition and constitutional procedures, he pushed through a legislative programme which satisfied his two associates and gave himself a five-year command in northern Italy and Gaul. In the event it lasted until 49 and enabled him to annex modern France (apart from the old Roman province in the south) and Belgium to the Roman empire. There were even expeditions across the Rhine and the English Channel. Before leaving Rome he had arranged for the elimination of Cicero, who had rejected several tempting overtures. Early in 58 the patrician demagogue and Tribune P. Clodius Pulcher, following a personal vendetta, was allowed to drive him into exile with the passive connivance of Pompey, despite earlier professions of friendship and support. Distraught and desperate, Cicero fled to Greece. Eighteen months later the tide had turned. Clodius had fallen out with Pompey, who, with Caesar's rather reluctant consent, arranged for a triumphal restoration. For a while thereafter Cicero tried to play an independent political hand, taking advantage of rifts in the triumviral solidarity. But these were patched up at the Conference of Luca (Lucca) in 56, and Cicero received a sharp warning from Pompey, which took prompt effect. A eulogy of Caesar's victories in the Senate, described by himself as a 'palinode', was his last important political gesture for several years. He continued active forensically, but his choice of clients now had to include creatures of the dynasts, some of them enemies of his own. Meanwhile his personal relations with Caesar developed a new cordiality, and in 54 his brother Quintus went to Gaul to make a military reputation and, as he hoped, his fortune as one of Caesar's lieutenant-generals.

The year 55 saw Pompey and Crassus together again in the Consulship. Caesar's tenure in Gaul was extended for another quinquennium, and the Consuls were appointed to commands in Spain and Syria for a like period (Pompey remained in Italy, governing Spain through deputies). But the later fifties produced a realignment. Pompey was the devoted husband of Caesar's daughter Julia; she died in 54 and in the following year Crassus was defeated and killed by the Parthians. Caesar and Pompey were left in what began to look like confrontation. After the conquest of Gaul Pompey could no longer feel secure in his position of senior partner, while at the same time Cato and his friends were losing their hostility to Pompey in face of the threat from Caesar. The *rapprochement* between Pompey and Senate, which Cicero had once unsuccessfully tried to promote, came about under the pressure of events. In 52, at the behest of the Catonians, Pompey took power as sole Consul (the term Dictator was avoided) to restore law and order, which had broken down in a welter of street warfare and electoral corruption. This accomplished with no less efficiency than the clearance of the seas in 67, the question of Caesar's future came uppermost. After protracted manoeuvring the upshot was another civil war, which broke out at the beginning of 49, when Caesar led his troops across the river Rubicon into the homeland. Hardly more than two months later, after Caesar had encircled and captured a large republican army at Corfinium, Pompey, the Consuls, and a large part of the Senate crossed the Adriatic with their remaining troops, leaving Caesar in undisputed control of Italy and Rome.

Cicero had missed the political preliminaries. In 51 he found himself unexpectedly saddled with the government of a province (a thing he had twice avoided in the past), namely Cilicia, comprising almost all the southern seaboard of Asia Minor and a large part of the interior, together with the island of Cyprus. He entered it at the end of July for his year's tenure. He proved an excellent, if reluctant, governor and with the assistance of his brother and other experienced military men on his staff he even campaigned against the untamed people of the mountains with enough success to win the title of Imperator from his troops and a Supplication (Thanksgiving) from the Senate – the usual preliminaries to a Triumph. Arriving in Italy during the final stage of the crisis he pleaded for peace in public and in private. When that failed, after many waverings recorded in almost daily letters to Atticus, he sailed from Italy in June and is next heard of early the following year in Pompey's camp near Dyrrachium (Durazzo).

Caesar's victory at Pharsalia in August 48 was virtually the end of Pompey, who was killed shortly afterwards in Egypt, but it was not the end of the Civil War. Thinking it was, Cicero accepted Caesar's invitation (conveyed through his own son-in-law Dolabella) to return to Italy and spent an unhappy year in Brundisium (Brindisi) pending decisions on his future, while Caesar was involved in Egypt and Asia. On Caesar's return in September 47 his anxieties were relieved in a gracious interview and he was able to take up life again in Rome.

It was almost entirely a private life. Caesar showed him much kindness and he was on outwardly friendly social terms with most of Caesar's principal followers, but his advice was not required and he rarely appeared in the Forum or the Senate House. Paradoxically he now had most to fear from a republican victory. For Cato and others had established a new position of strength in Africa, where Caesar's lieutenant Curio had lost his life and army early in the war; and after that was destroyed by another

Caesarian victory at Thapsus in April 46, Pompey's sons were able to fight another day in Spain. Even their defeat in the hard-fought battle of Munda (March 45) was not the end.

Meanwhile, especially after his daughter's death in February 45, Cicero took refuge in literary work. In his young days he had published verse, with temporary acclaim, and many carefully edited speeches. The works *On the Orator* and *On the Republic* appeared in the fifties. In 46–44 he turned to philosophy. Without any pretensions to original thought, he put the ideas he found in his Greek sources into elegant Latin in a rapid succession of treatises which have made a greater impact on the minds of men to come than perhaps any other secular writings of antiquity.

Cicero had no prior knowledge of the conspiracy against Caesar's life in 44, though its leader M. Brutus was his intimate friend. But when Caesar fell in the Senate House on the Ides of March, Brutus waved his blood-stained dagger and shouted Cicero's name. Certainly the act had Cicero's whole-hearted approval. But a little while later he ruefully recognized that though the king was dead the monarchy survived. The conspirators, an assortment of republican loyalists and disgruntled place-seekers, had not planned ahead, and the Consul Mark Antony, who in Cicero's opinion ought to have been eliminated along with his colleague Caesar, soon made it evident that he intended to take Caesar's place. The 'liberators' were driven out of Rome by mob violence.

Disgusted at the scene Cicero set out in July for Greece, where his son was a student in Athens, but reports from Rome made him turn back. On 2 September he delivered in the Senate the first of a series of attacks on Antony which he jestingly called *Philippics*, after Demosthenes' speeches against Philip of Macedon. There were no immediate consequences and for some time Cicero again lay low. But by the end of the year the situation had been transformed. Antony was at Mutina (Modena) besieging the legal governor of Cisalpine Gaul, Decimus Brutus, who was one of Caesar's assassins. Soon he found himself opposed by three republican armies. Their commanders were the two Consuls of 43, Hirtius and Pansa, both Caesarians but hostile to Antony's ambitions, and Caesar's youthful great-nephew and adopted son, Caesar Octavianus, who had returned to Italy the previous April and emerged as Antony's rival for the loyalty of Caesar's veterans. At this time Cicero professed complete confidence in Octavian's loyalty to the Republic. Meanwhile, he himself had taken the lead in Rome as the acknowledged embodiment of the Senate and People's will to resist the new despotism. M. Brutus and his brother-in-law and co-conspirator

Cassius had left for the East, where they succeeded in taking over the entire Roman empire east of the Adriatic in the republican interest. The West, however, was in the hands of four Caesarian governors, none of whom, except perhaps Cornificius in Africa, was wholly reliable from Cicero's standpoint. It was his business to make the Senate a focus for their dubious loyalties and to maintain a stream of hortatory correspondence.

In April the situation at Mutina was resolved. Antony suffered two heavy defeats and was forced to raise the siege and escape westwards. But both Consuls lost their lives in the fighting. The game in Italy now lay in Octavian's hands, but Antony was not finished. Joined by a large contingent under his lieutenant Ventidius he crossed the Alps into southern Gaul, now governed by Caesar's former Master of the Horse, M. Lepidus. The news that they had joined forces caused consternation in Rome, where the war had seemed as good as won. In northern Gaul Cicero's family friend L. Plancus professed loyalty and was joined by Decimus Brutus. But the armies remained inactive until August or September, when Plancus, along with Pollio, the governor of Further Spain, joined the opposition. Decimus' men deserted and he was killed in flight.

In Italy Octavian had begun to assert himself, demanding the vacant Consulship – at nineteen years old! When the Senate refused, he marched his army on Rome and occupied the city without bloodshed. His election followed on 19 August. Then came a meeting with Antony and Lepidus in October at which a common front was established. The three dynasts became 'Triumvirs for the Constitution of the Republic' and parcelled out the western part of the empire between them. Funds were raised and vengeance satisfied by a revival of Sulla's Proscriptions. The victims were numerous, many of them eminent, and Cicero was naturally among the first. After an abortive attempt to escape by sea he was hunted down and killed at his villa near Formiae on 7 December. His brother and nephew met a similar fate.

In 42 the republican cause finally went down to defeat at Philippi, where Brutus and Cassius perished. Eleven years later monarchy was established by Octavian's victory over Antony at Actium.

The complexities of Cicero's career and personality hardly appear in a mere summary of events.[2] 'In his various phases he became what circumstances made him, sometimes paltry, sometimes almost heroic. His

2. A full account is given in my own biography, *Cicero* (Duckworth, 1971), from which the following quotation is taken (pp. 279 ff.).

ambition was rooted in insufficiency. Carrying all his life a set of traditional ideas which he never consciously questioned, he seldom ignored his code, but was easily swayed and perplexed by side issues and more or less unacknowledged personal inducements. His agile mind moved on the surface of things, victim of their complexity. Always the advocate, he saw from ever-shifting angles, and what he saw he rarely analysed.

'Often confused himself, he perplexes us. He failed to realize that self-praise can defeat its end. Alongside the image of the wise and dauntless patriot which he tried to project into posterity has arisen the counter-image of a wind-bag, a wiseacre, a humbug, a spiteful, vain-glorious egotist. And that is not because, as some of his admirers have urged, the survival of his private correspondence has placed him at a disadvantage. His published speeches bewray him to a generation intolerant of his kind of cliché. The flabbiness, pomposity, and essential fatuity of Ciceronian rhetoric at its too frequent worst does him more damage than any epistolary "secrets". No other antique personality has inspired such venomous dislike. His modern enemies both hate and despise him – from titanic Mommsen, obsessed by scorn of political inadequacy, romantic worshipper of "complete and perfect" Caesar, to Kingsley Amis's young schoolmaster who had the bad luck to be reading the Second Philippic in class.[3] The living Cicero was hated by some, but not despised. His gifts, matching the times, were too conspicuous. And many opponents were disarmed; Mommsen himself might have capitulated to a dinner-party at Tusculum.'

Cicero's Family

In later life, after the death of his parents and a cousin, Lucius Cicero, to whom he was much attached, Cicero's family circle at one time or other included the following:

1. His wife Terentia. She was rich and well connected, possibly even of noble family; we hear only of a half-sister, a Vestal Virgin who probably belonged to the patrician Fabii. The marriage seems to have worked well for many years, but after Cicero's return from exile there

3. 'The last forty minutes had been spent in taking, or rather hauling, the Junior Sixth through not nearly enough of *In Marcum Antonium II*. For a man so long and thoroughly dead it was remarkable how much boredom, and also how precise an image of nasty silliness, Cicero could generate. "Antony was worth twenty of you, you bastard," Patrick said' (*Take a Girl like You*, Chapter V).

are signs of strain. The differences seem to have mainly had to do with money. In 46 they ended in divorce. Terentia is alleged to have lived to 103 and twice remarried.

2. His daughter Tullia. Probably born in 76 or 75 rather than 79 or 78, as usually supposed. Cicero was devoted to her and distraught with grief at her death in February 45. On her marriages see below.

3. His son Marcus, born in 65. He turned out a disappointment to his father, an unremarkable young man who was happier commanding a troop of cavalry than studying philosophy. He escaped the Proscriptions, being in Greece at the time, and served in Brutus' army. Later Octavian made him Augur, Consul in 30, and governor of Asia. He also gained the reputation of being the hardest drinker in Rome.

4. A brother Quintus, about two years his junior. Following in Cicero's wake he held the usual offices up to Praetor and was Proconsul in Asia from 61 to 59. In 54 he took service under Caesar in Gaul, but like his brother followed Pompey in the Civil War. Pardoned by Caesar after Pharsalia, he perished in the Proscriptions of 43. His relations with his brother were close and generally affectionate until 48. The story of their quarrel and superficial reconciliation can be found in Chapter 19 of my biography. A number of Cicero's letters to him written between 59 and 54 survive.

5. Quintus' wife Pomponia, sister of Atticus (see below). The marriage took place in 70 or thereabouts and ended with divorce in 45. It was never a success. Pomponia was several years older than her husband and apparently of a shrewish disposition. Cicero's letters contain many references to their domestic difficulties.

6. Their son, the younger Q. Cicero, born about the end of 67. Much more gifted intellectually than his cousin, he grew up to be a thorn in his elders' flesh. Also perished in the Proscriptions.

7. Tullia had three husbands, all young men of noble family. She was betrothed to the first, C. Calpurnius Piso Frugi, in 67 and married in 62. He was Quaestor in 58, but died the following year before Cicero's return. He seems to have been a model son-in-law, and Cicero writes warmly of his loyalty in the bad times.

8. Tullia probably married Furius Crassipes in 55. They were divorced within a few years, but nothing is known of the circumstances.

9. Tullia married P. Cornelius Dolabella in 50, a rake and a Caesarian. Divorce followed in 46, but Cicero remained on good terms with him until he allied himself with Antony, having succeeded Caesar as

Consul in 44. He committed suicide in the East in 42 to avoid capture by Cassius.

10. In January 45 Tullia bore a son, who lived only a few months. He was called Lentulus after Dolabella's adoptive name.

11. Not long after divorcing Terentia Cicero married his young and wealthy ward, Publilia. Another divorce followed after a few months. She had a brother(?), Publilius, and a mother living.

12. Pomponia's brother, T. Pomponius Atticus. He married Pilia in 56; her brother, Pilius Celer, was a noted speaker and a Caesarian. Their daughter, Caecilia Attica, was probably born in 51.

Atticus

Titus Pomponius (the *cognomen* Atticus was a personal acquisition) was born about November 110. His family was, like Cicero's, equestrian, but Roman as far back as it could be traced. Their friendship began in their schooldays. After his father's death, in 86 or a little later, the young Pomponius made his home in Athens for about twenty years, though often returning to Rome on visits. He seems never to have considered a political career, though on terms of close friendship with some leading nobles, especially Cato and his connections, including the orator Hortensius and M. Brutus. From his long residence in Athens and his love of things Hellenic he came to be called Atticus, 'the Athenian'.

In about 65 Rome again became his permanent domicile, though he made frequent and lengthy visits to an estate in Epirus, opposite the island of Corfu. It is to these absences and to Cicero's sojourns in his Italian villas and abroad that we owe the correspondence. Atticus' life was spent in cultural and antiquarian pursuits (he was the author of a work on Roman history and several chronicles of Roman noble families), on the management of his large fortune, and on obliging his friends. Much has sometimes been made of his adherence to the philosophy of Epicurus. No doubt it appealed to his temperament, though he was certainly no fervent disciple like his contemporary Lucretius. The Epicureans attached great importance to friendship. Despite wide differences of nature and circumstance his friendship with Cicero stood the test of time and his services were innumerable, especially in matters of business and in the dissemination of Cicero's literary works through his staff of slave-copyists. Epicurus also discouraged political activity. Apart from a demonstration in support of Cicero in 63 Atticus took no open part in politics (it seems that he did not even like voting at elections) and aimed at keeping on good terms with everybody, though his personal views were steadily conservative. In 'Caesar's War' he stayed in Italy and in 43 he befriended Antony's family and friends in Rome. To that he owed his escape from Proscription and his ability to save several others.

After Cicero's death he lived on until 32 in excellent relations with both Octavian and Antony. His daughter, Caecilia Attica, married the former's right-hand man, M. Agrippa, and their daughter Vipsania was the first wife of the future Emperor Tiberius and mother of his ill-fated son.

I have traced the story of Atticus' relations with Cicero in detail in the introduction to my annotated edition of their correspondence. The following estimate was based upon Cicero's letters and a brief biography by Atticus' younger friend, Cornelius Nepos:

'It is easy to be less than fair to a man who made so bland a success of safe living in troubled times and who, unlike Montaigne, has left no self-portrait to engage posterity in his favour. There was more in Atticus than "the quintessence of prudent mediocrity" (Tyrrell and Purser). The basis of his many friendships must have been a singularly attractive personality. Its hallmark was the *humanitas* which Cicero so often associates with him, that untranslatably Roman amalgam of kindness and culture, width of mind and tact of manner. Atticus never quarrelled with Pomponia in his life and spoke Greek as though Athenian born. A delightful talker, who liked to walk as he talked, he loved sparkle in others and doubtless evoked it. Many a Roman frown, even Brutus' "solemn old countenance", will have relaxed when Atticus thought it time to say "halis spoudês" ("no more gravity", "trêve de sérieux"). Intellectually omnivorous, he was as ready to take an interest in a treatise on Homeric accentuation as in the latest city scandal. His social qualities were finished by a palatable salt of idiosyncrasy – some quaint turns of speech, his rich man's "nèarness" excused by good taste, his exaggerated cult of antiquity and *mos maiorum*. Moving much among his social superiors, he deferred to no man's arrogance. There was a formidable side to Atticus, and Nepos' testimony that his friends respected quite as much as they loved him can be read between the lines of many a letter. "He never told a lie and could not tolerate lying in others": that too we can believe, though Atticus' conception of lying did not include prudent dissimulation. The reader of Cicero's correspondence needs no pious biographer to tell him that Atticus was a man of his word, indefatigable in pursuit of whatever he undertook. His moral code, however limited, was steadily and strictly observed: "In the things that really matter – uprightness, integrity, conscientiousness, fidelity to obligation – I put you second neither to myself nor to any other man." Cicero could flatter, but this does not sound like flattery. That deficiency in "noble rage" (Strachan-Davidson), which in modern estimates has tended to discount so many virtues, might have gone unnoticed in a smaller epoch. But greatness had not yet deserted the air that fed Roman blood and made Latin speech. All evasions notwithstanding, Cicero had his portion, which no Mommsenian spleen shall take away; in the end he ran his risks and "glaubte an Glauben". Atticus, with his comity and learning, his business morals and sagacious benevolence, his warm heart and cool head, represents a meaner species.'

The Letters

The Roman, at any rate the upper-class Roman, was a letter-writer. In ancient Greece a man's circle was apt to be mainly confined to a single small town and the countryside adjoining. He travelled comparatively seldom. But the well-to-do Roman was likely to have connections up and down Italy as well as in the provinces. He himself spent much time in his country houses. Business, public or private, might take him abroad for long periods. Although there was no postal system, bearers could usually be found – his own slaves, his friends' slaves, casual travellers, or the couriers of business companies.

Hardly any specimens of this activity survive except for Cicero's correspondence – purely private letters, written without any idea of future publication and published, apparently, almost exactly as they stood (the omission in one letter to Atticus of a scandalous story about Quintus junior may have been deliberate, but it is hard to find any other evidence of expurgation, let alone falsification). As such they are uniquely interesting even apart from their enormous value as a source of historical and other kinds of information. In them the modern reader comes close to the writer's personality and lives in his remote yet familiar world as in no other ancient book. Any translation of these letters that does not transmit life and actuality is a failure.

They have come down in two large collections, those to Atticus and the so-called *Letters to Friends*, both in sixteen 'Books', and two much smaller ones, to Q. Cicero and to M. Brutus. Many more were extant in antiquity of which only stray fragments now survive. Except for a few of the earliest letters to Atticus they were all written in the last twenty years of Cicero's life. The date and circumstances of their publication are doubtful. We know that Atticus preserved Cicero's letters to himself during his lifetime and allowed friends to read them. The view once held, that these were not published until the middle of the first century A.D., is maintained in the introduction to my edition and still appears to me the most probable. The rest of the correspondence will have come out much earlier. It was probably edited piecemeal by Cicero's faithful freedman and secretary, Tiro, who also edited his speeches and wrote his biography.

The collection of 'Letters to Friends' (*Epistulae ad Familiares*) did not originally appear as such. Some of its 'Books' consist entirely or mainly of letters to or from a single correspondent: Lentulus Spinther in 'Book' I, Appius Claudius Pulcher in 'Book' III, Caelius in 'Book' VIII, Terentia in 'Book' XIV, Tiro in 'Book' XVI. 'Book' XIII consists of letters of recommendation, 'Books' X–XII of correspondence relating to the struggle with Antony in 44–43. The other 'Books' show more or less of internal cohesion. The title 'Letters to Friends' seems to be no older than the Renaissance.

The 'friends' are a motley group. Some of them, as Trebatius Testa, Caelius, and Papirius Paetus, really were familiars, to whom Cicero could write as informally, though not as intimately, as to Atticus or to his brother. With powerful aristocrats like Cato, Lentulus Spinther, and Appius Pulcher he was on no such easy footing, and his letters to them are in as elaborate a style as his published works. The high sentiments, stately flatteries, and courteously veiled rebukes might have transposed naturally into eighteenth-century English, but put a modern translator at a disadvantage.

In the familiar letters two special problems of translation call for a word of comment. Cicero was a famous wit and regarded jokes as an essential ingredient of familiar letter-writing. Most of them take the form of puns or other word-plays which can only seldom be satisfactorily reproduced in another language. One does one's best and hopes for tolerance. The second difficulty is Cicero's habit, especially when writing to his friend 'the Athenian', of interlarding his Latin with scraps of Greek, sometimes quotations from Homer or other writers, sometimes not. In the latter case a translation which simply ignores the change of language robs the letters of one of their most characteristic elements. To use French (or some other foreign language) systematically, as was done by G. E. Jeans, leads to grotesque results. I compromised. When I could think of no convenient French (or Latin) expression I let Cicero's Greek go unmarked (the quotations, of course, mark themselves); occasionally, by way of compensation, I used such an expression when Cicero uses Latin.

The letters contain much to puzzle even specialists. In the more intimate ones, in default of the other side of the correspondence, Cicero's allusions often leave his modern readers guessing. The text too, much of it preserved in late fourteenth- and fifteenth-century manuscripts, presents many uncertainties over which scholars have racked their brains to more or less purpose. It has naturally been impossible to deal at all fully with such points in this volume or to discuss alternative readings and interpretations. For these I must refer back to the text and commentary of my edition.

BIBLIOGRAPHICAL NOTE

THE most recent edition of the entire correspondence, with commentary, is my own in the Cambridge Classical Texts and Commentaries series (C.U.P., 10 vols, 1965–80). Previously the only complete modern commentary was that of Tyrrell and Purser (1904–33), a mine of honest misinformation. There are a number of English translations, the most recent being the one published in the Penguin Classics series in 1978 (*Cicero's Letters to Atticus* and (2 vols) *Cicero's Letters to his Friends*). My *Cicero* (Duckworth, 1971) may be regarded as a biographical and historical companion to the correspondence. As a general history of the period T. Rice Holmes, *The Roman Republic* (3 vols, Oxford University Press, 1923), can still be recommended. Mommsen's *History of Rome*, however outmoded its ideological bias, keeps its fascination as a work of genius. Among contributions by living scholars R. Syme's *Roman Revolution* (O.U.P., 1939) is an established classic (largely, however, concerned with the period after Cicero's death). Anything by E. Badian and P. A. Brunt is of value, but much of their work is for specialists. The same goes for E. S. Gruen's challenging *Last Generation of the Roman Republic* (University of California Press, 1974). Notable for penetrating analysis of the problems and determinants underlying late-republican politics is the work of Christian Meier, especially *Res Publica Amissa* (Wiesbaden, Steiner, 1966) and *Caesars Bürgerkrieg* (1964: republished in *Entstehung des Begriffs Demokratie*, Frankfurt am Main, Suhrkamp Verlag, 1970); unfortunately it has not been translated.

Gaston Boissier's *Cicéron et ses amis* (1865; Engl. tr. 1897) can never be superseded as a delightful and sympathetic account of the man and his milieu. Numerous biographies exist in various languages, recently including M. Gelzer, *Cicero: ein biographischer Versuch* (Wiesbaden, Steiner, 1969); D. Stockton, *Cicero: A Political Biography* (O.U.P., 1971); E. Rawson, *Cicero* (Penguin Books, 1975); and my own Cicero (Duckworth, 1971).

CICERO:
SELECTED LETTERS

CICERO TO ATTICUS

Rome, November 68

KNOWING me as well as you do, you can appreciate better than most
how deeply my cousin Lucius' death has grieved me, and what a loss it
means to me both in public and in private life. All the pleasure that one
human being's kindness and charm can give another I had from him. So
I do not doubt that you too are sorry; for you will feel my distress, and you
yourself have lost a family connection and a friend, one who possessed
every good quality and disposition to serve others, and who loved you both
of his own accord and from hearing me speak of you.

You write to me of your sister. She will tell you herself how anxious I
have been that my brother Quintus should feel towards her as a husband
ought. Thinking that he was rather out of temper I sent him a letter
designed to mollify him as a brother, advise him as my junior, and scold
him as a man on the wrong track; and from what he has since written to
me on a number of occasions I feel confident that all is as it ought to be
and as we should wish.

About letter dispatches, you find fault with me unjustly. Pomponia has
never told me of any person to whom I could give one, and furthermore I
myself as it happens have had no one going to Epirus and we don't yet
hear of you in Athens. Then as to the Acutilius business,[1] I had discharged
your commission as soon as I got back to Rome after you left. But, as it
turned out, there was no urgency, and reckoning that you were quite
capable of making up your own mind I preferred Peducaeus to write and
advise you rather than myself. And really, considering I lent my ears day

1. A financial dispute with Atticus.

after day to Acutilius, with whose style of conversation I dare say you are well acquainted, I should not have found it too onerous to write to you about his grumbles when I made light of listening to them, which *was* just a little tedious. But let me tell you that only one letter has reached me from *you*, my accuser, though you have more time for writing and more opportunities to send.

You say that even if a certain person[2] were out of humour with you I ought to bring him round. I understand your meaning and have not been remiss, but he is marvellously hipped. I did not fail to say the proper things about you, but I felt I ought to decide how far to press in the light of your wishes. If you will explain them to me you will see that, while I did not want to pay more attention to the matter than you did yourself, I shall pay no less than you desire.

On the Tadius matter, Tadius tells me that he has heard from you to the effect that there is no need to worry any longer as the estate is his by usucapion.[3] We are surprised you don't know that nothing can be alienated by usucapion from a legal tutelage, which is said to be the girl's position.

I am glad you are pleased with your purchase in Epirus.[4] Yes, do please look after my commissions[5] and anything else that may strike you as suitable to my place in Tusculum, so far as you can without putting yourself to too much trouble. It is the one place where I rest from all troubles and toils.

We are expecting Quintus back any day. Terentia has a bad attack of rheumatism. She is very fond of you and of your sister and mother, and sends her best love, as does my darling little Tullia. Take care of yourself and your affection for me; and be sure of my brotherly affection in return.

2. L. Lucceius.
3. Establishment of title by possession. The Tadius matter is complicated.
4. Atticus had recently bought his estate at Buthrotum.
5. Concerning the purchase of *objets d'art*.

2

CICERO TO ATTICUS

Rome, August 67

I had been active of my own accord before, but your two very sedulous letters to the same purpose were a powerful stimulus. Add to that constant exhortation from Sallustius to do my utmost with Lucceius for the restoration of your old friendship. But after all I could do I have failed, not only to re-establish his former sentiments towards you but even to get out of him *why* his sentiments have changed. To be sure he flourishes that arbitration business of his and other grievances which I knew existed even before you left, but there must surely be something else which has taken deeper root in his mind, something that cannot so easily be removed either by your letters or by my ambassadorial effort as by yourself in person – not only what you say but your old familiar face; that is, if you think it worth the trouble, as you certainly will if you take my advice and don't wish to belie your own good heart. You may think it odd that I seem so pessimistic now after writing to you earlier that I expected him to do as I told him. The fact is, you can hardly believe how much stiffer I find his attitude and more obstinate in this dudgeon. But your return will cure it, or else whichever is to blame will be the sufferer.

When you wrote in one of your letters that you supposed I was already elected you little knew the worries of a candidate[6] in Rome at the present time, with all kinds of injustices to plague him. No one knows when the elections will take place. But you'll hear all this from Philadelphus.

Please send the things you have got for my Academy as soon as possible. The very thought of the place, let alone the actual use of it, gives me enormous pleasure. Mind you don't hand over your books to anybody. Keep them for me, as you say you will. I am consumed with enthusiasm for them, as with disgust for all things else. It's unbelievable in so short a time how much worse you will find them than you left them.

6. For the Praetorship.

3

CICERO TO ATTICUS

Rome, shortly before 17 July 65

The position as regards my candidature,[7] in which I know you are deeply interested, is as follows, so far as can be foreseen up to date: Only P. Galba is canvassing, and he is getting for answer a good old Roman 'No', plain and unvarnished. It's generally thought that this premature canvass of his has rather helped my prospects, for people are commonly refusing him on the ground that they are obligated to me. So I hope to draw some advantage when the word goes round that a great many friends of mine are coming to light. I was thinking of starting my canvass just when Cincius says your boy will leave with this letter, i.e. 17 July, at the tribunician elections in the Campus. As apparently certain rivals I have Galba, Antonius, and Q. Cornificius. When you read this last I fancy you will either laugh or cry. Now get ready to slap your forehead: some folk think Caesonius may stand too! As for Aquilius, I don't expect he will. He has both said he won't and entered a plea of ill health and alleged his monarchy over the law courts in excuse.[8] If Catiline's jury finds that the sun doesn't shine at midday,[9] he will certainly be a candidate. I don't think you will be waiting for me to write about Aufidius and Palicanus.

Of the present candidates[10] Caesar[11] is regarded as a certainty. The other place is thought to lie between Thermus[12] and Silanus. They are so poorly off for friends and reputation that it doesn't seem to me an absolute impossibility to put Turius in their light, but I am alone in thinking so. From my point of view the best result would seem to be for Thermus to get in with Caesar, since he looks like being as strong a candidate as any of the present lot if he is left over to my year; the reason being that he is Curator of the Flaminian Way,[13] which will easily be finished by then. I

7. For the Consulship of 63.
8. These phrases are ironical.
9. Catiline was facing trial for extortion in Africa. He was acquitted.
10. For the Consulship of 64.
11. i.e., L. Julius Caesar. He was elected.
12. Perhaps identical with the man actually elected, C. Marcius Figulus. D. Junius Silanus (step-father of M. Brutus) was elected the following year.
13. The great north road of Italy, from Rome to Ariminum (Rimini). It was apparently under repair or improvement.

should be happy to tack him on to Consul Caesar now. Such in outline is my present idea of the position as to candidatures. For my part I shall spare no pains in faithfully fulfilling the whole duty of a candidate, and perhaps, as Gaul looks like counting heavily in the voting, I shall run down to join Piso's[14] staff in September, in the dead period after the courts have closed, returning in January. When I have made out the attitudes of the nobles I shall write to you. I hope the rest is plain sailing, at any rate as far as these local competitors are concerned. *You* must answer for the other phalanx, since you are not so far away, I mean our friend Pompey's. Tell him I shall not be offended if he doesn't turn up for my election![15]

Well, that's how it all stands. But I have something to tell you for which I very much hope you will forgive me. Your uncle Caecilius, having been defrauded by P. Varius of a large sum of money, has taken proceedings against Varius' cousin, Caninius Satyrus, for articles alleged to have been fraudulently conveyed to him by Varius. The other creditors are joined with him, including Lucullus, P. Scipio, and L. Pontius, who they expect will be receiver if it comes to a distraint. But this talk of a receiver is ridiculous. Now for the point. Caecilius asked me to appear against Satyrus. Well, hardly a day passes without this Satyrus calling on me. L. Domitius comes first in his attentions, I next. He made himself most useful both to me and to my brother Quintus when we were candidates. I was naturally most embarrassed in view of my friendship not only with Satyrus but with Domitius, on whom my hopes of success depend beyond any other man. I explained all this to Caecilius, making it clear at the same time that had the dispute been solely between himself and Satyrus I should have met his wishes. As it was, seeing that the whole group of creditors was involved, men moreover of the highest station who would easily maintain their common cause without help from anyone Caecilius might bring in on his own account, I suggested that it would be reasonable for him to make allowance for my obligations and my present position. I had the impression that he took this less kindly than I should have wished or than is usual among gentlemen, and from that time on he entirely dropped our friendly contacts which had begun only a few days previously.

May I ask you to forgive me over this, and to believe that it was good feeling that prevented me from appearing against a friend in great trouble, who had given me every support and service in his power, in a matter most gravely affecting his good name? If however, you like to take a harsher

14. C. Calpurnius Piso (Consul in 67) was governor of Transalpine and Cisalpine Gaul.
15. Cicero was afraid that Pompey might put up a candidate of his own.

view, you may assume that the exigencies of my candidature made the stumbling-block. *I* consider that even if it were so I might be pardoned, 'since for no hide of bull nor slaughtered beast ...'[16] You know the game I am playing and how vital I think it not only to keep old friends but to gain new ones. I hope you now see my point of view in the matter – I am certainly anxious that you should.

I am quite delighted with your Hermathena.[17] It's so judiciously placed that the whole hall is like an offering at its feet. Many thanks.

4

CICERO TO ATTICUS

Rome, shortly after Letter 3

I have the honour to inform you that I have become the father of a little son, L. Julius Caesar and C. Marcius Figulus being Consuls.[18] Terentia is well. It's a long time since I had a line from you. I have already written to you in detail about my prospects. At the moment I am proposing to defend my fellow-candidate Catiline. We have the jury we want, with full co-operation from the prosecution.[19] If he is acquitted I hope he will be more inclined to work with me in the campaign. But should it go otherwise, I shall bear it philosophically.

I need you home pretty soon. There is a decidedly strong belief abroad that your nble friends are going to oppose my election. Clearly you will be invaluable to me in gaining them over. So mind you are in Rome by the beginning of January as you arranged.

16. *Iliad*, XXII. 159: 'Since for no beast for sacrifice or ox-hide were the twain striving ... but they ran for the life of god-like Hector.'

17. A bust of Athene (Minerva) on a square pedestal or post (herm).

18. i.e., just elected. The mock-pompous opening travesties the ordinary dating of a year by its Consuls; not, however, to fix a day, but to announce the result of the elections. Some editors omit the words as spurious.

19. See n. 9. For some reason Cicero withdrew at the last moment. The prosecutor (Cicero's future enemy P. Clodius) was in collusion with the defence.

5

METELLUS CELER TO CICERO

Cisalpine Gaul, c. 12 January 62

Q. Metellus Celer, son of Quintus, Proconsul, to M. Tullius Cicero greetings.

I hope you are well!

In view of our reciprocal sentiments and the restoration of our friendly relations I had not expected that I should ever be held up by you to offensive ridicule in my absence, or that my brother Metellus[20] would be attacked at your instance in person or estate because of a phrase.[21] If his own honourable character did not suffice for his protection, the dignity of our family and my zeal on behalf of you and your friends and the commonwealth should have been support enough. Now it seems that he has been beset, and I deserted, by those whom it least behoved.

So I wear the black of mourning[22] – I, in command of a province and an army conducting a war![23] Well, you and your friends have managed it so, without reason or forbearance. It was not like this in our forbears' time, and it will not be surprising if you all come to be sorry.[24] I did not think to find your own disposition so changeable towards me and mine. In the meantime neither domestic unhappiness nor any man's ill-usage shall turn me away from the commonwealth.

20. Q. Caecilius Metellus Nepos. Since entering office as Tribune on 10 December 63 he had demonstrated hostility to Cicero and his handling of the Catilinarian crisis. See next letter.

21. Probably the one reported in para. 7 of Cicero's reply ('that one who had punished others' etc.).

22. Customary when (e.g.) a close relative faced prosecution on a capital charge. Many Romans put on mourning for Cicero when threatened by Clodius in 58. Metellus Nepos had been suspended from office by the Senate.

23. Against Catiline.

24. Perhaps a hint of what might happen when Pompey returned from the East.

6

CICERO TO METELLUS CELER

Rome, mid January 62

From M. Tullius Cicero, son of Marcus, to Q. Metellus Celer, son of Quintus, Proconsul, greetings.

I hope all is well with you and the army.[25]

You write that you had not expected ever to be held up to offensive ridicule by me, in view of our reciprocal sentiments and the restoration of friendly relations. What that means, I cannot precisely tell. But I suspect you have heard a report to the effect that, while arguing in the Senate that there were very many who regretted my saving of the commonwealth, I remarked that relatives of yours, to whom you could not say no, had prevailed upon you to suppress what you had decided you ought to say in the Senate in commendation of myself. In making this observation, I added that you and I had made a division of duty in the preservation of the commonwealth: my part was to guard Rome from domestic plots and the enemy within the gates, yours to protect Italy from armed force and underground conspiracy.[26] This partnership of ours in so vital and splendid a task had been impaired by relatives of yours, who feared you might make me some gesture of mutual goodwill in response to the ungrudging warmth of my tributes to yourself.

When in the course of my remarks I explained how eagerly I had been looking forward to your speech and how egregiously I had been astray, my speech caused some amusement and a moderate amount of laughter ensued – not directed at you, but rather at my mistake, and at the artless candour with which I admitted my desire to be praised by you. Really there could be nothing but compliment to you in my saying that at the very height of my glory I still hankered for some testimonial from *your* lips.

As for your reference to 'our reciprocal sentiments', I do not know how *you* define reciprocity in friendship. *I* conceive it to lie in goodwill equally

---

25. It was usual to include the army in this formula when writing to a commanding general.
26. As Praetor in 63 Celer had raised troops in northern Italy and cut off Catiline's retreat to Gaul.

received and returned. If I were to say that I forwent a province[27] for your sake, you would think *me* less than sincere. It suited my purpose to do so, and I draw more pleasure and profit every day from my decision. What I do say is, that having announced the relinquishment of my province at a public meeting, I lost no time in planning how to transfer it to you. Of the lottery among the board of Praetors I say nothing. I only invite you to surmise that I was privy to all my colleague's actions in the matter. Be pleased to recall what followed, how promptly I called the Senate together on the day the lottery had taken place, and at what length I spoke about you. You said to me yourself that my speech was flattering to you to the point of being less than complimentary to your colleagues. Moreover, the senatorial decree[28] passed that day contained a preamble which, as long as the document survives, will plainly testify to the friendly office I did you. Then, after you left Rome, I would ask you to recollect my speeches in the Senate with reference to yourself, my deliverances at public meetings, and the letters I sent you. When you have put all this together, I leave to your own judgement whether your conduct on the occasion of your recent visit[29] to Rome adequately 'reciprocated' mine at all these points.

You refer to 'the restoration of friendly relations'. I fail to understand why you should speak of a restoration of relations which have never been impaired.

You write that your brother Metellus should not have been attacked by me because of a phrase. Now in the first place I would ask you to believe that your sentiment here, your fraternal spirit redolent of good feeling and natural affection, has my warm approval. Secondly, if in any matter I have opposed your brother on public grounds, I ask you to forgive me – in public spirit I call no man my superior. But if I have defended my existence as a citizen in face of a savage onslaught on his part, you should be content that *I* do not protest to *you* about your brother's ill-usage. When I learned that he was planning and preparing his entire programme as Tribune with

27. Macedonia and Cisalpine Gaul had been assigned by the Senate as consular provinces for 62. Cicero enlisted support against Catiline from his unreliable colleague C. Antonius by letting him have Macedonia instead of drawing lots. Later he announced that he would not take a province at all, leaving Cisalpine Gaul to be allotted to one of the eight Praetors. He goes on to imply that Antonius, instigated by himself, had manipulated the lottery in Celer's favour.

28. The decree (c. October 63) will have appointed Celer to a command in north Italy prior to his taking over the governorship of his province. Cicero's name would appear in the preamble with a complimentary reference to Celer's services as Praetor.

29. This visit must have taken place at the end of 63 while Celer was still Praetor.

a view to my destruction, I addressed myself to your lady wife Claudia[30] and your sister Mucia[31] (her friendly disposition towards me as a friend of Cn. Pompeius had been plain to me in many connections) and asked them to persuade him to give up his injurious design. And yet, on the last day of the year, as I am sure you have heard, he put upon me, Consul and saviour of the commonwealth, an insult which has never been put on any holder of any magistracy, no matter how disloyal: he deprived me of the power to address an assembly before retiring from office. This affront, however, redounded greatly to my honour. In face of his refusal to let me do more than take the oath,[32] I swore in loud tones the truest and finest oath that ever was, and the people likewise in loud tones swore that I had sworn the truth.

Even after receiving so signal an insult I sent common friends to Metellus that very same day to urge him to change his attitude. He replied that his hands were no longer free; and in fact he had declared at a public meeting a little while previously that one who had punished others without a hearing ought not to be given the right to speak himself. What sense of responsibility, what civic virtue! To judge the preserver of the Senate from massacre, of Rome from arson, of Italy from war, worthy of the same penalty as was inflicted by the Senate with the approbation of all honest men upon those who had designed to set fire to Rome, slaughter magistrates and Senate, and kindle a terrible conflict![33] Accordingly, I stood up to your brother Metellus face to face. On the Kalends of January we had a political disputation in the Senate which let him feel that he had to deal with a man of courage and resolution. In a speech on 3 January he named me in every sentence with threats; he had thoroughly made up his mind to bring me down by hook or by crook – not through due process of law, but by aggressive violence. If I had not offered a spirited and manly resistance to his indiscretions, nobody could have believed that my record as a courageous Consul was aught but a freak of chance.

If you were unaware of Metellus' intentions towards me, you must recognize that your brother has kept you in the dark about matters of the

---

30. See Glossary of Persons under 'Clodia'.

31. Actually half-sister, married to Pompey.

32. The usual oath taken by a retiring magistrate, that he had observed the laws during his term of office. Cicero neatly adapted it to the occasion by swearing that he alone had saved Rome and the Republic.

33. The senate had decreed a public Thanksgiving in honour of Cicero's services almost in these terms.

highest consequence. On the other hand, if he told you something of his plans, you ought to appreciate how mild and easy-going I show myself in not expostulating with you on this very subject. And if you recognize that I was not upset by a 'phrase' of Metellus but by the bitter hostility of his purpose and attitude towards me, I must ask you now to note my for-bearance – if that is the right word for laxity and weakness in the face of the most severe provocation. I have never once spoken in the Senate for a motion against your brother; on all such occasions I have kept my seat and supported those who appeared to me to make the most lenient proposal. I will add something else: although I could not be expected, after what had passed, to be active in the matter, I was not sorry to see my enemy relieved[34] (because he was your brother) by a senatorial decree, and I even assisted, so far as in me lay, to bring this about.

Thus I made no attack upon your brother, but repelled *his* attack on me; and my disposition towards you, so far from being 'changeable', has been eminently stable, so much so that my feelings remained the same even when friendly actions on your part were no longer forthcoming. Even now, though you have written to me in almost menacing terms, this is the answer I have to make: I not only pardon your irritation, I highly commend it – my own experience of the power of a brother's affection is my monitor. In return, I ask you to be fair in your judgement of a similar feeling on my part, and to take the view that, if I have been the victim of a bitter, savage, and unprovoked attack by a member of your family, it was not incumbent on me to give way – that, on the contrary, I was entitled in such a situation to your support and that of the army you command.

I have ever wanted you to be my friend, and have tried to let you see that I am a very good friend of yours. My sentiments remain the same, and shall, as long as you so desire. I shall sooner give up my resentment against your brother out of affection for you than abate a jot of the goodwill between us out of animosity towards him.

---

34. Perhaps the decree allowed Nepos to leave Italy, as in fact he did.

7

CICERO TO POMPEY

Rome, April 62

From M. Tullius Cicero, son of Marcus, to Cn. Pompeius Magnus,[35] son of Gnaeus, Imperator, greetings.

I hope all is well with you and the army, as it is with me.

Like the rest of us I was immeasurably delighted with your dispatch,[36] in which you have held out the bright prospect of a peaceful future; such a prospect as I have ever been promising to all and sundry in reliance on your single self. I must tell you, however, that it came as a severe blow to your old enemies, nowadays your friends;[37] their high hopes dashed, they despond.

Your personal letter to me evinces but little of your friendly sentiments towards me, but you may be sure that it gave me pleasure all the same. My chief joy is apt to lie in the consciousness of my services to others. If these fail of a like response, I am perfectly content that the balance of good offices should rest on my side. I have no doubt that if my own hearty goodwill towards you does not suffice to win your attachment, the public interest will join us in confederacy.

Not to leave you in ignorance of the particular in which your letter has disappointed me, let me speak plainly, as becomes my character and our friendly relations. My achievements[38] have been such that I expected to find a word of congratulation upon them in your letter, both for friendship's sake and that of the commonwealth. I imagine you omitted anything of the sort for fear of giving offence in any quarter.[39] But I must tell you that what I have done for the safety of the country stands approved

35. Pompey's cognomen 'Magnus' ('the Great'), conferred by his victorious troops in 81 and confirmed by Sulla, was used officially, and in a formal address like this it would have been discourteous to omit it. Otherwise Cicero does not normally use it simply as a name, without further implications.

36. To the magistrates and Senate, no doubt announcing the writer's return to Italy in the near future. He actually arrived at the end of the year.

37. Who these were is disputed. Probably Caesar and perhaps Crassus were in mind, also subversives generally who hoped to see Pompey take their part against the senatorial establishment.

38. These had been described in a lengthy letter sent to Pompey the previous December.

39. i.e. to people like Caesar who condemned the execution of the Catilinarian conspirators.

in the judgement and testimony of the whole world. When you return, you will find that I have acted with a measure of policy and a lack of self-regard which will make you well content to have me as your political ally and private friend – a not much lesser Laelius to a far greater Africanus.[40]

8

CICERO TO ATTICUS

Rome, 25 January 61

Three letters from you have now come to hand, the first by M. Cornelius, given him I think at Tres Tabernae, the second forwarded to me by your host at Canusium, the third dispatched from the boat 'as they loosed the cable': all of them, to speak euphuistically, not only sprinkled with the salt of courtesy but also distinguished by tokens of affection. In them you challenged a reply, but I have been rather slow in making one because I can't find a trustworthy carrier. There are so few who can carry a letter of any substance without lightening the weight by perusal. And then, I don't feel sure that any and every traveller to Epirus is on his way to you. For I imagine that no sooner had you sacrificed at the altar of your Amalthea[41] than you set off for the siege of Sicyon,[42] though even that I am not sure about, I mean when you are going to join Antonius or how much time you are spending in Epirus. Accordingly I dare not trust letters of a more or less confidential sort to either Achaeans[43] or Epirotes.

Since you left me there are things that well deserve a letter of mine, but I must not expose such to the risk of getting lost or opened or intercepted. First then you may care to know that I have *not* been given first voice in

40. Scipio Africanus the Younger, destroyer of Carthage in 146. His lifelong friend was C. Laelius, called Sapiens ('the Wise'). Both figure in Cicero's Dialogues.

41. Like a general before a campaign. Atticus' estate contained a shrine to the nymph of this name. See Letter 10, p. 48.

42. i.e., 'You left Buthrotum almost immediately in order to visit C. Antonius and ask him to put pressure on the town of Sicyon' – which owed Atticus money.

43. Inhabitants of Greece proper.

the Senate, the pacificator of the Allobroges being put in front of me[44] – at which the House murmured but I myself was not sorry. I am thereby relieved of any obligation to be civil to a cross-grained individual[45] and left free to maintain my political standing in opposition to his wishes. Moreover the second place carries almost as much prestige as the first, while one's inclinations are not too much fettered by one's sense of the consular favour. Catulus comes third, Hortensius, if you are still interested, fourth. The Consul himself is of petty and perverse mentality, given to the sort of peevish sneer that raises a laugh even in the absence of any wit. His *moue* is funnier than his *mot*. He is politically inactive and stands aloof from the optimates, having neither will to make him politically useful nor courage to make him dangerous. His colleague however is most complimentary to me personally and a zealous champion of the right side. At present their differences are slight enough, but I am afraid that a certain infected spot may spread. I expect you have heard that at the national sacrifice[46] in Caesar's residence a *man* in woman's clothes got in, and that after the Vestals had repeated the ceremony Q. Cornificius (he took the lead, in case you think it was one of us)[47] raised the matter in the Senate. It was then referred back by senatorial decree to the Vestals and College of Pontiffs, who pronounced that the occurrence constituted a sacrilege. Then by senatorial decree the Consuls promulgated a bill. And Caesar sent his wife[48] notice of divorce. Such being the position, Piso out of friendship for P. Clodius is working for the rejection of the bill which he is himself proposing, and proposing moreover under a senatorial decree on a matter of religion. Messalla is so far taking a strong and stringent line. The honest men[49] are yielding to Clodius' pleas and dropping out. Gangs of roughs are in formation. I myself, though I was quite a Lycurgus[50] to start with, am softening every day. Cato presses and prods. All in all, I am afraid that

---

44. The Consulars spoke each year in an order determined by the Consul presiding at the first meeting. C. Piso may be called 'pacificator of the Allobroges' (the principal tribe of Narbonese Gaul, now in revolt against Rome) in irony, as having oppressed them during his governorship. Cicero had defended him in 63 against a charge of unjustly executing a provincial. But he may have made proposals in the Senate for a peaceful settlement.

45. i.e., the Consul, M. Pupius Piso.

46. The festival of the Good Goddess (see Glossary of Terms).

47. i.e., a Consular.

48. Pompeia, with whom Clodius was supposed to have had a rendezvous. Hence Caesar's explanation: 'Caesar's wife must be above suspicion.'

49. See Glossary of Terms.

50. i.e., all for stern measures, probably with reference to an Athenian orator who made a hobby of prosecutions, rather than the Spartan lawgiver.

what with neglect (?) by the honest men and resistance by the rascals these proceedings may be productive of great mischief in the body politic.

As to that friend[51] of yours (you know whom I mean? The person of whom you write to me that he began to praise when he no longer dared to criticize), he professes the highest regard for me and makes a parade of warm affection, praising on the surface while below it, but not so far below that it's difficult to see, he's jealous. Awkward, tortuous, politically paltry, shabby, timid, disingenuous – but I shall go more into detail on another occasion. As yet I am not sufficiently *au fait* with the topic, and I dare not entrust a letter on such high matters to this who knows what of a messenger.

The Praetors[52] have not yet drawn lots for their provinces. The matter stands where it stood when you left. I shall put in my speech[53] the topographical description of Misenum and Puteoli which you ask for. I had noticed that '3 December' was an error. Of the things you praise in the speeches I had, let me tell you, a pretty good opinion, though I did not dare to say so before; now I assure you they look to me far more Attic than ever in the light of your approbation. I have made some additions to the Metellus one, and shall send you the volume, since affection for me has made you an amateur of oratory.

What news have I to tell you? Why yes, Consul Messalla has bought Autronius' house for HS 13,400,000. You wonder what concern it is of yours. Only that after this transaction I am considered to have made a good bargain,[54] and folk have begun to realize that it's legitimate to make a respectable show in the world with purchases financed by one's friends. That Teucris[55] is an infernal slow-coach, but I have hopes of her. Please settle things over there. Expect a less guarded letter from me by and by. 25 January, M. Messalla and M. Piso being Consuls.

51. Pompey.

52. Including Q. Cicero.

53. Probably a speech of 62 in reply to Q. Metellus Nepos which Cicero was now editing.

54. Cicero had recently used borrowed money to buy a mansion on the Palatine Hill from Crassus.

55. C. Antonius, Cicero's colleague as Consul and now governor of Macedonia, had promised him a loan. Teucris seems to have been an intermediary, but the name (= 'woman of Troy') may be fictitious.

9

CICERO TO ATTICUS

Rome, 13 February 61

I am afraid it's not in the best of taste to tell you how busy I am, but in fact I am so harassed that I have hardly found time even for these few lines, and stolen it at that from most pressing business.

I have already given you a description of Pompey's first public speech – of no comfort to the poor or interest to the rascals; on the other hand the rich were not pleased and the honest men were not edified. So – a frost. Then an irresponsible Tribune, Fufius, egged on by Consul Piso, called Pompey out to address the Assembly. This took place in the Flaminian Circus, on market-day just where the holiday crowd was gathered. Fufius asked him whether he thought it right for a jury to be selected by a Praetor to serve under the same Praetor's presidency, that being the procedure determined by the Senate in the Clodius sacrilege case. Pompey then replied, very much *en bon aristocrate*, that in all matters he held and had always held the Senate's authority in the highest respect – at considerable length too.

Subsequently Consul Messalla asked Pompey in the Senate for his views about the sacrilege and the promulgated bill. He then addressed the Senate, commending in general terms all decrees of that body, and remarked to me as he sat down beside me that he hoped he had now replied sufficiently to questioning on these matters. When Crassus saw that Pompey had netted some credit from the general impression that he approved of my Consulship, he got to his feet and held forth on the subject in most encomiastic terms, going so far as to say that it was to me he owed his status as a Senator and a citizen, his freedom and his very life. Whenever he saw his wife or his house or the city of his birth, he saw a gift of mine. In short, he worked up the whole theme which I am in the habit of embroidering in my speeches one way and another, all about fire, sword, etc. (you are their Aristarchus and know my colour-box), really most impressively. I was sitting next to Pompey and I could see he was put out, whether at Crassus gaining the credit which might have been his or to realize that my achievements are of sufficient consequence to make the Senate so willing to hear them praised – praised too by a man who had all the less reason to offer me such incense in that everything I have written glorifies Pompey at his expense. This day's work has brought me very close to Crassus, not but what I was glad enough to take whatever tribute Pompey more or less obliquely vouchsafed.

As for myself – ye gods, how I spread my tail in front of my new audience, Pompey! If ever periods and *clausulae* and enthymemes and *raisonnements*[56] came to my call, they did on that occasion. In a word, I brought the house down. And why not, on such a theme – the dignity of our order, concord between Senate and Knights, unison of Italy, remnants of the conspiracy in their death-throes, reduced price of grain, internal peace? You should know by now how I can boom away on such topics. I think you must have caught the reverberations in Epirus, and for that reason I won't dwell on the subject.

Affairs in Rome stand thus: The Senate is quite an Areopagus,[57] thoroughly resolute, strict, and courageous. When the day came for the bill to be put to the Assembly under the terms of the senatorial decree, there was a flocking together of our goateed young bloods, the whole Catilinarian gang with little Miss Curio[58] at their head, to plead for its rejection. Consul Piso, the proposer of the bill, spoke against it. Clodius' roughs had taken possession of the gangways. The voting papers were distributed without any 'ayes'. Suddenly up springs Cato to the platform and gives Consul Piso a spectacular dressing down, if one can apply such a term to a most impressive, powerful, in fact wholesome speech. He was joined by our friend Hortensius and many honest men besides, Favonius' contribution being especially notable. At this rally of optimates the Assembly was dismissed, and the Senate summoned. A full house voted a decree instructing the Consuls to urge the people to accept the bill. Piso fought against it, and Clodius went on his knees to every member individually, but Curio, who moved the rejection of the decree, only got about 15 votes against a good 400 on the other side. So that was that. Fufius then vetoed the decree. Clodius is making pathetic speeches, full of abusive attacks on Lucullus, Hortensius, C. Piso, and Consul Messalla. Me he simply accuses of having 'fully informed myself'.[59] The Senate is

---

56. Four Greek rhetorical terms are only approximately rendered.

57. The ancient Athenian court of justice sitting on 'Ares' Hill'.

58. Curio the younger. Velleius the historian calls him 'a spendthrift of money and chastity – his own and other people's'.

59. Cicero's enemies used to twit him with this phrase in allusion to his underground activities in collecting information about Catiline's plot.

resolving to take no action on praetorian provinces, embassies or other business until the bill has been put to the Assembly.

So much then for affairs in Rome – though there is one thing more I may mention, which has come to me as a surprise. Messalla is an excellent Consul, courageous, steady, conscientious; I am the object of his praise, regard, and imitation. The other has just one redeeming vice; he is lazy – somnolent, ignorant, a complete *fainéant*, but in disposition so *méchant* that he has turned against Pompey ever since that public speech in which he eulogized the Senate. Naturally he has become extremely unpopular with all the honest men. His behaviour is prompted quite as much by sympathy with subversion and subversive movements as by his friendship with Clodius. But he has no kindred spirit among the magistrates except Fufius. We have a good lot of Tribunes. Cornutus in particular is a mock-Cato. In a word, ***.

Now to return to private matters. Teucris has carried out her promise. On your side please discharge the commission you undertook. My brother Quintus, having bought the remaining three quarters of the building in Argiletum for HS 725,000, is trying to sell his place at Tusculum in order, if possible, to buy the Pacilius house in Rome. I have made my peace with Lucceius.[60] He's clearly a bad case of candidate-fever. I shall put my shoulder to the wheel. Let me have an account as full as you can make it of your doings and whereabouts and the shape of things over there.

Ides of February.

IO

CICERO TO ATTICUS

Rome, beginning of July 61

You ask me what happened over the trial for it to turn out so contrary to everybody's expectations, and you also want to know how it was that I took less than my usual part in the fray. I shall answer you Homerically,[61] cart before horse.

60. Apparently Cicero too had fallen out with him. He became a candidate for the Consulship of 59.

61. Perhaps in allusion to the *Odyssey*, in which Odysseus' earlier adventures occupy the middle of the poem.

Well then, so long as I had the Senate's authority to defend, I took so brisk and vigorous a 'part in the fray' that crowds flocked around me shouting enthusiastic applause. If ever you gave me credit for courage in public life, you would surely have admired me in that affair. When Clodius had betaken himself to speech-making at meetings and used my name to stir up ill-feeling, ye gods, what battles, what havoc I made! The onslaughts on Piso, Curio, the whole bunch! How I pilloried irresponsible age and licentious youth! Upon my sacred word, I longed to have you by, not only as an adviser to follow but as a spectator of those memorable bouts. But then Hortensius conceived the idea of getting Fufius to propose a law on the sacrilege differing from the consular bill only in respect of the constitution of the jury, on which however everything turned, and worked hard for its acceptance because he had persuaded himself and others that no jury on earth could acquit Clodius. I saw we had got a jury of paupers, and drew in my horns, saying nothing in evidence but what was so generally known and attested that I could not leave it out.

If therefore you want to know the reason for the verdict of not guilty (to come back from cart to horse), it was the needy and disreputable quality of the jury, and *that* was due to Hortensius' miscalculation. Afraid that Fufius might veto the law proposed under the senatorial decree, he failed to see how much better it would have been to leave Clodius under the stigma of an impending trial than to commit him to an unreliable tribunal. His hatred made him impatient to bring the case to court. He said that a sword of lead would be sharp enough to cut Clodius' throat.

But if you want to know what sort of a trial it was, it was a trial with an incredible outcome; so that others beside myself (who did so from the first) are now criticizing Hortensius' tactics after the event. The challenging of the jury took place amid uproar, with the prosecutor throwing out the most unsavoury characters like an honest Censor, while the defendant put all the more respectable elements on one side like a soft-hearted trainer.[62] As soon as the jury took their seats, honest men feared the worst. A more raffish assemblage never sat down in a low-grade music hall. Fly-blown Senators, beggar Knights, and Paymaster Tribunes who might better have been called 'Paytakers'. Even so there were a few honest men whom the accused had not been able to drive off at the challenge. There they sat, gloomy and shamefaced (?) in this incongruous company, sadly uncomfortable to feel themselves exposed to the miasma of disreputability.

62. Of gladiators. Apparently the better sort of these were sometimes kept out of specially dangerous fights.

In these circumstances the strictness and unanimity of the court as various matters were referred to it during the preliminaries was quite astounding. The defendant met with nothing but rebuffs, the prosecutor was repeatedly given more than he asked. In short Hortensius triumphed in his perspicacity, and nobody but looked on Clodius, not as a man standing his trial, but as one convicted twenty times over. When I myself was called as a witness, you must have heard from the shouts of Clodius' supporters how the jury rose in a body and surrounded me, pointing to their bare throats as if offering their lives to P. Clodius in exchange for mine. I felt the incident as a much finer tribute than the action of your compatriots[63] in not letting Xenocrates take the oath when he gave evidence, or of our Roman jurymen who refused to look at Metellus Numidicus' accounts when they were taken round in the usual way[64] – yes indeed, this was a far grander gesture. Accordingly, when they heard the jury clamouring in my defence as though I were the salvation of Rome, the accused and all his counsel collapsed in despair. Next morning a crowd gathered at my house as large as took me home the day I laid down the Consulship. Our splendid Areopagites[65] loudly declared that they would not come unless they were given a guard. This being put to the court, there was only one vote against asking for a guard. The matter was brought before the Senate, which passed a solemn, elaborate decree, commending the jury and instructing the magistrates to take the necessary steps. Nobody thought the fellow would reply to the indictment.

'Now tell me, Muses nine ... how first the fire did fall.'[66] You know Baldhead,[67] him of the Nanneius sale (?), my encomiast, of whose complimentary speech I wrote to you. Inside a couple of days, with a single slave (an ex-gladiator at that) for go-between, he settled the whole business – called them to his house, made promises, backed bills, or paid cash down. On top of that (it's really too abominable!) some jurors actually received a bonus in the form of assignations with certain ladies or introductions to youths of noble family. Yet even so, with the honest men making themselves very scarce and the Forum crowded with slaves, 25 jurors had the courage to take the risk, no small one, preferring to sacrifice their lives rather than the whole community. To 31 on the other

---

63. As though Atticus, 'the Athenian', actually was one. Cicero was fond of this pleasantry.
64. At his trial for extortion.
65. i.e., the jury.
66. *Iliad*, XVI. 112.
67. i.e., Crassus.

hand light purses mattered more than light reputations. Meeting one of them afterwards, Catulus asked him why they had wanted us to provide them with a guard – or was it that they were afraid of having their pockets picked? There then, as briefly as I can give it, you have the quality of the trial and the explanation of the verdict.

You go on to ask about the general situation now and my own in particular. I can only answer that, unless some god or other takes pity on us, the settlement of the Republic which you attribute to my policy and I to divine providence, and which seemed unshakably established upon the unity of all honest men and the prestige of my Consulship, has slipped through our fingers in this one trial, if one can call it a trial in which thirty of the most irresponsible rascals in Rome pocket their bribes and play ducks and drakes with religion and morality, in which Talna and Plautus and Spongia and the other riff-raff find that an offence was not committed when every man and beast too knows it was. And yet, to offer you some comfort on public affairs, rascality does not exult so merrily in victory as bad men had expected after the infliction of so grave an injury upon the body politic. They quite supposed that with the collapse of religion and good morals, of the integrity of the courts and the authority of the Senate openly triumphant villainy and vice would wreak vengeance on the best in our society for the pain branded by the severity of my Consulship upon the worst. Yet once again it was I – I don't feel that I am bragging offensively when I talk about myself in your hearing, especially in a letter which I don't wish to be read to other people – well, as I say, it was I yet again who revived the drooping courage of the honest men, fortifying and raising them one by one. Then by denouncing and harassing the venal jurors I effectively stopped the mouths of all sympathizers and backers of the winning side. I drove Consul Piso from pillar to post, and deprived him of Syria, which had already been pledged to him. I recalled the Senate to its earlier strict temper and roused it from despondency. Clodius I quashed face to face in the Senate in a set speech of impressive solemnity and also in an exchange of amenities which went somewhat as follows – you can sample it here and there, but the rest cannot retain its force and piquancy without the thrill of battle which you folks[68] call *le feu de l'action*:

When we met in the Senate on the Ides of May and my turn came, I spoke at length about the political situation on the highest level, bringing in with happiest effect that stock piece urging members not to collapse or flag because of a single blow. I said that I did not think the reverse was

68. Again = 'Athenians'.

such as to call either for disguise or undue alarm. We should be judged arrant fools if we ignored it and arrant cowards if we let it frighten us. Lentulus[69] had been twice acquitted, Catiline twice also, and now a jury had let loose a third enemy upon the state. 'Clodius, you are mistaken. The jury has not preserved you for the streets of Rome, but for the death-chamber. Their object was not to keep you in the community but to deprive you of the chance of exile. And so, gentlemen, take heart and maintain your dignity. The political consensus of honest men still holds. They have gained the spur of indignation, but lost nothing of their manly spirit. No fresh harm has been done, but harm already there has come to light. The trial of a single wretch has unmasked more like him.' But what am I thinking of? I have nearly put my speech into my letter. To come back to our exchange:

Our little Beauty[70] gets on his feet and accuses me of having been at Baiae – not true, but anyhow, 'Well,' I reply, 'is that like saying I intruded on the Mysteries?'[71] 'What business has an Arpinum man with the waters?' 'Tell that to your counsel,'[72] I retorted; 'he was keen enough to get certain of them that belonged to an Arpinum man' (you know Marius' place of course). 'How long,' cried he, 'are we going to put up with this king?' 'You talk about kings,' I answered, 'when Rex[73] didn't have a word to say about you?' (he had hoped to have the squandering of Rex's money). 'So you've bought a house,' said he. I rejoined, 'One might think he was saying that I had bought a jury.' 'They didn't credit you on oath.' 'On the contrary 35 jurymen gave *me* credit and 31 gave *you* none – they got their money in advance!' The roars of applause were too much for him and he collapsed into silence.

As for my personal position, it is as follows: With the honest men I stand as I did when you left, with the dregs of the city populace much better than when you left. It does me no harm that my evidence[74] apparently failed to carry weight. My unpopularity has been reduced by a sort of pain-less blood-letting, especially as all who sympathize with the outrage acknowledge that a perfectly clear case was bought off from the jury.

---

69. P. Cornelius Lentulus Sura, Catiline's principal lieutenant.

70. Or 'Pretty-Boy'. Cicero uses the diminutive of Pulcher ('handsome'), Clodius' cognomen.

71. Literally 'was in a secret place', alluding to Clodius' intrusion on the Good Goddess' festival.

72. i.e., the elder Curio, who had acquired Marius' villa near Baiae in Sulla's Proscriptions.

73. Q. Marcius Rex, Consul in 68, was Clodius' brother-in-law, recently deceased. Clodius did not benefit under his will.

74. Disproving Clodius' alibi.

There is a further point: this wretched starveling rabble that comes to meetings and sucks the treasury dry imagines that I have no rival in the good graces of our Great One.[75] And it is a fact that we have been brought together by a good deal of pleasant personal contact, so much so that those conspirators of the wine-table, our goateed young bloods, have nicknamed him Cn. Cicero. Accordingly I get wonderful ovations at the games and the gladiators, without a single shepherd's whistle.

Now we are waiting for the elections, into which, to everybody's disgust, our Great Man has pushed Aulus' son[76] using neither prestige nor personal influence to get him in, but those engines with which Philip[77] said any fortress could be stormed provided there was a way up for a donkey with a load of gold on its back. That second fiddle of a Consul is said to have undertaken the business, and to be keeping distributing agents at his house. *I* don't believe that, but two vexatious decrees, which are thought to be aimed at the Consul, have now been passed at the instance of Cato and Domitius, one permitting magistrates' houses to be searched, the other declaring it an offence against the state to harbour distributing agents in one's house. Moreover Lurco the Tribune, an office at declared enmity with the lex Aelia, has been dispensed from its provisions and those of the lex Fufia[78] too, to enable him to propose a law on bribery which he had promulgated – his lameness makes a fine omen! So the elections have been put off till 27 July. The novel feature in his law is that any person promising money in a tribe shall not be punishable provided he does not pay it; but if he does, he shall be liable for HS 3000 to every tribe for life. I said that P. Clodius had already complied with this law, being in the habit of promising and then not paying. But note! That consular office of which I have had so much to say, which Curio once used to call an apotheosis, will be worth no more than a rat's tail if this fellow is elected. Therefore I suppose one must take to letters, as you do, and not care a button for their Consulships.

You say you have decided not to go to Asia.[79] For my part I would rather you had been going, and I have some fear of awkwardness arising over it.

75. See n. 35.

76. i.e., L. Afranius, whose father's *praenomen* was Aulus. But the point of the nickname is uncertain (possibly from the first two letters of the name: *A.f.* = *Auli filius*).

77. Philip II of Macedon.

78. These two laws, sometimes mentioned as one, restricted the legislative powers of Tribunes.

79. The Roman province, of which Q. Cicero was now governor. Cicero had hoped that Atticus would take a position on his staff.

Still I can't blame your decision, especially as I have not gone out to a province myself.

I shall make do with the mottoes that you have put in your Shrine of Amalthea, especially as Thyillus has forsaken me and Archias has written nothing *à mon sujet*. I'm afraid that having composed a Greek poem for the Luculli he may now be thinking in terms of Caecilian drama.[80]

I have thanked Antonius on your behalf, and have given the letter to Mallius. The reason why I have not written to you more often in the past is that I had no suitable bearer and was not sufficiently sure of your address. I have given you a fine write-up.

If Cincius brings me any affair of yours, I shall see to it; but at present he is more concerned with one of his own, in which I am doing what I can for him. If you are going to be in one place, you may expect plenty of letters from me. But send even more yourself. I should be grateful for a description of your Shrine of Amalthea, its furnishings and layout; and would you send me any poems or narratives you have about her? I have an *envie* to make one on my place at Arpinum. I shall be sending you a sample of my writings. I have nothing quite finished.

II

CICERO TO ATTICUS

Rome, 20 January 60

I must tell you that what I most badly need at the present time is a confidant – someone with whom I could share all that gives me any anxiety, a wise, affectionate friend to whom I could talk without pretence or evasion or concealment. My brother, the soul of candour and affection, is away. *[81] is not a *person* at all – only 'sea-shore and air' and 'mere solitude'. And you whose talk and advice has so often lightened my worry

---

80. i.e., Archias might write a poem in praise of one of the Caecilii Metelli instead of writing about Cicero. 'Caecilian drama' plays on the name of the early comic dramatist Caecilius Statius.

81. The manuscripts have 'Metellus', which seems to be a mistake for some other name, though it is conceivable that Cicero is replying to a reference by Atticus to the Consul, Metellus Celer. The quoted words must come from a Latin play.

and vexation of spirit, the partner in my public life and intimate of all my private concerns, the sharer of all my talk and plans, where are you? I am so utterly forsaken that my only moments of relaxation are those I spend with my wife, my little daughter, and my darling Marcus. My brilliant, worldly friendships may make a fine show in public, but in the home they are barren things. My house is crammed of a morning, I go down to the Forum surrounded by droves of friends, but in all the multitude I cannot find one with whom I can pass an unguarded joke or fetch a private sigh. That is why I am writing and longing for you, why I now fairly summon you home. There are many things to worry and vex me, but once I have you here to listen I feel I can pour them all away in a single walk and talk.

Of private worries with all their pricks and pains I shall say nothing. I won't commit them to this letter and an unknown courier. They are not *very* distressing (I don't want to upset you), but still they are on my mind, nagging away, with no friendly talk and advice to set them at rest. As for the state, I am ready enough to do my part, but time and again the medicine itself injures the patient. I need only summarize what has taken place since your departure for you to cry out perforce that Rome is doomed. I believe it was after you left that the Clodian drama came on to the stage. I thought I saw there a chance to cut back licence and teach the young folk a lesson. So I played *fortissimo*, put my whole heart and brain into the effort, not from any personal animus but in the hope, I won't say of reforming our society, but at least of healing its wounds.

Then came the calamity of a bought, debauched trial. Mark what followed. A Consul[82] was thrust upon us whom only philosophers like you and me could look at without a sigh. There was a blow! The Senate passed a decree on electoral bribery and another on the courts, but no law was carried through. The Senate was abused, the Knights estranged because of the provision 'whoever as juror . . .'[83] Thus the year saw the overthrow of the two foundations of the constitution which I (and I alone) had established. The authority of the Senate was thrown in the dust and the harmony of the orders dissolved. Now this fine new year is upon us. It has begun with failure to perform the annual rites of the Goddess of Youth, Memmius having initiated M. Lucullus' wife into rites of his own. Menelaus took this hard and divorced the lady – but the shepherd of Ida

82. Afranius.
83. The Knights had previously been immune from prosecutions for judicial corruption.

in olden days only flouted Menelaus, whereas our modern Paris has wiped his boots on *Agamemnon as well.*[84]

There is a Tribune called *C. Herennius,* whom perhaps you don't even know, though you *may* know him because he belongs to your tribe and his father Sextus used to disburse your gratuities. He is trying to make a plebeian out of P. Clodius and proposing that the assembly of the whole people should vote on Clodius' matter in the Campus Martius.[85] I gave him my usual warm reception in the Senate, but he is a complete pachyderm.

Metellus is an excellent Consul and a good friend of mine, but he has lost face by having promulgated the same proposal about Clodius, as a matter of form. As for Aulus' son, gods above, what a lazy, poor-spirited warrior! All he is fit for is to offer himself as a daily butt for Palicanus' abuse, which is what he does. An agrarian law has been promulgated by Flavius, an irresponsible affair, pretty much the same as the Plotia.[86] But all the while not so much as the shadow of a statesman is to be found. The man who might have been one, my friend – for so he is, let me tell you – Pompey, lives up to that lovely embroidered gown[87] of his by holding his tongue. From Crassus not a word that might lose him popularity. The others you know. They seem fools enough to expect to keep their fishponds after losing constitutional freedom. The one man who cares for that, with more resolution and integrity, it seems to me, than judgement or intelligence, is Cato. He has now been over two months tormenting the unfortunate tax-farmers, who were his devoted friends, and won't let the Senate give them an answer. So we are unable to pass any decrees on other matters until the tax-farmers are given their answer,[88] which I suppose will mean that the deputations will be put off.

You see now what heavy seas we are in, and if between these lines such as they are you read other things which I leave unwritten, rejoin us at long last. The conditions here to which I am asking you to return are such that anyone might wish to run away from them, but I hope you value my affection enough to want to get back to *that,* even with all the accompany-

---

84. The rites of the goddess Juventas (Youth) were in the charge of the Lucullus family. It is implied that Memmius (Paris) had been involved with the wives of both M. Lucullus (Menelaus) and his elder brother Lucius (Agamemnon).

85. In order to qualify for office as Tribune, Clodius (a patrician) had to become a plebeian (this was finally arranged by means of an adoption).

86. Nothing is known of this law.

87. At Caesar's instance Pompey had been authorized to wear triumphal insignia, including the special embroidered gown, at public shows.

88. They wanted to be released from a public contract which had turned out unprofitably.

ing disagreeables. As to being registered in your absence, I shall see that a notice is published and displayed everywhere. But registration at the very end of the census period is real businessman's style. So let us see you as soon as may be. Keep well. 20 January, Q. Metellus and L. Afranius being Consuls.

12
CICERO TO ATTICUS

Antium, April 59

I promised you in an earlier letter that there would be work to show for this spell away from home, but I am no longer very positive on the point. I have taken so kindly to idleness that I can't tear myself away from it. So I either amuse myself with books, of which I have a goodly store at Antium, or I count the waves – the weather is unsuitable for fishing mackerel. To writing I feel a downright repugnance. The Geography which I had purposed is really a big undertaking. Eratosthenes, whom I had meant to follow, is sharply censured by Serapio and Hipparchus. What if Tyrannio joins in? And really the material is hard to set out, monotonous, not so easy to embellish as it looked, and (the main point) I find any excuse good enough for doing nothing. I am even considering whether I might not settle down here at Antium and see this whole period through. I had sooner have been *duovir*[89] here than Consul in Rome. You were wiser than I in getting a house in Buthrotum. Yet I can assure you there is not much to choose between that town and this community of Antium. One can hardly believe that there could be a place so near Rome where many of the inhabitants have never seen Vatinius, where no member of the Board of Twenty[90] has a single well-wisher besides myself, where nobody disturbs me and everybody likes me. Yes, this is surely the place to practise politics. In Rome that is impossible, and what is more I am sick of it. So I shall compose *histoires inédites* which I shall read to nobody but you, in the vein of Theopompus or a lot more savage even.

89. One of the two chief magistrates of Antium, corresponding to the Consuls in Rome.
90. Commission set up by Caesar to supervise land distribution.

And my sole form of political activity now is to hate the rascals, and even that I do without spleen – rather with a certain relish in *.

But to come to business, I have written to the City Quaestors about Quintus' affair.[91] See what they have to say, whether there is any hope of denarii or whether we must let ourselves be foisted off with Pompey's cistophores. Also make up your mind what's to be done about the wall. What else? Oh yes, let me know when you think of leaving Rome.

13

CICERO TO ATTICUS

Formiae, c. 26 April 59

How you whet my appetite about your talk with Bibulus, your discussion with Ox-Eyes,[92] and that apolaustic dinner party too! So come expecting greedy ears. But the most serious danger we now have to fear in my opinion is that when our Sampsiceramus[93] realizes that his name is mud in every man's mouth and sees that these proceedings are very liable to be upset, he may start plunging. For my part I have so lost my manly spirit that I prefer to be tyrannized over in peace and quiet such as is now rotting our fibre than to fight with the rosiest prospect of success.

You are always urging me to composition, but it's out of the question. It's not a country house I have here but a public exchange, so many of the good folk of Formiae come in ***. But never mind the multitude – after 10 o'clock the common run doesn't bother me. But my closest neighbour is one C. Arrius, or rather room-mate, for that is what he has now become. He actually says he won't go to Rome because he wants to philosophize with me here all day long. Then on the other side there is Catulus' friend Sebosus. Where is a man to turn? I would go to Arpinum right away upon my word, only it's clearly most convenient for me to expect you at Formiae – up to 6 May that is, no longer, for look at the kind of people I am

91. The question was whether Q. Cicero was to be paid his allowances as governor in Roman or Asiatic currency.

92. The Greek word *boôpis* is a stock Homeric epithet for Hera. Cicero uses it as a nickname for Clodia, who *had* large, brilliant eyes; also Hera was the wife of her brother, Zeus.

93. Ruler of a principality in Syria, hence a nickname for Pompey.

condemned to listen to! What a marvellous opportunity for anyone who might be interested in buying my place here while these fellows are on my carpet! And yet you say, and very fine too, 'Let's attack something big, something that needs plenty of thought and time.' However, I shan't disappoint you nor spare my pains.

14
CICERO TO ATTICUS

Formiae, 29 April or 1 May 59

Dinner was over and I had already begun to nod when (29 April) I received your letter about the Campanian Domain. In a word, it gave me such a shock at first that sleep became impossible, but rather from activity than distress of mind. The points which occur to me as I turn the matter over are more or less as follows: In the first place, from what you wrote in your previous letter, that you had heard from a friend of Caesar's that something would be proposed which nobody would disapprove of, I had expected something on a pretty large scale. This doesn't have that appearance. Then (I'm comforting myself, you see) all expectation of land allotment seems to have been channelled into the Campanian Domain, and that, at seven acres per man, cannot support more than 5,000 grantees; so they are bound to lose the support of the multitude left over. Moreover if anything could further inflame better-class sentiment, roused already as it evidently is, assuredly this will do it; especially since after the abolition of customs duties in Italy and the distribution of the Campanian Domain the only internal revenue left is the five per cent[94] – and that will probably be swept away by the shouts of our footmen at a single scratch assembly.

What our friend Gnaeus is up to now I simply do not know:

> On tiny pipes no longer now he blows,
> But, mouthband off, he puffs and blasts amain,[95]

seeing that he's allowed himself to be pushed even to this length. Hitherto he has quibbled, taking the line that he approves of Caesar's legislation,

94. A tax on the manumission of slaves.
95. From Sophocles (fr. 768).

but that Caesar himself must take responsibility for his procedure. Thus he (Pompey) was in favour of the agrarian bill, but whether opportunity was given for a veto or not was no concern of his. He was in favour of settling the King of Egypt's affair[96] at long last, but whether or not Bibulus had been watching the skies[97] at the time it was not his business to inquire. As for the tax-farmers, he had wished to oblige the Equestrian Order, but could not be expected to prophesy all that would happen if Bibulus went down to the Forum at that juncture. Very well, my good Sampsiceramus, but what are you going to say now? That you have arranged a revenue for us in Mt Antilibanus, and taken away our rents in Campania? How are you going to make that sound convincing? Perhaps the answer will be: 'I'll keep you under with Caesar's army.' Oh no you won't. It won't be that army of yours that will keep me under so much as the ingratitude of the honest men as they are called, who have never made me the slightest return or recompense, material or even verbal. But if I had urged myself in that direction I should surely have found some method of opposition before now. Things being as they are, my mind is made up. Since your friend Dicaearchus and my favourite Theophrastus are so much at loggerheads, your man rating the active life far and away the best and mine the contemplative, I mean to figure as one who has humoured them both. For I think I have done quite enough to satisfy Dicaearchus; now I turn to the other school, which not only permits me to rest from my labours but scolds me for labouring in the first place. So, Titus mine, let me throw myself into my studies, those wonderful studies which I ought never to have left and to which I must now at last return.

You write of my brother Quintus' letter. He wrote to me in the same strain, 'in like a lion, out like a –'[98] well, I don't quite know what to call it. In his opening lines he laments having to stay on in a way that would move a heart of stone; then again he so far relaxes as to ask me to correct and publish his history. But please pay attention to the point about excise duty on transferred goods.[99] He says that he has referred the question to the Senate on the advice of his council. Evidently he had not read my letter in which, after thorough reflection and inquiry, I propounded to him that

96. The restoration of King Ptolemy XII, 'The Piper'. See Letter 23.

97. The announcement by a magistrate of his intention to 'watch the skies' (for omens from lightning) was generally regarded as a ban on prospective assembly, since by reporting an unfavourable omen he could make it illegal for the assembly to transact business. Caesar, however, took no notice of this form of obstruction.

98. Beginning of *Iliad*, VI. 181: 'In front a lion, behind a snake, in the middle a Chimaera.'

99. i.e., transferred from one harbour to another and so paying double duty.

no tax is due. If any provincials have already come to Rome from Asia on this matter I should be grateful if you would see them and, if you think fit, explain to them my views on it. If they can reach a settlement, then, to keep the good cause alive in the Senate, I shall not fail the tax-farmers. Otherwise, to be frank with you, on this matter my sentiments are rather with the entire province of Asia and the local businessmen, who are also very closely concerned. I feel that what I suggest is very important to us. But you will see to it.

Tell me about the Quaestors. Are they boggling even about paying in cistophores?[100] I ask because if nothing else is forthcoming, when we have tried all we know, I shouldn't despise even that last resort.

We shall see you at Arpinum and welcome you in country style since you have scorned our seaside hospitality.

15

CICERO TO ATTICUS

Rome, between 7 and 14 July 59

I have many things on my mind, arising from the grave political crisis and these dangers that menace me personally. They are legion, but nothing distresses me more than Statius'[101] manumission.

> That my commands – no, set commands aside, that my displeasure
> Should count with him for nothing![102]

And yet I don't know what to do, and, after all, the talk is more than the thing itself. Moreover I can't even be angry with those I really love. I am only pained, deeply pained. My other troubles are set in great affairs. Clodius' threats and the combats I have to expect give me only moderate concern, for I think I can either face them with all honour or decline them without embarrassment. Perhaps you will say that we have had enough

---

100. See Letter 12, fin.
101. Quintus' dependence on this slave had become a scandal.
102. From Terence's comedy *Phormio*, 232.

of honour – *le siècle du gland est passé*[103] – and implore me to think of security. Oh dear, why are you not here? Nothing, I am sure, would escape you, whereas I perhaps am blind and hold too fast to that which is good.

The truth is that the present régime is the most infamous, disgraceful, and uniformly odious to all sorts and classes and ages of men that ever was, more so upon my word than I could have wished, let alone expected. These 'popular' politicians have taught even quiet folk to hiss. Bibulus is *in excelsis*,[104] I don't know why, but they laud him as though he were the man who 'singly by delaying saved our all'.[105] My beloved Pompey, to my great sorrow, has been the author of his own downfall. They hold nobody by goodwill; that they may find it necessary to use terror is what I am afraid of. For my part I do not fight what they are doing on account of my friendship with him, and I do not endorse it, for that would be to condemn all that I did in days gone by. I take a middle way.

Popular sentiment has been most manifest at the theatre and the shows. At the gladiators both the Showmaster and his guests (?)[106] were overwhelmed with hisses. At the Games of Apollo Diphilus the actor attacked poor Pompey quite brutally: 'To our misfortune art thou Great'[107] – there were a dozen encores.

> 'But that same manhood bitterly
> In time to come shalt thou lament.'

The whole audience vociferated applause as he spoke that, and the rest also. Indeed these lines might seem to have been written for the occasion by an enemy of Pompey. 'If neither law nor custom can constrain', etc., was recited to a loud accompaniment of shouting and clapping. When Caesar entered, applause was non-existent. He was followed by Curio junior, who received the sort of ovation that Pompey used to get in the days before freedom fell. Caesar took it badly, and a letter is said to be winging its way to Pompey in Capua. They hate the Knights, who stood up to applaud Curio, they are at war with the whole community. They

103. A Greek saying: 'We don't eat acorns any more.' The French rendering (from Voltaire) is due to G. E. Jeans.

104. The Consul Bibulus had shut himself up in his house, from which he 'watched the skies' and issued manifestos against the 'Triumvirs'.

105. Ennius' well-known line on Hannibal's opponent in the Second Punic War, Fabius Cunctator (*Annals*, 370).

106. Probably the Showmaster is Gabinius and his guests are the 'Triumvirs'.

107. This and the following quotations come from an unknown Latin tragedy.

threaten the Roscian law,[108] even the corn law. It's a pretty kettle of fish. I myself should have preferred their game to run its course in silence, but I am afraid that may not be possible. Public opinion won't endure it any longer, yet endured apparently it must be. But now there is only one universal cry, though with hatred rather than power behind it.

Dear Publius is threatening me, most hostile. The business is looming, and you will naturally make haste back to meet it. I think I have very firm backing in my old consular army of all honest men, including the moderately honest. Pompey signifies goodwill towards me out of the ordinary. He also assures me that Clodius will not say a word about me, wherein he does not deceive me but is himself deceived. When Cosconius[109] died I was invited to take his place. That would have been what is called stepping into the breach – a signal public disgrace and worse than useless even as regards 'security'. For they are unpopular with the honest men, I with the rascals. I should have kept my own unpopularity and accepted other people's as well. Caesar wants to have me on his staff.[110] That would be a more respectable evasion of the danger, which however I do not decline. It comes to this, I would rather fight. But my mind is not made up. Again I say, 'If only you were here!' However, if the need arises I shall send for you.

What else now, let me see. This, I think. I am certain that Rome is finished. Why go on mincing words?

But I write this in haste and I am really afraid of saying too much. In future letters I shall either put everything down in plain terms, if I get hold of a thoroughly trustworthy messenger, or else, if I write obscurely, you will none the less understand. In such letters I shall call myself Laelius and you Furius.[111] The rest shall be in veiled language.

I am sedulous here in my attentions to Caecilius. I hear Bibulus' edicts have been sent to you. They have put Pompey in a passion of rage and chagrin.

108. A law of 67 assigning the first fourteen rows in the theatre to the Knights (the Senate sat in the orchestra).
109. A member of Caesar's agrarian Board of Twenty.
110. In Gaul; see Introduction.
111. After C. Laelius Sapiens and L. Furius Philus, friends of the younger Scipio Africanus.

Rome, after 25 July 59

On politics I need not go into detail. The republic is finished. Its plight is all the sadder than when you left because at that time it looked as though the authoritarian régime was agreeable to the masses and, though odious, not actually lethal to their betters; whereas now it is all at once so universally detested that we tremble to think where it will erupt. We know by experience the violent temper and recklessness of these men, who in their rage against Cato have brought Rome to ruin; but they did seem to be using a mild form of poison, so that we might reasonably hope for a painless death. But now I am afraid that what with the hisses of the crowd and the talk of the respectable and the outcry in the country, they are thoroughly exasperated. For my part, as I often remarked to you in conversation as well as in writing, I used to hope that the political wheel had turned so smoothly that we could hardly hear the sound or see the track upon the ground. And so it would have been, if folk had had the patience to wait for the storm to pass over. But after sighing for a long while in secret they at last began to groan, and now finally to cry out in universal protest.

So there is our poor friend,[112] unused to disrepute, his whole career passed in a blaze of admiration and glory, now physically disfigured and broken in spirit, at his wit's end for what to do. He sees the precipice if he goes on and the stigma of a turncoat if he turns back. The honest men are his enemies, the rascals themselves are not his friends. See now how soft-hearted I am. I could not keep back my tears when I saw him addressing a public meeting on 25 July about Bibulus' edicts. How magnificently he used to posture on that platform in other days, surrounded by an adoring people, every man wishing him well! How humble and abject he was then, what a sorry figure he cut in his own eyes, to say nothing of his audience! What a sight! Only Crassus could enjoy it, not so others. He was a fallen star, one looked upon him as a man who had *slid* rather than moved of his own volition. I suppose that if Apelles had seen his Venus or Protogenes his Ialysus[113] daubed with filth, he would have

112. Pompey.
113. Cicero had seen this painting of a legendary hero in Rhodes.

felt a pang as sharp as mine at the sight of this figure, painted and embellished with all the colours of my art, now suddenly made ugly. In view of the Clodius affair[114] nobody expects me to be his friend, yet my affection for him was more than any injury could dissipate. Naturally Bibulus' Archilochian edicts against him are so agreeable to the public that one can't get past the place where they are posted for the crowd of readers. To their subject they are so painful that his mortification is making him look ill. To me I must say they are unpleasant, both because they torment too savagely a man for whom I have always had a regard and because I am afraid that impetuous as he is, a fierce fighter not accustomed to insults, he may give free rein to his mortification and anger.

Where Bibulus will end up I don't know. As things stand at the moment he is in wonderfully high repute. When he postponed the elections till October, a thing which generally runs counter to the popular wish, Caesar thought he might stir up a public meeting with a speech into going for Bibulus' house. After a long, highly inflammatory harangue he could not raise a murmur. In short, they realize that they have no support in any section of society, which makes the danger of violence all the greater.

Clodius is hostile. Pompey continues to assure me that he will do nothing against me. It would be dangerous for me to believe that, and I am getting ready to defend myself. I hope to have strong support from all classes. I miss you, and the facts of the case call for your return to meet the crisis. Your presence at the pinch will strengthen me vastly in policy and courage and actual defensive power. I am well satisfied with Varro. Pompey talks marvellously. I hope I shall at least come off with much honour or actually avoid any unpleasantness.

See that you keep me informed on your side of your doings and amusements and your dealings with the good people of Sicyon.

114. Pompey had collaborated in arranging for Clodius' adoption by a plebeian and consequent election as Tribune.

CICERO TO ATTICUS

En route, *c. 24 (?) March 58*

I hope I may see the day when I shall thank you for making me go on living. So far I am heartily sorry you did. But I beg you to come to me as soon as possible at Vibo,[115] where I am going. I have changed direction for many reasons. But if you come there, I shall be able to make a plan for my whole journey and exile. If you do not do that, I shall be surprised; but I am confident you will.

18

CICERO TO HIS FAMILY

Brundisium, 29 April 58

From Tullius to his dear Terentia and Tullia and Marcus greetings.

I send you letters less often than I have opportunity, because, wretched as every hour is for me, when I write to you at home or read your letters I am so overcome with tears that I cannot bear it. If only I had been less anxious to save my life! Assuredly I should have seen no sorrow in my days, or not much. If fortune has spared me for some hope of one day recovering some measure of well-being, my error has not been so total. But if these present evils are to stay, then, yes, I want to see you, dear heart, as soon as I can, and to die in your arms, since neither the Gods whom you have worshipped so piously nor the men to whose service I have always devoted myself have made us any recompense.

I have stayed in Brundisium for thirteen days with M. Laenius Flaccus, a very worthy gentleman. He has disregarded the danger to his own property and status in his concern for my safety, and refused to be deterred

---

115. Cicero was on his way into exile. In fact, Atticus did not join him in south Italy.

by the penalties of a wicked law[116] from carrying out the established duties of hospitality and friendship. I pray that one day I may be able to show him my gratitude. Grateful I shall always be. I am leaving Brundisium on 29 April and making for Cyzicus by way of Macedonia.

Ah, what a desperate, pitiful case is mine! What now? Shall I ask you to come – a sick woman, physically and spiritually exhausted? Shall I *not* ask then? Am I to live without you? Perhaps I should put it like this: if there is any hope of my return, you must build it up, and help in the campaign. On the other hand if all is over, as I fear, then come to me any way you can. Be sure of one thing: if I have you, I shall not feel that I am utterly lost. But what is to become of my Tulliola? You at home must take care of that – I have nothing to suggest. But assuredly, however matters turn out, the poor little girl's marriage and good name must be a primary consideration. Then there is my son. What will he do? I hope that *he* will always be with me, my darling child. I cannot write any more now. Grief clogs my pen.

How you have fared I do not know – whether you still have something left, or, as I fear, have been stripped of all. Yes, I trust that Piso[117] will always be faithful. You need not worry about the freeing of the household. In the first place, the promise made to your people was that you would treat each case on its merits (Orpheus, in fact, is loyal so far, none of the others very noticeably so). The position of the other slaves is that if it turned out that my property was no longer mine, they would be my freedmen, provided they could make good their claim to the status; whereas, if I still had a hold on them, they would remain my slaves except for just a few. But these are minor matters.

You urge me to hold my head high and hope for restoration. I wish the facts may give ground for reasonable hope. Meanwhile, as matters wretchedly stand, when am I going to get your next letter? Who will bring it to me? I should have waited for it at Brundisium if the sailors had let me, but they did not want to lose the fair weather.

For the rest, dearest Terentia, bear up with all the dignity you can muster. It has been a good life, a great career. The good in me, nothing bad, has brought me down. I have done nothing wrong, except that when I lost the good things of life I did not lose life itself. But if it was more for our children's happiness that I should live, let us bear what remains,

---

116. Clodius' bill, as amended, allowed Cicero to live at a distance of not less than 400 (or 500) miles from Rome, but provided that his outlawry should begin from the date of its passage.

117. Tullia's husband, C. Calpurnius Piso Frugi.

intolerable though it be. And yet, while I tell you to be strong, I cannot tell myself.

I am sending Clodius Philhetaerus back, because he is hampered by eye-trouble. He is a faithful fellow. Sallustius is the most forward of all. Pescennius is full of kindly feeling towards me; I think he will always be attentive to you. Sicca had told me that he would stay with me, but has left Brundisium.

Take care of your health as best you can, and believe that your unhappiness grieves me more than my own. My dear Terentia, loyalest and best of wives, my darling little daughter, and Marcus, our one remaining hope – goodbye.

29 April, from Brundisium.

19
CICERO TO HIS BROTHER

Thessalonica, 13 June 58

From Marcus to his brother Quintus greetings.

My brother, my brother, my brother! Were you really afraid that I was angry with you for some reason and on that account sent boys to you without a letter, or even did not want to see you? *I* angry with *you*? How *could* I be? As though it was *you* who struck me down, *your* enemies, *your* unpopularity, and not *I* who have lamentably caused *your* downfall! That much-lauded Consulship of mine has robbed me of you, and my children, and my country, and my possessions; I only hope it has robbed you of nothing but myself. Sure it is that you have never given me cause for anything but pride and pleasure, whereas I have brought you sorrow for my calamity, fear of your own, loss, grief, loneliness. *I* not want to see *you*? No, it was rather that I did not want to be seen by you! You would not have seen your brother, the man you left in Rome, the man you knew, the man who saw you off and said goodbye with mutual tears – you would not have seen any trace or shadow of *him*; only a likeness of a breathing corpse.

Would that you had seen me or heard of me dead before this happened!

Would that I had left you as the survivor not of my life only but of my standing! But I call all the Gods to witness that one saying called me back from death – everyone told me that some part of your life was bound up in mine. I was wrong, criminally wrong. If I had died, the fact itself would stand as ample proof of my brotherly love for you. Instead, through my fault you have to do without me and stand in need of others while I am alive, and my voice, which has often defended strangers, is silent when my own flesh and blood is in danger.[118]

As for the fact that my boys came to you without a letter, since you see that anger was not the reason, the reason was surely inertia and an endless stream of tears and grieving. You can imagine how I weep as I write these lines, as I am sure you do as you read them. Can I help thinking of you sometimes, or ever think of you without tears? When I miss you, I do not miss you as a brother only, but as a delightful brother almost of my own age,[119] a son in obedience, a father in wisdom. What pleasure did I ever take apart from you or you apart from me? And then at the same time I miss my daughter, the most loving, modest, and clever daughter a man ever had, the image of my face and speech and mind. Likewise my charming, darling little boy, whom I, cruel brute that I am, put away from my arms. All too wise for his years, the poor child already understood what was going on. Likewise your son, your[120] image, whom my boy loved like a brother and had begun to respect like an elder brother. As for my loyalest of wives, poor, unhappy soul, I did not let her come with me so that there should be someone to protect the remnants of our common disaster, our children.

However, I did write to you as best I could and gave the letter to your freedman Philogonus. I expect it was delivered to you later. In it I urge and ask of you, as in the verbal message brought you by my boys, to go straight on to Rome and make haste. To begin with, I wanted you to stand guard in case there may be enemies whose cruelty is not yet satisfied by our downfall. Secondly, I was afraid of the outburst of grief which our meeting would have brought on. As for parting, I could not have borne it, and I feared the very thing you say in your letter, that you might not endure to be separated from me. For these reasons the heavy affliction of not seeing you, which seems the bitterest, saddest thing that could happen to

118. Quintus had reason to fear that a charge might be brought against him in connection with his record as governor of Asia.

119. Text doubtful.

120. 'My' (*meam*), according to the manuscripts.

brothers so affectionate and close as we are, was less bitter and sad than our meeting would have been, and still more our parting.

Now if you can do what I, whom you always thought a strong man, am unable to do, then stand up and brace yourself for the struggle you may have to sustain. I should hope (if any hope of mine counts for anything) that your integrity, the affection in which you are held in the community, and in some degree also the pity felt for myself will bring you protection. If, however, it turns out that your hands are free of that danger, you will doubtless do what you think can be done, if anything, about me. I get many letters from many people on the subject and they make themselves out to be hopeful. But for my own part I can't see any grounds for hope, when my enemies are in power and my friends have either deserted or actually betrayed me. Perhaps the idea of my coming home frightens them as involving blame for their own villainy. But please see how things stand in Rome and make them clear to me. In spite of all, I shall go on living as long as you need me, if you find you have to go through an ordeal. Live any longer in this kind of life I cannot. No worldly wisdom or philosophic instruction is strong enough to endure such anguish. I know I had the opportunity to die a more honourable and useful death, but that is only one of many chances I let slip. If I were to bewail past mistakes, I should only be adding to your sorrow and exposing my own folly. One thing I ought not and cannot do, and that is to linger on in so miserable and dishonourable an existence any longer than your predicament or a well-grounded hope shall demand. Once I was happy indeed, in my brother, children, wife, means, even in the very nature of my wealth,[121] the equal of any man that ever lived in prestige, moral standing, reputation, influence. Now in my abject ruin I cannot bear to mourn myself and mine much longer.

Why then did you write to me about a bill of exchange?[122] As though your resources were not supporting me at present. Ah, how well I see and feel what a wicked thing I did! You are about to pay your creditors with your heart's blood and your son's, while I squandered to no purpose the money which I received from the Treasury on your behalf.[123] However,

---

121. Apart from his inherited fortune this was mainly derived from legacies left by grateful clients.

122. Quintus will have offered to negotiate a bill in Rome, the money to be paid to his brother in Thessalonica.

123. See n. 91.

both M. Antonius and Caepio[124] were paid the sums you had mentioned. As for me, what I have is enough for my present purposes. Whether I am restored or given up for lost, no more is needed.

If you have any trouble, I advise you to go to Crassus and Calidius. How much faith you should put in Hortensius I don't know. He behaved to *me* most villainously and treacherously, while pretending the warmest affection and sedulously keeping up our daily intercourse. Q. Arrius joined him in this. Through their policies and promises and advice I was left in the lurch and fell into my present plight. But you will keep all this under cover, lest it tell against you. Be careful of one thing (and for that reason I think you should conciliate Hortensius himself through Pomponius): that epigram about the lex Aurelia which was attributed to you when you were standing for the Aedileship,[125] mind it doesn't get established by false evidence.[126] My principal fear is that when people realize how much pity your entreaties and your escape from a prosecution is going to arouse for us, they will attack you the more vigorously. I think Messalla[127] is on your side. Pompey, I think, is still pretending. If only you don't have to put all this to the test! I should pray to the Gods for that if they had not given up listening to my prayers. None the less, I do pray that they may be content with these boundless afflictions of ours, which, however, are free from any stigma of wrong-doing. The whole tragedy is that fine actions have been cruelly penalized.

My brother, I need not commend my daughter (and yours) and our Marcus to your care. On the contrary, I grieve to think that their orphaned state will bring you no less sorrow than me. But while you are safe, they will not be orphans. I swear that tears forbid me to write of other things – so may I be granted some salvation and the power to die in my country! Please look after Terentia too, and write back to me on all matters. Be as brave as the nature of the case permits.

Ides of June, Thessalonica.

124. Better known as M. Brutus.

125. In 66.

126. It can be supposed that the epigram was offensive to Pompey and Crassus, since the lex Aurelia of 70, revising the Roman jury system, was passed in their Consulship with their support. Cicero seems to have feared that Hortensius might confirm its attribution to Quintus out of spite. As an opponent of the law he would be a credible witness.

127. The Consul of 61, as generally supposed. Perhaps more probably Hortensius' nephew Messalla Rufus, Consul in 53.

20

CICERO TO ATTICUS

Thessalonica, 5 August 58

Though I wrote to you that I should stay in Epirus, I changed my mind when I saw that my chances were thinning and fading away, and have not moved from Thessalonica. I had decided to stay there until I heard something from you about what you said in your last letter, namely that some move would be made about my case in the Senate after the elections, Pompey having told you so. Well, the elections are over and you don't write a word to me, so I shall regard that as equivalent to writing that there is nothing doing, and I shall not take it too hard that for no very long time I have been amused by hope. As for the change likely to turn to my advantage which you wrote that you saw coming, those who come from Rome say that nothing of the kind will happen. The remaining hope lies in the Tribunes-Designate. If I wait for that, you will have no reason to think that I have failed in what I owe to my cause and my friends' good-will.

You repeatedly take me to task for bearing what has happened to me so hard, but you ought to forgive me when you see how I am tried beyond anything you ever witnessed or heard of. You say you hear that grief has actually disturbed the balance of my mind. No, my mind is sound enough. If it had only been equally so in the hour of danger, when I experienced the cruellest malice from those who I thought cared most about my welfare! The moment they saw me a little unnerved and inclined to waver, they pushed me on, employing all their wickedness and perfidy to bring about my downfall.[128]

As matters stand I must go to Cyzicus, where letters will reach me less often. So I hope you will be all the more careful to send me full reports of everything you think I ought to know. Be good to my brother Quintus. If I leave him out of danger (ah me!), I shall not feel I am altogether lost. Dispatched Nones of August.

---

128. This is aimed especially at Hortensius (cf. the foregoing letter to Quintus). How much warrant Cicero had for such accusations is uncertain.

21

CICERO TO ATTICUS

Rome, about 10 September 57

As soon as I arrived in Rome and came by a suitable person to take a letter to you, I considered it my first duty to congratulate you on my return. I had found you, to be quite frank, neither bolder nor wiser than myself as an adviser, nor, I may add, excessively sedulous in guarding me from harm in default of observances on my part to make you so. But I also found that, having in the early days shared my error, or rather infatuation, and participated in my false alarm, you felt our severance most keenly, and devoted a vast amount of time and zeal and patience and labour to bringing about my return. And so I sincerely assure you that in the plenitude of longed-for joy and congratulation one thing has been wanting to make my cup flow over: to see you, or rather to hold you in my arms. Once I win that happiness, if ever I let it go and if I do not also claim all the arrears of your delightful company that are owing to me, I shall really consider myself hardly worthy of this restitution of my fortunes.

Of my general position it can so far be said that I have attained what I thought would be most difficult to recover, namely my public prestige, my standing in the Senate, and my influence among the honest men, in larger measure than I had dreamed possible. But my private affairs are in a very poor way – you are aware how my property has been crippled and dissipated and pillaged – and I stand in need not so much of your resources, which I count as my own, as of your advice in pulling together what is left and putting it on a sound footing.

I shall now give you a brief account of such matters as I think you will particularly like to learn from my pen, though I expect you have already been informed in letters from your own people or for that matter by report and general rumour.

I left Dyrrachium on 4 August, the very day on which the law for my recall was put to the vote. I landed at Brundisium on the Nones of August. My little Tullia was there to welcome me. It was her birthday and also, as it happened, the foundation day of the colony of Brundisium and of the temple of your neighbour the Goddess of Weal, a coincidence which attracted popular notice and was joyfully celebrated by the townsfolk. On 11 August (?), while at Brundisium, I learned by letter from Quintus that the law had been carried in the Assembly of Centuries amid remarkable demonstrations of enthusiasm by all ranks and ages and with an extraordinary concourse of country voters. Thence I set out, after receiving the most flattering marks of regard from the townspeople, and as I travelled along I was joined by congratulatory deputations from all quarters.

So I arrived at the outskirts of Rome. Not a man whose name was known to my nomenclator, no matter what his rank, but came out to meet me, except for enemies who could neither conceal nor deny the fact that they were such. When I reached the Porta Capena I found the steps of the temples thronged by the common people, who welcomed me with vociferous applause. Like numbers and applause followed me to the Capitol. In the Forum and on the Capitol itself the crowd was spectacular. In the Senate on the following day, the Nones of September, I made a speech of thanks to the House.

Two days later I spoke again. The price of grain had risen very high, and a crowd flocked first to the theatre and then to the Senate, clamouring at Clodius' instigation that the shortage was my doing. The Senate met during those days to consider the grain situation, and there was a general demand, not only from the populace but from the honest men too, that Pompey be asked to take charge of supplies. He himself was eager for the commission, and the crowd called on me by name to propose it. I did so in a full-dress speech. In the absence of all the Consulars except Messalla and Afranius, because, as they alleged, it was not safe for them to speak, the Senate passed a decree as proposed by me, to the effect that Pompey should be asked to undertake the matter and appropriate legislation be introduced. The decree was recited immediately, and the people applauded after the silly new-fangled fashion when my name was read out. I then addressed them at the invitation of all magistrates present except for one Praetor[129] and two Tribunes.

The following day there was a large attendance in the House, including all the Consulars. Pompey was given everything he asked. In asking for fifteen Lieutenant-Commissioners he named me first, and said that I should be his *alter ego* for all purposes. The Consuls drafted a law giving Pompey control over grain supplies throughout the world for a period of five years. Messius proposed an alternative bill which gives him control over all moneys and in addition a fleet, an army, and authority in the provinces superior to that of their governors. Our consular law now looks quite modest; Messius' is felt to be intolerable. According to himself

129. P. Clodius' brother Appius.

Pompey favours the former, according to his friends the latter. The Consulars are seething, Favonius at their head.[130] I hold my tongue, a course to which I am the more inclined because the Pontiffs have not yet given any answer about my house. If they lift the religious sanction,[131] I have a splendid site and the Consuls, under senatorial decree, will estimate the value of the building. If not, they will pull down the temple, let out a contract in their own name, and make an estimate for the whole.

So stand my affairs:

> 'Unsettled', when our luck is in;
> When out, we call it 'fair'.[132]

My financial position, as you know, is in very far from good order. Moreover, there are certain private matters which I don't trust to a letter. My brother is a paragon of affection, courage and loyalty, and I love him as I ought. I am looking forward to seeing you and beg you to make haste; and when you do come, come prepared to give me the benefit of your advice. It is a sort of second life I am beginning. Already, now that I am here, secret resentment and open jealousy are setting in among some of those who championed me when I was away. I need you badly.

22

CICERO TO ATTICUS

Rome, 23 November 57

I am sure you are dying to know what's afoot here, and also to know it from me – not that news of what goes on in full public view is any more reliable from my pen than when it comes to you from the letters or reports of others, but I should like you to see from a letter of my own how I react

130. Ironical. Favonius' official rank was humble, ex-Quaestor or at most ex-Tribune.
131. After demolishing Cicero's house on the Palatine Clodius had consecrated part of the site to the goddess Liberty. To allow Cicero to rebuild, this consecration had to be annulled by the Pontiffs and the shrine to Liberty pulled down. Had the Pontiffs maintained the consecration, the temple would still have been pulled down and replaced by another.
132. Line from an unknown Latin play. Shuckburgh rendered from Milton 'For happy though but ill, for ill not worst.'

to developments, and my attitude of mind and general state of being at the present time.

On 3 November an armed gang drove the workmen from my site, threw down Catulus' portico[133] which was in process of restoration by consular contract under a senatorial decree and had nearly reached the roof stage, smashed up my brother's house by throwing stones from my site, and then set it on fire. This was by Clodius' orders, with all Rome looking on as the firebrands were thrown, amid loud protest and lamentation – I won't say from honest men, for I doubt whether they exist, but from all and sundry. Clodius was running riot even before, but after this frenzy he thinks of nothing but massacring his enemies, and goes from street to street openly offering the slaves their freedom. Earlier on, when he would not stand trial, he had a difficult, obviously bad case, but still a case. He could have denied the charges or blamed others or even have defended this or that action as legitimate. But after this orgy of wrecking, arson, and loot, his followers have left him. It is all he can do to keep Decius (?) the undertaker or Gellius, and he takes slaves for his advisers. He sees that if he slaughters everybody he chooses in broad daylight, his case, when it comes to court, won't be a jot worse than it is already.

Accordingly, on 11 November as I was going down the Via Sacra,[134] he came after me with his men. Uproar! Stones flying, cudgels and swords in evidence. And all like a bolt from the blue! I retired into Tettius Damio's forecourt, and my companions had no difficulty in keeping out the rowdies. Clodius himself could have been killed, but I am becoming a dietician, I'm sick of surgery. When he found that everyone was calling for him to be bundled off to trial or rather to summary execution, his subsequent behaviour was such as made every Catiline look like an Acidinus.[135] On 12 November he tried to storm and burn Milo's house in the Cermalus, bringing out fellows with drawn swords and shields and others with lighted firebrands, all in full view at eleven o'clock in the morning. He himself had made P. Sulla's house his assault base. Then out came Q. Flaccus with some stout warriors from Milo's other house, the Anniana,[136] and killed off the most notorious bandits of the whole Clodian

133. Built by the elder Catulus close to Cicero's house. It had been demolished by Clodius and replaced with one of his own.

134. Street adjoining the north side of the Forum.

135. A proverbially respectable personage, Consul in 179.

136. Milo inherited this house from his adoptive father T. Annius. It was on the road from the Forum up to the Capitol just across the valley from the Cermalus (the northern height of the Palatine).

gang. He had every wish to kill their principal, but *he* had gone to earth in the recesses (?) of Sulla's house. Senate on the 14th. Clodius at home. Marcellinus first-rate, and the rest backed him up vigorously. But Metellus talked out the time with a filibuster, abetted by Appius and also, I must add, by that friend of yours,[137] about whose consistency of conduct you write most truly. Sestius was beside himself. Clodius later threatened reprisals against the city if his elections[138] were not held. Milo on his side posted up Marcellinus' proposal, which the latter had read out from script, calling for a trial to cover my whole case – the site, the fires, and my own narrow escape, all to take place before the elections. He also put up an announcement that he would watch the skies[139] on all comitial days. Public speeches followed, a seditious one by Metellus, a reckless one by Appius, a quite frantic one by Publius. What it all came to was that, unless Milo declared contrary auspices in the Campus Martius, the elections would be held.

On 19 November Milo went to the Campus before midnight with a large following. Though Clodius had a picked force of runaway slaves at his back, he did not dare go to the Campus. Milo stayed till noon, to the public's enormous glee and his own great *réclame*. The campaign of the three brethren[140] became a fiasco. They found their violence outmatched and their fury treated with contempt. However, Metellus asked Milo to declare the auspices to him next day in the Forum. No need, he said, to go at night to the Campus. He himself would be in the Comitium at daybreak. So, on the 20th, in came Milo to the Comitium while it was still dark. As dawn broke, there was Metellus scurrying along the byways to the Campus. Milo caught him up between the Woods[141] and made his declaration, on which Metellus turned tail, to the accompaniment of a deal of coarse jeering from Q. Flaccus. The 21st was market-day, and for a couple of days there was no assembly.

On the morning of the 22nd I am writing this between two and three o'clock. Milo is already in position on the Campus. My neighbour Marcellus (the candidate)[142] is snoring loud enough for me to hear him. I am told that Clodius' forecourt is pretty well deserted – a handful of ragamuffins

137. Hortensius.
138. To the Curule Aedileship, for which Clodius was a candidate.
139. See n. 97.
140. Clodius, his brother Appius, and their half-brother Metellus Nepos.
141. The place called 'Between two Woods' was on the lower ground between the two heights of the Capitol.
142. Probably C. Marcellus, Consul in 50.

without a lantern. Clodius' party complain that it's all been my plan. Little do they know our heroic Milo, what a resourceful as well as gallant fellow he is. His spirit is amazing. I pass over certain recent brilliancies, but the sum and substance is as follows: I don't believe there will be any elections. I think Publius will be brought to trial by Milo, unless he is killed first. If he now puts himself in Milo's way in a rough-and-tumble I don't doubt that Milo will dispatch him with his own hands.[143] He has no qualms about doing so, and makes no bones about it. He is not scared of what happened to me, for *he* is never going to follow anybody's envious and treacherous advice or put his trust in a sluggish nobility.

My *heart* is high, higher even than in my palmy days, but my purse is low. None the less, with the help of my friends and against his opposition, I am repaying my brother's generosity, so far as my resources allow, so as not to be left entirely penniless. With you away I don't know what line to take as to my position in general. So make haste.

23
CICERO TO LENTULUS SPINTHER

Rome, 15 January 56

From M. Cicero to P. Lentulus, Proconsul, greetings.

Nothing was settled in the Senate on the Ides of January because a large part of the day was taken up by an altercation between Consul Lentulus[144] and Tribune Caninius. I spoke at length that day myself, and I think I made a very considerable impression on the Senate when I dwelt on your

143. This is practically what happened four years later.
144. Marcellinus. The matter at issue was the restoration of Ptolemy XII ('The Piper') to the throne of Egypt, from which he had been expelled by his subjects. The Senate had originally commissioned Lentulus Spinther, as governor of Cilicia (including Cyprus), to effect this, but in January the custodians of the Sibylline prophecies produced an oracle forbidding the employment of a 'host'. This was no doubt also a move against Pompey, who came more and more under suspicion of wanting to handle the restoration himself. The business dragged on until August. In the end Lentulus did nothing, and Ptolemy was reinstated by the enterprising governor of Syria, A. Gabinius, in 55.

attachment to that Order. We therefore thought best to make only short speeches on the day following, feeling that we had regained the House's goodwill – I had clear evidence of that both during my address and in approaches and appeals to individuals. Accordingly three proposals were put forward: first Bibulus', that the king be restored by a Commission of Three, second Hortensius', that he be restored by you without an army, and third Vulcatius', that he be restored by Pompey. There was a demand that Bibulus' motion should be split. So far as it concerned the religious issue it was agreed, opposition on this point being now out of the question, but on the Commission of Three it was heavily defeated. Hortensius' motion stood next, when Tribune Lupus began to insist that, having himself consulted the House earlier concerning Pompey, he had the right to take a vote before the Consuls. His speech was received with loud protests from all sides – it was unfair and without precedent. The Consuls did not give way, but neither did they put up much of a fight. They wanted the sitting talked out, which is what happened, because it was plain to them that Hortensius' motion would get a thumping majority despite much open canvassing in support of Vulcatius – which again was not to the liking of the Consuls, who had wished Bibulus' motion to win the day. The argument was prolonged till nightfall, and the House rose.

I happened to be dining with Pompey that evening. It was a better moment than had ever come my way before, because we had just had our most successful day in the Senate since your departure. So I talked to him, and I could flatter myself that I led his mind away from all other notions and focused it upon upholding your position. When I listen to him talking, I quite acquit him of all suspicion of selfish aims. But when I look at his friends of all classes, I see what is now plain to everyone, that this whole business has for a long while past been bedevilled by certain individuals, not without the connivance of the king himself and his advisers.

I am writing this on 15 January before daybreak. The Senate is to meet today. At the meeting, as I hope, we shall maintain our position, so far as practicable in the general ambience of treachery and unfair play. As for the role of the People,[145] I think we have so managed that no proceedings in that quarter are possible without violation of the auspices and the laws, in fact without violence. Yesterday a senatorial resolution[146] in very impressive terms went through on these matters, and although Cato[147]

145. i.e. the popular legislative assembly.
146. *auctoritas*, a decree of the Senate vetoed by a Tribune, but recorded.
147. C. Porcius Cato.

and Caninius cast vetoes, it was placed on record. I think you have been
sent a copy. On other matters I shall write to tell you whatever takes place,
and shall use all my care, pains, diligence, and influence to ensure that
things go as much as possible on the right lines.

24

CICERO TO LENTULUS SPINTHER

Rome, January (?) 56

From M. Cicero to P. Lentulus, Proconsul, greetings.

For many years I have been on friendly terms with A. Trebonius,[148] who
has important business concerns, both extensive and in good order, in
your province. In the past he has always been very well regarded in the
province on account of his personal distinction and of recommendations
from myself and his other friends; and he now trusts that this letter from
me will put him in your good graces in view of your affection for me and
the close relations between us. May I earnestly request you not to
disappoint him, and commend to you all his business affairs, his freedmen,
agents, and household? May I ask you in particular to confirm T.
Ampius'[149] decisions with respect to his property, and to treat him in all
matters in such a way as to let him understand that my recommendation
has been more than formal?[150]

---

148. Distinguish from Caesar's assassin, C. Trebonius.
149. Lentulus' predecessor as governor of Cilicia.
150. Cicero prided himself as a writer of letters of recommendation. Book XIII of *Letters to
Friends* is made up of them.

CICERO TO HIS BROTHER

Rome, 12–15 February 56

From Marcus to his brother Quintus greetings.

I gave you the earlier news in my last. Now for the sequel: On the Kalends of February there was a move to postpone the embassies[151] to the Ides. No conclusion reached that day. On 2 February Milo appeared to stand trial[152] with Pompey as supporting counsellor. M. Marcellus spoke (I had asked him) and we came off creditably. Case adjourned to 7 February. Meanwhile the embassies were postponed to the Ides and the House was asked to consider the Quaestors' provinces and the Praetors' establishments. But business was interrupted by numerous complaints about the state of the commonwealth and nothing done. C. Cato gave notice of a bill to relieve Lentulus of his command, and his son put on mourning.

Milo appeared on 7 February. Pompey spoke – or rather tried to speak, for no sooner was he on his feet than Clodius' gang raised a clamour, and all through the speech he was interrupted not merely by shouting but by insults and abuse. When he wound up (and I will say he showed courage; he was not put off, delivered all he had to say, sometimes even managing to get silence by his personal authority) – well, when he wound up, Clodius rose. Wishing to repay the compliment, our side gave him such an uproarious reception that he lost command of thoughts, tongue, and countenance. That lasted till half past one, Pompey having finished just after midday – all manner of insults, ending up with some highly scabrous verse to the address of Clodius and Clodia. Pale with fury, he started a game of question and answer in the middle of the shouting: 'Who's starving the people to death?' 'Pompey,' answered the gang. 'Who wants to go to Alexandria?' Answer: 'Pompey.' 'Whom do you want to go?' Answer: 'Crassus' (who was present as a supporter of Milo, wishing him no good). About 2.15 the Clodians started spitting at us, as though on a signal. Sharp rise in temperature! They made a push to dislodge us, our side counter-charged. Flight of gang. Clodius was hurled from the rostra, at

151. Delegates from abroad appeared before the Senate in February.
152. On a charge of breach of the peace (*de vi*) brought by Clodius.

which point I too made off for fear of what might happen in the free-for-all. The Senate was convened in its House, and Pompey went home. I did not attend, however, not wishing to keep mum about so remarkable an incident nor yet to offend the honest men by standing up for Pompey, who was under fire from Bibulus, Curio, Favonius, and Servilius junior. The debate was adjourned to the following day. Clodius had the trial postponed to Quirinus' Day.[153]

On 8 February the Senate met in the temple of Apollo[154] in order that Pompey could be present. Pompey spoke strongly – nothing concluded that day. 9 February, Senate in temple of Apollo. A decree was passed pronouncing the doings of 7 February contrary to public interest. That day C. Cato delivered a broadside against Pompey – a set speech like a prosecuting counsel's with Pompey in the dock. He said many highly laudatory things about me, which I could have done without, denouncing Pompey's treachery towards me. The ill-wishers listened in rapt silence. Pompey replied warmly, making oblique allusion to Crassus and saying plainly that he intended to take better care of his life than Africanus had done, whom C. Carbo murdered.[155]

So I think big things are on the way. Pompey has information (and talks about it to me) that a plot against his life is on foot, that Crassus is backing C. Cato and supplying Clodius with funds, and that both are getting support both from Crassus and from Curio, Bibulus, and his other enemies. He says he must take very good care not to be caught napping, with the meeting-going public pretty well alienated, the nobility hostile, the Senate ill-disposed, and the younger generation ill-conditioned. So he is getting ready and bringing up men from the country. Clodius on his side is reinforcing his gang in readiness for Quirinus' Day. With the same date in view we have much the advantage even with Milo's own forces, but a large contingent is expected from Picenum and Gaul, which should further enable us to make a stand against Cato's bills concerning Milo and Lentulus.

On 10 February Sestius was charged with bribery by an informer, Cn. Nerius of the tribe Pupinia, and on the same day with breach of the peace by a certain M. Tullius. He was unwell, so, as was only proper, I called on

---

153. Quirinalia, a festival in honour of Quirinus (the deified Romulus, founder of Rome) on 17 February.

154. Outside the ancient city boundary. As holding *imperium* Pompey could come inside only by special dispensation.

155. In 129. But murder was never proved.

him immediately and promised him my services without reservation. And I have acted accordingly, contrary to what people were expecting in the belief that I was justifiably annoyed with him. So I figure in his eyes and everyone else's as an eminently forgiving and grateful character. And I shall so continue. The same informer Nerius has named as 'tied' witnesses[156] Cn. Lentulus Vatia and C. Cornelius of the tribe Stellatina. The same day the Senate passed a decree to the effect that the political clubs and caucuses should be dissolved and a bill put through providing that persons not complying with this ordinance be liable to the same penalty as those guilty of breach of peace.

On 11 February I defended Bestia on a bribery charge before Praetor Cn. Domitius in mid Forum. There was a large crowd in court. In the course of my speech I came to the occasion on which Bestia saved Sestius' life when he was lying covered with wounds in the temple of Castor. I took the favourable opportunity to lay down a foundation for my defence of Sestius against the charges which are being got up against him and pronounced a well-deserved eulogy, which was received with great approval by all. Sestius was highly pleased. I tell you all this because you have often referred in your letters to the desirability of preserving good relations with him.

I am writing this before dawn on 12 February. This evening I shall be dining with Pomponius at his wedding.[157]

In the rest of my affairs it is as you foretold when I was far from hopeful – my prestige and influence flourishes. This restitution, in which we both share, is due, my dear brother, to your patience, courage, devotion, and, let me add, your personal charm.

Piso's house (the Liciniana) near the wood[158] has been rented for you, but I hope you will be moving into your own in a few months' time, after the Kalends of July. The Lamiae have taken your house in Carinae – nice, clean tenants. Since your letter from Olbia I have heard nothing from you. I am anxious to know how you are and how you amuse yourself, and above all to see you as soon as possible.

Take care of your health, my dear brother, and don't forget that it's Sardinia where you are, winter time though it be.[159]

15 February

156. Witnesses who, once named, were obliged to give their evidence.
157. To Pilia.
158. Reading uncertain.
159. The climate of Sardinia was notoriously unhealthy, more so, naturally, in summer than in winter. Quintas was there as Pompey's Legate on grain business.

CICERO TO HIS BROTHER

En route *to Anagnia,* 9 *April 56*

From Marcus to his brother Quintus greetings.

I sent you a letter[160] the other day telling you that our Tullia was betrothed to Crassipes on 4 April, along with the rest of the news, public and private. Subsequent items are as follows: On the Nones of April the Senate decreed HS40,000,000 to Pompey as Grain Commissioner. The same day there was a warm debate on the Campanian Land[161] – the shouting in the House was like at a public meeting. The shortage of funds and the high price of grain made the question more acute. I must not fail to mention that M. Furius Flaccus, a Roman Knight and a scoundrel, was expelled from the Capitoline College and the Guild of Mercury,[162] he being present and throwing himself at the feet of every member in turn.

On 6 April I gave a dinner for Crassipes to celebrate the engagement. Your and my boy Quintus (a very good boy) could not come because of a very slight indisposition. On the 8th I went to see him and found him quite recovered. He talked to me at length and in the nicest way about the disagreements between our ladies. It was really most entertaining. Pomponia has been grumbling about you too, but we will talk of this when we meet.

On leaving the boy I went over to your site. Work was going ahead with a crowd of builders. I said a few animating words to Longilius the contractor, and he convinced me that he wants to give us satisfaction. Your house will be splendid. One can see more now than we could judge from the plan. Mine too will be built rapidly.

I dined that evening at Crassipes' and after dinner had myself carried to Pompey's villa, not having been able to meet him during the day because he had been away – I wanted to see him because I was leaving Rome next day and he had a trip to Sardinia in view. So I met him and asked him to send you back to us as soon as possible. 'Straight away,' said he. He would

160. Not extant.

161. See Glossary of Terms. A move was afoot to cancel the distribution on the ground that Caesar's laws were passed illegally.

162. The *Capitolini* were in charge of the Capitoline Games held every Ides of October. The *Mercuriales* were a corporation of merchants.

be leaving, he said, on 11 April and taking ship from Labro[163] or Pisae. Now as soon as he arrives, my dear fellow, be sure to take the next boat, provided the weather is suitable.

On 9 April I dictated this letter before daylight and am writing the rest on the road, expecting to stay the night with T. Titius near Anagnia. Tomorrow I intend to stay at Laterium, and then, after five days in the Arpinum area, go on to Pompeii. I shall have a look at my Cumae place on the way back, and so to Rome (since Milo's trial has been scheduled for the Nones of May) on the 6th, then, as I hope, to see you, my dearest and sweetest of brothers. I thought it best to hold up the building at Arcanum pending your arrival.

Be sure to keep well, my dear fellow, and come back as soon as you can.

27
CICERO TO LUCCEIUS

Cumae (?), c. 12 April 55

From M. Cicero to L. Lucceius, son of Quintus, greetings.

Although I have more than once attempted to take up my present topic with you face to face, a sort of shyness, almost awkwardness, has held me back. Away from your presence, I shall set it out with less trepidation. A letter has no blushes.

I have a burning desire, of a strength you will hardly credit but ought not, I think, to blame, that my name should gain lustre and celebrity through your works. You often promise me, it is true, that you will comply with my wish; but I ask you to forgive my impatience. The quality of your literary performances, eagerly as I have always awaited them, has surpassed my expectation. I am captivated and enkindled. I want to see my achievements enshrined in your compositions with the minimum of delay. The thought that posterity will talk of me and the hope, one might say, of immortality hurries me on, but so too does the desire to enjoy in my lifetime the support of your weighty testimony, the evidence of your goodwill, and the charm of your literary talent.

163. No place of this name is otherwise recorded.

As I write these words, I am not unaware of the heavy burden weighing upon you of projects undertaken and already commenced. But seeing that you have almost finished your account of the Italian War and the Civil War,[164] and remembering that you told me you were embarking on subsequent events, I feel I should be failing myself if I did not suggest two alternatives for your consideration. Would you prefer to weave my affairs along with those of the rest of the period into a single narrative, or might you not rather follow many Greek precedents, as Callisthenes with the Phocian War, Timaeus with the War of Pyrrhus, and Polybius with that of Numantia, all of whom detached their accounts of these particular wars from their continuous histories? Just so, you might deal with the domestic conspiracy apart from wars against external enemies. From my point of view there seems little to choose, so far as my credit is concerned. But there is my impatience to be considered; and here it does make a difference, if, instead of waiting until you reach the place, you immediately seize upon the entire subject and period. Furthermore, if your whole mind is directed upon a single theme and a single figure, I can already envisage the great gain in general richness and splendour.

Not that I am unconscious of the effrontery of what I am about, first in laying such a burden upon you (pressure of work may refuse me), and secondly in asking you to write about me eulogistically. What if the record does not appear to you so eminently deserving of eulogy? But the bounds of delicacy once passed, it is best to be frankly and thoroughly brazen. Therefore I ask you again, not mincing my words, to write of this theme more enthusiastically than perhaps you feel. Waive the laws of history for this once. Do not scorn personal bias, if it urge you strongly in my favour – that sentiment of which you wrote very charmingly in one of your prefaces, declaring that you could no more be swayed thereby than Xenophon's Hercules by Pleasure.[165] Concede to the affection between us just a little more even than the truth will license.

If I prevail upon you to undertake the task, I persuade myself that the material will be worthy of your ready and skilful pen. I fancy a work of moderate length could be made up, from the beginning of the plot down

---

164. i.e. from the beginning of the war between Rome and her Italian allies in 91 down to Sulla's final victory over the Marians in 82.

165. Prodicus the Sophist's allegory of the Choice of Hercules is retailed by Xenophon in his *Memoirs of Socrates* (11.1.21). Cicero refers to it in his treatise *On Duties* (1.118). – This passage ought not to be taken too literally. It is an exhibition of false modesty – Cicero did not really believe that the wine of his achievements needed any bush – and a compliment to Lucceius, as showing how much store Cicero set upon his praise.

to my return from exile. In it you will also be able to make use of your special knowledge of political changes, in explaining the origins of the revolutionary movement and suggesting remedies for things awry. You will blame what you judge deserving of reproof and give reasons for commending what you approve; and if, according to your usual practice, you think proper to deal pretty freely, you will hold up to censure the perfidy, artifice, and betrayal of which many were guilty towards me. Moreover, my experiences will give plenty of variety to your narrative, full of a certain kind of delectation to enthrall the minds of those who read, when you are the writer. Nothing tends more to the reader's enjoyment than varieties of circumstance and vicissitudes of fortune. For myself, though far from desirable in the living, they will be pleasant in the reading; for there is something agreeable in the secure recollection of bygone unhappiness.[166] For others, who went through no personal distress and painlessly survey misfortunes not their own, even the emotion of pity is enjoyable. Which of us is not affected pleasurably, along with a sentiment of compassion, at the story of the dying Epaminondas on the field of Mantinea, ordering the javelin to be plucked from his body only after he had been told in answer to his question that his shield was safe, so that even in the agony of his wound he could meet an honourable death with mind at ease? Whose sympathies are not aroused and held as he reads of Themistocles' flight and death?[167] The actual chronological record of events exercises no very powerful fascination upon us; it is like the recital of an almanac. But in the doubtful and various fortunes of an outstanding individual we often find surprise and suspense, joy and distress, hope and fear; and if they are rounded off by a notable conclusion, our minds as we read are filled with the liveliest gratification.

So I shall be especially delighted if you find it best to set my story apart from the main stream of your work, in which you embrace events in their historical sequence – this drama, one may call it, of what I did and experienced; for it contains various 'acts', and many changes of plan and circumstance. Nor am I apprehensive of appearing to angle for your favour with the bait of a little flattery when I declare that you of all others are the writer by whom I desire my praises to be sung. After all, you are not ignorant of your own worth; a man like you knows better than to see sycophancy in admiration rather than jealousy in its absence. Nor am I myself so foolish as to ask any author to immortalize my name but one

166. cf. Virgil's *forsan et haec olim meminisse iuvabit*.
167. The manuscripts say 'and return'. But Themistocles never returned from his exile.

who in so doing will gain glory for his own genius. Alexander the Great did not ask Apelles to paint his portrait and Lysippus to sculpt his statue in order to curry favour with these artists, but because he believed the work would redound to his own fame as well as theirs. Those artists, however, only made a physical likeness known to people unacquainted with the original; and even in default of such memorials famous men would lose none of their celebrity. Agesilaus of Sparta, who would not allow representations of himself in paintings or sculpture, is no less pertinent to my case than those who took pains over the matter. Xenophon's one little volume in eulogy of that king has achieved far more than all the portraits and statues under the sun.

There is a further reason why a place in your works as compared with those of other writers will bring my mind a more lively satisfaction and my memory more signal honour. You will confer upon me the benefit not only of your literary skill, as Timaeus did upon Timoleon or Herodotus upon Themistocles, but of your authority as a famed and admired public man, tried and notably approved in public affairs of the greatest moment. Not only shall I gain a herald, such as Alexander when he visited Sigeum said Homer was to Achilles, but a witness – the weighty testimony of a great and famous man. For I am of one mind with Naevius' Hector, who delights, not in praise merely, but, he adds, 'from one that praisèd is'.[168]

Suppose, however, I am refused; that is to say, suppose something hinders you (for I feel it would be against nature for you to *refuse* any request of mine), I shall perhaps be driven to a course often censured by some, namely to write about myself – and yet I shall have many illustrious precedents. But I need not point out to you that this *genre* has certain disadvantages. An autobiographer must needs write over-modestly where praise is due and pass over anything that calls for censure. Moreover, his credit and authority are less, and many will blame him and say that heralds at athletic contests show more delicacy, in that after placing garlands on the heads of the winners and loudly proclaiming their names, they call in another herald when it is *their* turn to be crowned at the end of the games, in order to avoid announcing their own victory with their own lips. I am anxious to escape these drawbacks, as I shall, if you take my case. I beg you so to do.

In case it may surprise you that I urge you so earnestly and at such length *now*, when you have repeatedly promised me that you will compose the record of my public career, its policies and events, and spare no pains,

168. The verse is from Naevius' (lost) play *Hector's Departure*.

my motive is, as I wrote in the first place, impatience. I cannot wait to see the world learning about me in my lifetime from your books and to enjoy my modicum of glory myself before I die.

If it is not troubling you too much, please write back and tell me what you intend to do. If you undertake the case, I will prepare notes on all points.[169] If you put me off, I shall talk to you personally. Meanwhile, do not be idle. Give a thorough polish to the work you have in hand. And love me well.[170]

28
CICERO TO ATTICUS

Antium, end of June (?) 56

Come now! Do you really think there is anyone whom I would sooner have read and approve my compositions than yourself? Why then did I send this one to anybody else first? Because the person[171] to whom I sent it was pressing me and I did not have two copies. There was also the fact (I might as well stop nibbling at what has to be swallowed) that I was not exactly proud of my palinode. But good night to principle, sincerity, and honour! You will scarcely credit the treachery of our public leaders, as they set up to be and *would* be if they had a grain of honesty about them. I had seen it, knew it, led on by them as I was, deserted, thrown to the wolves. Yet even so I was disposed to agree with them in politics. They proved to be what they had always been. At long last, and by your advice, I have come to my senses.

You will say that you recommended what I should *do*, not that I should write as well. The truth is, I wanted to bind myself irrevocably to this new alliance so as to make it quite impossible for me to slip back to those people who won't give up their jealousy even when they ought to be sorry for me. However, I have observed moderation in my 'apotheosis', as I told you

169. i.e. factual statements for Lucceius to embellish.

170. Writing to Atticus, Cicero describes this letter as 'a very pretty piece of writing'. It bore no fruit that we know of.

171. Probably Pompey. The composition which Cicero calls his palinode was probably his speech 'On the Consular Provinces', which lauded Caesar's achievements in Gaul.

I should. I shall give myself more rein if *he*[172] receives the offering cordially and if, on the other hand, it wrings the withers of certain gentlemen who object to my owning a villa[173] which once belonged to Catulus without recollecting that I bought it from Vettius, and say in the same breath that I ought not to have built my house and that I ought to sell it. But what's that compared with the fact that when I made speeches in the Senate on lines which even they approved they were delighted none the less that I had spoken against Pompey's wishes? *Il faut en finir.* Since the powerless won't be my friends, let me try to make myself liked by the powerful. You will say that I might have thought of that sooner. I know you wanted me to do so, and that I have been a prize donkey. But now it's time for me to love myself since *they* won't love me whatever I do.

Thank you very much for keeping a close eye on my house. Crassipes is forestalling your welcome-home dinner. 'Straight from the road to the suburbs?'[174] Well, it seems more convenient. I'll come to you the next day, naturally. It can't make any odds to you. But we shall see.

Your people have painted my library together with the book-cases and labels. Please commend them.

29

CICERO TO ATTICUS

Antium, end of June (?) 56

Egnatius is in Rome, but I took up Halimetus' (?)[175] affair with him strongly at Antium. He assured me that he would speak seriously to Aquilius. So you will see him if you wish. I hardly think I can oblige Macro. There is the auction, you see, at Larinum on the Ides and for the two days following. As you think such a lot of Macro, I must ask you to forgive me. But don't fail to dine with me on the 2nd with Pilia. You really must. On the Kalends I propose to dine at Crassipes' place in the suburbs in lieu of

172. Caesar.

173. At Tusculum. Catulus is probably the elder of the two Catuli.

174. Suburban villas (*horti*, usually translated 'gardens') seem to have been associated with 'fast' living.

175. The name is probably corrupt.

an inn, and thus cheat the decree![176] Then home after dinner so that I can be ready for Milo in the morning. I shall see you there then, and shall warn you beforehand. All my household wish to be remembered to you.

30
CICERO TO M. MARIUS

Rome, late August 55

From M. Cicero to M. Marius greetings.

If some bodily distress or the frailty of your health has kept you from coming to the show,[177] I give credit to chance rather than to your own good sense. On the other hand, if you thought these objects of public wonderment unworthy of your notice, and chose not to come though your health would have permitted, why, I rejoice both at your freedom from physical distress and at your health of mind, in that you have disregarded these spectacles at which others idly marvel – always provided that you have reaped the fruits of your leisure. You have had a wonderful opportunity to enjoy it, left almost on your own in that delightful spot.[178] And after all, I don't doubt that throughout the period of the show you have spent the mornings browsing over your books in that bedroom of yours with its window that you let into the wall to overlook the bay of Stabiae. Meanwhile those who left you there were watching the public pantomimes half-asleep.[179] As for the rest of the day, you have been spending it in such diversions as you have provided to suit your own taste

176. Probably sumptuary, restricting expenditure on food in public places.

177. Given by Pompey in his second Consulship to inaugurate his stone theatre (the first built in Rome) and the temple of Venus Victrix. Pliny the Elder and Cassius Dio write of their magnificence.

178. Elsewhere Cicero writes of Marius as his neighbour at Pompeii. But Marius' villa may have been two or three miles to the south above modern Castellammare di Stabia.

179. The weather in high summer was naturally oppressive. Valerius Maximus (11.6.4) says that streams of running water were channelled through the theatre to mitigate the heat.

while we have had to endure what Sp. Maecius[180] presumably thought proper.

To be sure, the show (if you are interested) was on the most lavish scale; but it would have been little to your taste, to judge by my own. To begin with, certain performers honoured the occasion by returning to the boards, from which I thought they had honoured their reputations by retiring.[181] Your favourite, our friend Aesopus, gave a display which everyone was willing should be his finale. When he came to take an oath[182] and got as far as 'if I knowingly swear false', he lost his voice! I need not give you further details – you know the other shows.[183] They did not even have the sprightliness which one mostly finds in ordinary shows – one lost all sense of gaiety in watching the elaborate productions. These I don't doubt you are very well content to have missed. What pleasure is there in getting a *Clytemnestra* with six hundred mules or a *Trojan Horse* with three thousand mixing-bowls[184] or a variegated display of cavalry and infantry equipment in some battle or other? The public gaped at all this; it would not have amused you at all. If you were listening to your man Protogenes[185] during those days (so long as he read you anything in the world except my speeches), you have certainly had a good deal better time of it than any of us. As for the Greek[186] and Oscan[187] shows, I don't imagine you were sorry to miss *them* – especially as you can see an Oscan turn on your town council,[188] and you care so little for Greeks that you don't even take Greek Street to get to your house! Or perhaps, having

---

180. Spurius Maecius Tarpa selected the plays to be produced at the show. He may have been Chairman (*magister*) of the Guild of Poets established in the third century: cf. Horace, *Satires*, 1.10.38, *Art of Poetry*, 386.

181. The common phrase *honoris causa*, 'by way of compliment', is echoed in another sense, 'for the sake of (their) repute'.

182. Perhaps as part of his role. Others suppose that actors had to take an oath before starting their performance (but why?).

183. i.e. comedies and mimes.

184. The first of these two tragedies was by Accius. Grammarians ascribe a *Trojan Horse* both to Livius Andronicus and to Naevius. The bowls are thought to have figured as part of the spoils of Troy.

185. No doubt a reader (*anagnostes*).

186. Probably Greek plays performed in Greek, as distinct from Latin adaptations of Greek originals; cf. *Letters to Atticus* 410 (XVI.5).I.

187. i.e. *Fabulae Atellanae*, a type of coarse farce with stock characters, like a Punch and Judy show.

188. 'Oscan' standing for 'Campanian'. *Graffiti* found in Pompeii show that a M. Marius stood for election as Aedile.

scorned gladiators,[189] you are sorry not to have seen the athletes! Pompey himself admits that they were a waste of time and midday oil![190] That leaves the hunts, two every day for five days, magnificent – nobody says otherwise. But what pleasure can a cultivated man get out of seeing a weak human being torn to pieces by a powerful animal or a splendid animal transfixed by a hunting spear? Anyhow, if these sights are worth seeing, you have seen them often; and we spectators saw nothing new. The last day was for the elephants. The groundlings showed much astonishment thereat, but no enjoyment. There was even an impulse of compassion, a feeling that the monsters had something human about them.[191]

As for me, these past days, during the plays (in case you picture me as a free man, if not a happy one), I pretty well ruptured my lungs defending your friend Caninius Gallus.[192] If only my public were as accommodating as Aesopus', upon my word I should be glad to give up my profession and spend my time with you and other congenial spirits. I was weary of it even in the days when youth and ambition spurred me forward, and when moreover I was at liberty to refuse a case I did not care for. But now life is simply not worth living. I have no reward to expect for my labours, and sometimes I am obliged to defend persons who have deserved none too well of me at the request of those who *have* deserved well.

Accordingly, I am looking out for any excuse to live as I please at long last; and you and your leisured manner of existence have my hearty commendation and approval. I resign myself to the rarity of your visits more easily than I otherwise should, because, even if you were in Rome, I am so confoundedly busy that I should not be able to enjoy the entertainment of your company, nor you of mine (if any entertainment it holds). When and if I slacken my chains (for to be loose of them entirely is more than I can ask), then, no question about it, I shall teach you the art of civilized living, to which you have been giving your undivided attention

189. i.e. some gladiatorial show (apparently a private allusion). The explanation that Marius had defied Clodius' gangs does not suit what is known of him.

190. *operam et oleum perdere* was a proverbial expression for a waste of time and money, *oleum* referring to 'midnight oil'. Here it is humorously applied to the oil used by athletes in anointing themselves.

191. Pliny's account (*Natural History,* VIII.21) that the whole crowd of spectators rose and cursed Pompey is evidently embroidered.

192. The charge may have referred to his activities as Tribune in 56. As an adherent of Pompey's he will have been one of a number of defendants for whom Cicero appeared at this period at the behest of Pompey and Caesar, some of them old enemies of his own.

for years! Only you must go on propping up that frail health of yours and looking after yourself, so that you can visit my places[193] in the country and run around with me in my little litter.

I have written at unusual length, out of an abundance, not of spare time, but of affection for you, because in one of your letters you threw out a hint, if you remember, that I might write something to prevent you feeling sorry to have missed the show. If I have succeeded in that, so much the better; but if not, I console myself with the thought that henceforth you will come to the shows and visit us, and that you won't forgo any prospect of pleasure to yourself on account of my letters.

31

CICERO TO HIS BROTHER

Rome, early February 54

From Marcus to his brother Quintus greetings.

Your tablets[194] clamorously demanded this letter. Otherwise, in actual material the day of your departure offers virtually no subject for my pen. But when we are together we are seldom at a loss for talk, and in the same way our letters must sometimes just ramble on.

Well then, the liberties of the good folk of Tenedos have been chopped by their own axe;[195] nobody came to their defence except myself, Bibulus, Calidius, and Favonius. You got an honourable mention from the men of Magnesia by Mt Sipylus; they said you were the only one to stand up to L. Sestius Pansa's demand.[196] If there is anything you ought to know on the remaining days, or for that matter if there is nothing, I shall still write you a daily line. On the 12th I shall not fail you, nor Pomponius either.

---

193. Possibly 'our places'; Marius too may have had more than one villa in the area. Cicero at this period had one at Pompeii and one at Cumae.

194. See Glossary of Terms.

195. The people of Tenedos seem to have petitioned the Senate for the status of a 'free' community, and to have been summarily refused. The exact origin of the proverbial expression 'axe of Tenedos' is variously explained, but has to do with the eponymous hero of the island, Tenes, who was supposed to have introduced a peculiarly drastic legal code.

196. Nothing is known of Pansa or his demand. He may have been a tax-farmer.

Lucretius' poetry is as you say – sparkling with natural genius, but plenty of technical skill.[197] If you read Sallust's *From Empedocles*,[198] I'll rate you both more and less than ordinary humanity.[199]

32

CICERO TO CAESAR

Rome, April 54

From Cicero to Caesar, Imperator, greetings.

Please observe how fully I am persuaded that you are my *alter ego*, not only in my own concerns but in those of my friends also. I had intended to take C. Trebatius with me wherever I might go, in order to bring him home again the richer by any and every benefit and mark of goodwill in my power to bestow. But Pompey has stayed on longer than I expected, and my own departure seems prevented, or at any rate delayed, by a certain hesitation on my part of which you are not uninformed.[200] So observe my presumption: I now want Trebatius to look to you for everything he would have hoped for from me, and I have assured him of your friendly disposition in terms really no less ample than I had previously been wont to use respecting my own.

But a remarkable coincidence has supervened, as though in evidence of the correctness of my opinion and in guarantee of your kindness. Just as I was talking rather seriously to our friend Balbus at my house on the subject of this very Trebatius, a letter comes in from you concluding as follows: 'I shall make M. Curtius' son[201] king of Gaul. Or, if you please,

197. According to St Jerome Cicero edited Lucretius' poem *On the Nature of the Universe* after the poet's death.

198. Presumably a Latin translation of the fifth-century philosopher-poet Empedocles. The identity of the translator is unknown.

199. Literally: 'I shall think you a man (*virum*), but not a human being.'

200. In 55 Pompey received a five-year command in Spain and in the autumn of 54 he appointed Cicero as one of his Legates. But neither he nor Cicero went there. The 'hesitation' is generally referred to apprehensions about Clodius' designs.

201. M. *Curti filium*, conjectured for M. *itfiuium* in the manuscripts. The person referred to is clearly the M. Curtius whom Cicero had asked Caesar to appoint Military Tribune in the following year (*Letters to his Brother Quintus* 18 (11.14).3).

make him over to Lepta,[202] and send me somebody else on whom to bestow my favours.' Balbus and I both raised our hands to heaven. It came so pat as to seem no accident, but divine intervention.

I send you Trebatius accordingly. I thought it right to do so of my own accord in the first instance, but at your invitation in the second. In embracing his acquaintance with all your usual courtesy, my dear Caesar, I should wish you to confer upon his single person all the kindnesses which I could induce you to wish to confer upon my friends. As for him, I will answer that you will find him – I won't use that old-fashioned expression[203] of which you rightly made fun when I wrote to you about Milo, I'll say it in plain Latin, in the language of sensible men: there is no better fellow, no more honest and honourable gentleman alive. Add to which, he is a leading light in Civil Law; his memory is extraordinary, his learning profound.

I do not ask on his behalf for a Tribunate or Prefecture or any other specific favour. It is your goodwill and generosity I bespeak; though if in addition you have a mind to decorate him with suchlike ambitious trinkets, I say nothing to deter you. In fine, I put him altogether, as the phrase goes, out of my hand into yours – the hand of a great conqueror and a great gentleman,[204] if I may become a trifle fulsome, though that's hardly permissible with you. But you will let it pass, I see you will.[205]

Take care of your health and keep that warm corner in your heart for me.

33
CICERO TO TREBATIUS

Rome, end of June (?) 54

From Cicero to Trebatius.

I am continually putting in a word for you, but with what effect I am anxious to hear from yourself. My greatest hope is in Balbus, to whom I

---

202. See Glossary of Persons. This is his first appearance in the Letters and Caesar's reason for mentioning him is unknown.
203. Or 'old saw'. What this was, or why Cicero wrote to Caesar about Milo, we do not know.
204. Literally 'pre-eminent both in victory' (i.e. with the sword) 'and loyalty' (to its pledges).
205. The good nature apparent in Caesar's letter will tolerate even flattery of himself.

write about you very earnestly and often. What surprises me is that I don't get a letter from you whenever one comes in from my brother Quintus. I hear there is not an ounce of either gold or silver in Britain. If that is true, my advice is to lay hold of a chariot[206] and hurry back to us at full speed! But if we can gain our end[207] even without Britain, contrive to make yourself one of Caesar's intimates. My brother will give you valuable assistance, and so will Balbus; but your greatest asset, believe me, is your own honourable character and hard work. You are serving under a very generous chief, your age is just right, your recommendation is certainly out of the ordinary. So the one thing you have to be afraid of is seeming to do yourself less than justice.

34
CICERO TO TREBATIUS

Rome, August (middle or late) 54

From Cicero to Trebatius.

Caesar has written to me very civilly, regretting that he has so far been too busy to get to know you very well, but assuring me that this will come. I told him in my reply how greatly he would oblige me by conferring upon you all he could in the way of goodwill, friendly offices, and liberality. But your letter gave me an impression of undue impatience; also it surprised me that you make so little account of the advantages of a Tribunate, especially one involving no military service. I shall complain to Vacerra and Manilius.[208] I dare not say a word to Cornelius.[209] He is responsible if you play the fool, since you give out that it was from him you learned your *wisdom*. Now why don't you press this opportunity, this chance? – you'll never find a better.

---

206. Caesar's second expedition to Britain was now in preparation. He describes how the Britons used their war-chariots in *Bell. Gall.* IV.33.
207. Trebatius went to Gaul to make his fortune.
208. Two of Trebatius' fellow-jurisconsults.
209. Q. Cornelius Maximus is mentioned in the *Digest* as Trebatius' teacher in law.

As for what you say about that Counsellor Precianus,[210] I go on commending you to him, for he writes himself that he has given you reason to be grateful. Let me know how that matter stands. I am looking forward to Britannic letters from you all.

35

CICERO TO HIS BROTHER

Rome, late August 54

From Marcus to his brother Quintus greetings.

When you get a letter from me in the hand of one of my secretaries you are to infer that I did not have a minute to spare; when in my own, that I had – a minute! For let me tell you that I have never in my life been more inundated with briefs and trials, and in a heat-wave at that, in the most oppressive time of the year. But I must put up with it, since you so advise. I shall not let it appear that *I* have disappointed your[211] joint hopes and plans; and if that prove difficult, at any rate I shall reap a rich harvest of influence and prestige from my labour. So I follow your wishes. I take care to offend nobody, to be highly regarded even by those who deplore our having become so closely involved with Caesar, and an object of much attention and friendly feeling from non-partisans or from those whose sympathies actually lie this way. There has been a debate in the Senate lasting a number of days on the bribery question. The most drastic action was called for, the candidates for the Consulship have gone to intolerable lengths. I did not attend. I have decided not to come forward to cure the ills of the body politic without powerful backing.

The day I write this letter Drusus has been acquitted of collusive prosecution by the Paymaster-Tribunes. The overall majority was four, the Senators and Knights having found him guilty. This afternoon I shall be defending Vatinius – an easy matter. The elections have been put off

---

210. Unknown. Possibly *Preciano* means 'in the Precius business'.
211. Quintus' and Caesar's.

to September. Scaurus' trial[212] will proceed straight away, and I shall not let him down.

I don't at all approve of Sophocles' *Banqueters*,[213] though I see you have made an amusing little play.

Now I come to what ought perhaps to have been put first. How pleased I was to get your letter from Britain! I dreaded the Ocean and the island coast. Not that I make light of what is to come, but there is more to hope than to fear, and my suspense is more a matter of anticipation than of anxiety. You evidently have some splendid literary material – the places, the natural phenomena and scenes, the customs, the peoples you fight, and, last but not least, the Commander-in-Chief! I shall be glad to help you, as you ask, in any way you wish, and I shall send you the verses you ask for (an owl to Athens!)[214]

But see here, you seem to be keeping me in the dark. Tell me, my dear fellow, how does Caesar react to my verses?[215] He wrote to me that he read the first Canto and has never read anything better than the earlier part, even in Greek, but finds the rest, down to a certain point, a trifle 'languid'. The truth, please! Is it the material or the style he doesn't like? No need for you to be nervous – my self-esteem won't drop a hair's-breadth. Just write to me *en ami de la vérité* and in your usual fraternal way.

36
CICERO TO HIS BROTHER

Rome, end of November 54

From Marcus to his brother Quintus greetings.

I have no answer to make to your earlier letter, which is full of spleen and grumblings (you say you gave another in similar vein to Labeo the previous day, but he has not yet arrived); for the letter which followed it obliterated all my vexation. I only warn and beg you amid these

212. For extortion in Sardinia.
213. Sophocles wrote a satyric play so entitled, but Cicero's meaning is obscure.
214. Like 'coals to Newcastle'. The owl was the bird of Athene.
215. A poem entitled 'On my vicissitudes', dealing with the author's exile and restoration.

annoyances and labours and privations to be mindful of our purpose when you went to Gaul. They were no trifling or ordinary advantages that we had in view. What would have seemed worth the price of our separation? Our object was to gain reliable, comprehensive support for our public position and status from the goodwill of a very fine and very powerful person. Our capital is invested in hope rather than in money; if that hope were to be abandoned, all else would be saved only to be lost later on. Accordingly, if you will frequently carry your mind back to our old reasoned purpose and hope, you will find it easier to put up with your military labours and the other irritants – which, however, you will lay aside when you so desire; but the time is not yet ripe for that, though it is already drawing near.

I would also advise you not to trust anything to a letter which might embarrass us if it became public property. There are many things of which I had sooner be ignorant than informed, if the information carries risk. I shall write to you at greater length when, as I hope, my boy is himself again and my mind is easy. On your part please see to it that I know to whom I ought to give the letter which I shall then be sending – should it be Caesar's couriers, so that he forwards it to you straight away, or Labienus'? For where those Nervii of yours live and how far they are away from us I don't know.

It gave me much pleasure to learn from your letter of the courage and dignity of Caesar's bearing in his great sorrow.[216] As for your command that I finish that poem addressed to him which I had begun, my time is much distracted and my mind far more so, but since Caesar knows from my letter to you that I have started on something, I shall go back to what I began and finish it during these leisure days of Supplications.[217] I am very glad that thanks to them our friend Messalla and the others have been relieved of annoyance,[218] and when you folk reckon him as certain of election along with Domitius you don't at all run counter to our opinion. I make myself responsible to Caesar for Messalla's behaviour. But Memmius pins hopes on Caesar's return to Italy, wherein I fancy

216. His daughter Julia's death.

217. See Glossary of Terms. This Thanksgiving was probably in connection with a Tiber flood.

218. The loss of 'comitial days' due to the Thanksgiving meant that the consular elections for 53, in which the four persons here mentioned were candidates, would not take place before the end of the year. Under the Roman system this had the effect of relieving the successful candidates from the threat of prosecution for electoral malpractice until the end of their terms of office.

he is making a mistake. Here at any rate he is in the cold. Scaurus was thrown over by Pompey some time ago.

Business has been adjourned and the elections brought to an Interregnum. There is talk of a Dictator, disagreeable to the honest men; what they are saying is to me still less agreeable. But the whole idea is viewed with alarm, and at the same time it's falling flat. Pompey categorically denies any desire for it. Talking to me himself earlier on he did not use to deny it. It looks as though Hirrus will make the proposal (Gods, what an ass he is! How he loves himself – in which regard he has no competitor!). He got me to frighten off Crassus Junianus,[219] who is at my service. Does he want it or doesn't he? Hard to tell, but if Hirrus is the mover, he will never persuade the world that he doesn't. At present they are talking of nothing else in the way of politics; certainly nothing is a-doing.

The funeral of Serranus, Domitius' son,[220] took place on 23 November, a very sad occasion. His father spoke a eulogy of my composition.

Now about Milo: Pompey does nothing to help him and everything to help Gutta.[221] He says that he will see to it that Caesar throws his weight that way. This appalls Milo, as well it may, and he is almost in despair should Pompey become Dictator. If he assists anyone vetoing the Dictatorship with his organized band, he fears Pompey's hostility, whereas if he doesn't give such assistance he's afraid it will be carried through by force. He is preparing some most magnificent Games, in fact they will cost as much as any that ever were – which is double and triple folly, for (a) nobody asked him, (b) he had previously given a splendid show, (c) he can't afford it; or rather more than triple because (d) he could have seen himself as a president, not as Aedile.[222]

That's about all. Take care of your health, my dearest brother.

---

219. A Tribune in 53. His full name seems to have been P. Licinius Crassus Junianus (Brutus) Damasippus.

220. Reading with Münzer *Domiti* for *domestici*. The deceased will have been a son of L. Domitius Ahenobarbus adopted by an Atilius Serranus.

221. Perhaps a nickname for Pompey's father-in-law Metellus Scipio. He and Milo were standing for the Consulship of 52.

222. *magister*. According to a recent suggestion, Milo had become president of an association such as the Capitolini or Mercuriales (see n. 162). My former translation 'executor' was traditional, but no such function existed in Rome.

CICERO TO ATTICUS

Rome, end of November 54

At last the letter I have been longing for! Delighted to hear you are back! I salute you as a man of your word, a paragon of punctuality. And what a lovely voyage! I was really nervous about that I assure you, remembering those tarpaulins on your last crossing. But if I am not mistaken I shall see you sooner than you say, for I imagine you thought your women-folk were in Apulia. When you find that this is not the case, what is to keep you in Apulia? Or do you have to spare some days for Vestorius[223] and resavour his Latin Atticism after the interval? No, no! Hurry back to Rome, come and look at the empty husks of the real old Roman Republic we used to know. For example, come and see money distributed before the elections tribe by tribe, all in one place openly, see Gabinius acquitted, get the whiff of a Dictatorship in your nostrils, enjoy the public holiday and the universal free-for-all, behold my equanimity, my amusement, my contempt for Selicius' 10 per cent,[224] and yes, my delectable *rapprochement* with Caesar. That does give me some satisfaction, the one plank left from the wreck. The way he treats my (and your) dear Quintus! Such distinction, such appreciation and favour! I couldn't do more if I were G.O.C. myself. He has just offered him the choice of a legion for the winter, so Quintus writes to me. Wouldn't you love such a man? If not, then which of your fine friends?

Now pay attention. Did I tell you that I have joined Pompey's staff[225] and shall be out of town after the Ides of January? I thought this would fit in nicely from several points of view. But I won't ramble on. The rest, I think, when we meet – might as well leave you *something* to wait for! My kindest regards to Dionysius; I have not only kept a place for him, but actually built one. In fact the prospect of his arrival makes no small addition to the great happiness I feel in your return. Do please stay with me your first night in Rome, you and your people.

---

223. A resident of Puteoli of whose lack of culture Cicero makes fun elsewhere. 'Atticism' plays on Atticus' name – Vestorius might have no pretensions to Attic wit or culture, but he was an 'Atticist' all the same.

224. Or perhaps 8¼ per cent (annual), depending on the interpretation of Cicero's expression.

225. As Legate, with nominal duties. Pompey was governing the Spanish provinces *in absentia*.

CICERO TO LENTULUS SPINTHER

Rome, December 54

From M. Cicero to Lentulus, Imperator, greetings.

I am glad to have your letter, which shows that you appreciate my *piety* towards you – I won't say my goodwill, for even this solemn, sacred word 'piety' seems to me inadequate for what I owe you. When you write that you are grateful for my efforts on your behalf, it must be out of the overflowing affection of your heart. *Grateful*, because I do what it would be rank villainy to leave undone? But you would have a much better and clearer impression of my sentiments towards you, if we had been together and in Rome all this time we have been separated. Take what you say you have in view (nobody can do it better than you, and I am eagerly looking forward to the prospect) – speeches in the Senate and general activity and conduct of public affairs, as to which I shall tell you my opinion and position presently and answer your enquiries – well, at least I should have found in you the wisest and most affectionate of guides, while you would have found in me an adviser of experience perhaps not altogether negligible, and of undeniable loyalty and goodwill. For your sake, it is true, I am duly delighted to think of you as Imperator, governing your province after a successful campaign at the head of a victorious army. But at least you could have enjoyed the due fruits of my gratitude fuller and fresher on the spot; and when it came to repaying certain people, some of them hostile to you, as you know, because you championed my restoration, others jealous of the grandeur and glory of the achievement – what a companion in arms I should have made you! To be sure, that inveterate enemy of his friends[226] who recompensed your signal favours by turning the feeble remnants of his violence against you[227] has done our work for us. The exposure of his recent operations[228] has robbed him of all independence in the future, let alone prestige. I could have wished that you had gained your experience in my case and

---

226. Domitius Ahenobarbus, now Consul along with Ap. Claudius Pulcher (see my commentary).

227. We do not know how Domitius had attacked Lentulus.

228. A scandalous electoral compact revealed by C. Memmius in September 54; see *Letters to Atticus* 91 (IV.17).2.

not in your own as well, but I am glad in a bad business to think that you have not paid so very heavy a price for a lesson in the unreliability of mankind which *I* learned to my bitter sorrow.

This seems a good opportunity for me to give an exposition of the whole topic by way of a reply to your enquiries. You write that you have heard by letter that I am in good relations with Caesar and Appius, and you add that you have nothing to say against that. But you intimate that you would like to know my reasons for defending Vatinius and speaking to his character. To give you a clear explanation I must trace the principles of my political conduct a little further back.

To begin with, thanks to your public endeavours, dear sir, I conceived myself as restored, not only to my family and friends, but to my country. I owed *you* an affection well nigh transcending reason and the most complete and signal personal devotion. To our country, which had lent you no slight assistance in your campaign for my restoration, I felt myself to owe as a matter of gratitude at least the loyalty which I had formerly rendered only as the common duty of a Roman, and not as due in respect of any special favour to myself. The Senate heard these sentiments from my own lips during your Consulship, and you perceived them in the talks and discussions we had together. Yet even in those early days there was much to give me pause. I saw how your efforts to complete my rehabilitation met with covert ill-will in some quarters and doubtful support in others. In the matter of my memorials[229] those who ought to have helped you did not; similarly with respect to the criminal violence with which I and my brother were driven out of our homes.[230] I must add that even in those items to which, necessary as they were to me after the ruin of my private fortune, I attached minimal importance, I mean the indemnification of my losses by authority of the Senate, they showed a less forthcoming attitude than I had expected. I saw all this – it was plain enough; but any bitterness was outweighed by gratitude for what they had done.

And so, notwithstanding my regard for Pompey, to whom by your own declaration and testimony I owed a very great deal – a regard founded not only upon his goodness to me but on affection and what I might call life-long predilection – I made no account of his wishes and held firmly by all my old political sentiments. When Pompey came into town

229. No doubt including the one referred to on pp. 102f.
230. See Letter 22.

to speak to character on behalf of P. Sestius[231] and Vatinius said in evidence that I had made friends with C. Caesar because of his success and good fortune, I said in Pompey's presence that I thought M. Bibulus' sad plight (as Vatinius regarded it) preferable to any man's Triumphs and victories. At another point in Vatinius' evidence I said that the same people who had not allowed Bibulus to leave his home had forced me to leave mine.[232] My whole cross-examination was nothing but a condemnation of Vatinius' career as Tribune. On this topic I spoke throughout with the greatest frankness and spirit, dwelling on the use of violence, the auspices, and the grants of foreign kingdoms. And I did so not only at this trial but in the Senate, consistently and often. On the Nones of April in the Consulship of Marcellinus and Philippus the Senate actually adopted a proposal of mine that the question of the Campanian land should be referred to a full House on the Ides of May. Was not that invading the innermost citadel of the ruling clique? And could I have shown myself more oblivious of my past vicissitudes or more mindful of my political record?

That speech of mine caused a sensation, not only where I had intended but in quite unexpected quarters.[233] After the Senate had passed a decree in accordance with my motion, Pompey (without giving me any indication of displeasure) left for Sardinia and Africa, and joined Caesar at Luca on the way. Caesar there complained at length about my motion – he had been stirred up against me by Crassus, whom he had seen previously at Ravenna. Pompey by general admission was a good deal upset. I heard this from various sources, but my principal informant was my brother. Pompey met him in Sardinia a few days after leaving Luca. 'You're the very man I want,' he told him. 'Most lucky our meeting just now. Unless you talk seriously to your brother Marcus, you are going to have to pay up on the guarantee[234] you gave me on his behalf.' In short, he remonstrated in strong terms, mentioning his services to me, recalling the many discussions he had had with my brother himself about Caesar's legislation and the pledges my brother had given him concerning my future conduct, appealing to my brother's personal knowledge of the fact that his own support for my restoration had been given with Caesar's

231. Tried on charges of violence in February 56, Cicero defending. He was acquitted.
232. As Consul in 59 Bibulus had spent most of the year shut up in his house. The remarks quoted here do not in fact occur in the extant speeches *pro Sestio* and *in Vatinium*.
233. Probably Caesar and Pompey are respectively indicated.
234. Pompey spoke metaphorically, Q. Cicero having in 57 made himself responsible for his brother's future political behaviour if restored from exile.

blessing. He asked him to commend to me Caesar's cause and prestige, with the request that I should refrain from attacking them if I would not or could not defend them.

Though my brother conveyed all this to me, Pompey also sent Vibullius with an oral message, asking me not to commit myself on the Campanian question till his return. Then I took stock. It was like a dialogue between me and my country. Would she not allow me, after all I had suffered and gone through for her sake, to behave with propriety and gratitude towards my benefactors and to honour my brother's pledge? Would she not let her loyal citizen, as I had always shown myself, be also a man of honour?

Now all the time I was acting and speaking in a manner liable to annoy Pompey, I received reports of how certain folk,[235] whose identity you should by now be able to guess, were talking. Fully as the course I was now following accorded with their past and present political sentiments, they were none the less expressing satisfaction at Pompey's disappoint-ment with me and at the prospect that Caesar would be my sworn enemy in future. This was wounding enough; but much more so was their behaviour to my enemy[236] – the enemy, I should rather say, of law, justice, and tranquillity, of Rome and all honest men. This individual they chose to embrace and caress, petting and cosseting him before my very eyes. It was not enough to raise my spleen, because that organ has entirely disappeared, but enough at any rate to let them think they were raising it. At this point I surveyed the whole range of my affairs, so far as I could with only human wit to guide me, cast up my accounts in full, and arrived at the grand total of my cogitations. That is what I shall try to set out for you in brief.

If I had seen the state in the control of rascals and villains, as we know happened in Cinna's time and at some other periods of its history, no reward, or danger either (and while rewards count for little with me, even the bravest of us are influenced by dangers), would have driven me on to their side, no matter how much they might have done for me personally. But the leading man in Rome was Cn. Pompeius. The power and glory he enjoyed had been earned by state services of the highest importance and by the most signal military achievements. From early manhood I had rejoiced in his success, and as Praetor and Consul had come forward to promote it. On his side, he had individually helped me

235. 'Optimates' like Hortensius, Bibulus, and Domitius.
236. Clodius.

with his influence and voice in the Senate, and in conjunction with yourself by planned effort in my cause. His only enemy in Rome was also
mine. All these points considered, I did not feel I need fear the reputation
of inconsistency if in certain speeches I changed my tack a little and rallied
in sentiment to the support of this great figure, my personal benefactor.

In this determination I could not but embrace Caesar, as you will
recognize, for his interest and prestige were bound up with Pompey's.
Here the old friendship which, as you are aware, existed between Caesar
and myself and my brother Quintus counted for much, and no less
Caesar's own gracious and generous attitude, which soon became plainly
apparent to us in his letters and friendly acts.[237] Moreover, patriotic considerations had great weight with me. It was not, I felt, the will of our
country that there should be a struggle with these men, especially after
Caesar's great achievements; I felt she was keenly anxious to avoid such
a struggle. But the weightiest element in thus persuading me was the
pledge concerning myself which Pompey had given to Caesar and which
my brother gave to Pompey.

I had besides to note in our community the phenomena which our
favourite Plato has characterized so wonderfully – the tendency for the
members of a political society to resemble its leaders.[238] I remembered
that from the very first day of my Consulship sure foundations were laid
for the strengthening of the Senate, so that no one ought to have been
surprised either at the courage or the moral power of that Order as
revealed on the Nones of December following.[239] Equally I remembered
that after my retirement from office down to the Consulship of Caesar
and Bibulus, so long as my views carried any considerable weight in the
Senate, all honest men were pretty much of one mind. Later, while you
were governor of Hither Spain and the state had no Consuls, only
traffickers in provinces[240] and servile instruments of sedition, accident
may be said to have flung my person as a bone of contention into the
midst of civil conflict and strife. At that crisis the consensus in my defence
of the Senate, of all Italy, of all honest men was truly remarkable, a thing

237. In the spring of 54 Q. Cicero left for Gaul to take up an appointment as Caesar's
Legate.

238. cf. *Laws*, 711 C. But Cicero's words are in fact an almost exact translation of a passage
in Xenophon's *Education of Cyrus* (VIII.8.5).

239. The day on which the Senate voted for the execution of the Catilinarian conspirators.

240. According to Cicero's version of events the Consuls of 58, Piso and Gabinius, were
bribed by Clodius with appointments to the provincial governorships of Macedonia and Syria
respectively.

transcending belief. I will not say what happened – the blame is complex and many shared in it – only this briefly, that it was generals, not an army, that I lacked. Granted that those who failed to defend me[241] were to blame, no less so were those who left me in the lurch;[242] and if those who were afraid should be in the dock, those who only pretended to be afraid are yet more deserving of censure.[243] At any rate there must be applause for my refusal to let my countrymen, whom I had preserved nd who were desirous of saving me, be thrown leaderless against armed slaves – for my decision to let the potential power of honest men united (had they been allowed to fight for me before I fell) be demonstrated rather when the opportunity came to raise me from the dust. You saw their spirit when you took action on my behalf; more, you confirmed and maintained it. In that campaign – so far from denying, I shall always remember and gladly proclaim it – you found certain very high-born personages more courageous in securing my reinstatement than they had shown themselves in preventing my exile. Had they chosen to hold to that policy, they would have recovered the respect of the community at the same time as they restored me to its membership. Your Consulship had put fresh heart into the honest men, roused from their apathy by your resolute and praiseworthy initiatives, especially when Cn. Pompeius joined the cause. Even Caesar, now that the Senate had recognized his splendid achievements by signal and unprecedented honours and marks of esteem, was moving towards a position of support for the authority of the House. No bad citizen would have had a loophole through which to injure his country.

Now pray mark the sequel. That embodiment of mischief, that pilferer of the secrets of women's worship, who treated the Good Goddess[244] with as little respect as his three sisters, escaped scot-free. A Tribune was ready to bring the agitator to trial and punishment at the hands of honest men. He was saved by the votes of those who thereby lost Rome what should have been a splendid example to posterity of the chastisement of sedition. Subsequently the same group allowed a memorial[245] – not

241. Not the mass of the 'honest men' but Pompey.

242. The 'optimate' leaders.

243. In Cicero's obstinately held opinion the behaviour of certain of his friends (especially Hortensius) at the crisis of March 58 amounted to deliberate treachery (see n. 128).

244. See n. 46.

245. cf. p. 98. It may have been a building started at the end of Cicero's Consulship to commemorate the suppression of the Catilinarian conspiracy. Clodius seems to have effaced the inscription and substituted one bearing his own name.

my memorial, for the funds employed were not victory-spoils of mine, I merely signed the contract for the work – allowed the *Senate's* memorial to be inscribed with the name of a public enemy in letters of blood. These people desired my restoration, and for that I am deeply beholden. But I could have wished that they had not merely taken a doctor's interest in the life of the patient, but a trainer's in his strength and physical appearance. Certain persons in my case have followed the example of Apelles, who applied the utmost refinement of his art to perfecting the head and bust of his Venus, but left the rest of the body a mere sketch – they made a finished job of the *capital*[246] section only, leaving the rest unfinished and rough.

In this connection I disappointed the expectations of the jealous as well as the hostile. Once upon a time they were told, and believed, a false story about one of the boldest and most stout-hearted men who ever lived, whose equal in grandeur and resolution of spirit I do not know, Q. Metellus,[247] son of Lucius. He, so they like to say, was a broken man after his return from exile. A likely tale! Had he not gone quite readily into banishment, endured it with notable cheerfulness, and been at no great pains to return? Was he broken as the result of an episode in which he had emerged superior to all his contemporaries, even the eminent M. Scaurus, in resolution and integrity? Be that as it may, they formed the same notion about me as they had been given, or surmised for themselves, about Metellus. They thought I should be a humbled man henceforth – whereas my country was making me actually prouder than I had ever been in my life! Had she not declared that she could not do without me, one single citizen? Metellus, after all, was brought back by the bill of a single Tribune, I by the whole state under the leadership of the Senate and with all Italy in attendance. The relevant law was promulgated by almost[248] the entire body of magistrates, moved by yourself as Consul at the Assembly of the Centuries with the enthusiastic support of all classes and individuals. In a word, all the forces of the commonwealth were mobilized to that one end.

Not that after this experience I made any pretensions, or make any today, to which the most jaundiced critic could fairly take exception. I merely endeavour to serve my friends, or even my acquaintances, with time and counsel and hard work. My way of life perhaps irritates those

246. Cicero plays on two meanings of *caput*, 'head' and 'status as a citizen'.
247. Numidicus (see Glossary of Persons).
248. See my edition. One Praetor (Clodius' brother Appius) and two Tribunes stayed out.

who look at its outward show and glitter, but cannot see the care and toil behind. One stricture, of which they make no secret, is that in my speeches in favour of Caesar I am more or less deserting the good old cause. Well, I have just advanced my reasons, but to these I would add another, not the least important, which I had begun to explain. Dear sir, you will not find again among our honest men that league of sentiment which you left behind you. Established in my Consulship, thereafter disturbed from time to time, shattered before you became Consul, and then restored by you in its entirety, it has now been forsaken by those who should have been its champions. Their faces, though faces can easily play the hypocrite, declare as much; more, they have shown it to be so by many a vote in Senate and courtroom – these men who in the world as we used to know it were called Optimates.

Accordingly, men of sense, of whom I hope I am and am considered to be one, have now completely to recast their views and sympathies. To cite Plato again, a very weighty authority with me; he tells us to push our political efforts as far as may be acceptable to our countrymen, but never to use force against parent or fatherland.[249] He gives his reason for keeping out of public affairs as follows: finding the people of Athens almost in its dotage, and seeing them without government either of persuasion or compulsion, he did not believe them amenable to persuasion and regarded compulsion as a sacrilege.[250] My situation was different. I was not dealing with a nation in its dotage, nor did I have a free choice whether or not to engage in public life, being inextricably involved. But I congratulated myself on having a cause to champion both expedient to myself personally and commendable to any honest man.[251] An added incentive was Caesar's quite remarkable, in fact amazing, generosity towards my brother and myself. He would have deserved my support however he was faring, but in so brilliant a career of success and victory I should think him worthy of homage even if he were not the good friend to us that he is. For I would have you believe that, apart from yourself and your fellow-architects of my restoration, there is no man to whose good offices I acknowledge myself so deeply beholden – and am glad to do so.

After this exposition your enquiries as to Vatinius and Crassus are easily

---

249. In *Crito*, 51c.

250. cf. Plato, *Epist.* 5. 322a, b.

251. The maintenance of Caesar in his command, championed by Cicero in his speech 'On the Consular Provinces' (summer of 56; Caesar's personal generosity came later).

answered – about Appius,[252] as about Caesar, you say you have no criticism to offer, and I am glad my action has your approval. To take Vatinius then, Pompey originally arranged a reconciliation between us immediately after his election to the Praetorship,[253] although I had made some very strong speeches in the Senate against his candidature – not so much to damage *him* as in support and compliment to Cato. Subsequently Caesar made a tremendous point of my undertaking his defence.[254] As for why I spoke for his character, I appeal to you not to ask me that question about Vatinius or any other defendant, otherwise I shall ask you a similar question when you come home. For that matter I can ask it while you are still abroad. Just call to mind the men for whom *you* have sent testimonials from the ends of the earth – don't be afraid, I do the same myself for the same people and shall so continue. To resume, I had another incentive to defend Vatinius, to which I referred in my speech at the trial. I said I was doing what the Parasite in the *Eunuch* recommends to the Captain:[255]

> When she says 'Phaedria', you must straight away
> Say 'Pamphila'. Should she want Phaedria in
> To dinner, you must counter 'Why not ask
> Pamphila for a song?' If she commends
> His handsome looks, you praise the girl's. In short,
> Give tit, my friend, for tat. The pin will prick.

So I drew the parallel. Certain high-born gentlemen, to whom I owed a debt of gratitude, were over-fond of an enemy of mine. In the Senate they would sometimes take him aside for a serious talk, sometimes salute him in hearty, hail-fellow-well-met style; this before my eyes. Well then, since they had *their* Publius, I hoped the gentlemen of the jury would allow *me* another Publius, with whom to sting those personages just a little in return for the mild provocation I had received! Nor did I merely *say* this; I often do it, Gods and men approving.

So much for Vatinius. Now as to Crassus: I was on very good terms with him, having in the interests of general harmony expunged by what I might call a deliberate act of oblivion all the grave wrongs he had done

252. A reconciliation between Cicero and Ap. Claudius had been effected by Pompey.
253. Early in 55. M. Cato's candidature was defeated by bribery and violence.
254. In 54, when Vatinius was accused of bribery. Cicero's witness to character seems to have been given in a second trial.
255. Terence, *The Eunuch*, 440 ff. Phaedria is a male character, Pamphila female.

me. I should have stomached his sudden defence of Gabinius,[256] whom he had attacked on the days immediately preceding, if he had gone to work without abusing me. But when I argued with him politely, he insulted me. I flared up. It was not, I think, just the irritation of the moment, which might not have carried me so far, but my suppressed resentment at the many injuries he had done me. I thought I had dissipated all that, but a residue was still there without my being aware of it, and now it all suddenly came to the surface. Here again certain persons, the same whom I so often indicate without naming names, expressed the greatest satisfaction at my plain speaking, and told me that now at last they felt I was restored to Rome the man I used to be; and outside the House too this fracas brought me many congratulations. And yet they went around saying how pleased they were to think that Crassus would be my enemy henceforward, and that his associates would never be my friends. These backbitings were brought to my knowledge by very worthy folk; and when Pompey pressed me as strongly as I have ever known him do to make it up with Crassus and Caesar wrote a letter making it plain that this quarrel has greatly upset him, why, I took account of my circumstances and of my heart as well. And Crassus, as though to make all Rome witness of our reconciliation, set out for his province virtually from my doorstep. He offered to dine with me, and did so at my son-in-law Crassipes' place in the suburbs. Accordingly I took up his cause at his urgent request and defended it in the Senate[257] as you say you have heard. Good faith required no less.

You now know my reasons for defending each particular cause or case, and the general position from which I take such part in politics as I may. I should like it to be clear to you that my attitude would have been just the same if I had had a completely open and untrammelled choice. I should not be in favour of fighting such formidable power, nor of abolishing the pre-eminence of our greatest citizens, even if that were possible. Nor should I be for sticking fast to one set of opinions, when circumstances have changed and the sentiments of honest men are no longer the same. I believe in moving with the times. Unchanging consistency of standpoint has never been considered a virtue in great

---

256. When Gabinius restored Ptolemy the Piper to his throne in 55, Cicero attacked him in the Senate. According to Dio Cassius (xxxix.60.1) the Consuls, Pompey and Crassus, came to his defence, calling Cicero 'exile', but no doubt the insult came from Crassus, not Pompey.

257. In January 54; cf. *Letters to Friends* 25 (*Fam.* 5.8).

statesmen. At sea it is good sailing to run before the gale, even if the ship cannot make harbour; but if she *can* make harbour by changing tack, only a fool would risk shipwreck by holding to the original course rather than change and still reach his destination. Similarly, while all of us as statesmen should set before our eyes the goal of peace with honour to which I have so often pointed, it is our aim, not our language, which must always be the same.

Therefore, as I have just stated, my politics would be exactly what they now are, even if my hands were completely free. But since I am attracted to this standpoint by favours from some quarters and pushed to it by injuries from others, I am by no means loath to take and express the political views which I deem most conducive to the public welfare as well as my own. I take this line the more openly and frequently because my brother Quintus is Caesar's Legate, and because Caesar has always received my slightest intervention, even purely verbal, on his behalf with such display of gratitude as to make me feel that he is deeply obliged to me. I use all his influence, which is very powerful, and his resources, which you know to be very large, as though they were my own. In fact, I do not think I could have foiled the designs of evil men against me in any other way than by adding to the means of defence which have always been at my disposal the goodwill of the powers that be.

Had I had you with me here, my belief is that I should have followed this same course. I know your natural temperance and moderation. I know that your warm friendship towards myself has no cast of malice towards others, that on the contrary you are as frank and straightforward as you are high-minded and unselfish. I have seen certain persons behave to you as you could once see them behaving to me. Surely my motives would have been yours. But when eventually I can avail myself of your presence, you will be my director in all things, with the same care for my standing as you had for my existence as a citizen. As for me, you may be sure of finding in me a partner and companion in all things, in your every act, opinion, and desire. No object in all my life will be so precious to me as to make you happier every day in the services you have rendered me.

You ask me to send you the products of my pen since you left Rome. There are some speeches, which I shall give to Menocritus – don't be alarmed, there are not very many of them! I have also composed – I am tending to get away from oratory and go back to the gentler Muses who please me best, as they always have from my youth – composed, as I was saying, three volumes in the form of an argument and dialogue *On the Orator*, in the manner (so at least I intended) of Aristotle. I think your son will find them of some use. They do not deal in the standard rules, but embrace the whole theory of oratory as the ancients knew it, both Aristotelian and Isocratic. I have also written a poem in three books *On my Vicissitudes*. I should have sent you this before, if I had thought right to publish it, for it is, and will be to all eternity, evidence of your services and of my gratitude. But I was inhibited by the thought, not so much of those who might feel themselves aspersed (*that* I have done sparingly and gently), but of my benefactors – if I had named them all, there would have been no end to it. All the same I shall see that you get these volumes too, if I can find a reliable bearer. All this part of my daily life I submit to you. Everything I may achieve in the way of literature and study, my old delights, I shall be most happy to bring to the bar of your judgement. You have always cared for these things.

What you say about your domestic concerns and the commissions you give me lie so close to my heart that I desire no reminder; a *request* I can scarcely take without real pain. You say you were unable to settle my brother Quintus' business, because sickness prevented you from crossing over to Cilicia[258] last summer, but that you will now use your best efforts to settle it. The fact is that my brother considers with good cause that once he has annexed this property his fortunes will have been laced on a firm foundation, thanks to you. I hope you will keep me abreast, as intimately and as often as you can, of your own affairs and of your (and my) dear boy's studies and exercises. And I would have you believe that you are to me the dearest and most valued friend that ever man had, and that I shall make it my business to prove this, not only to you, but to all mankind, indeed to all posterity.

Appius was in the habit of saying in private, and later said publicly in the Senate, that, if passage was given to a curiate[259] law, he would draw lots for a province with his colleague; but if there was no curiate law, he would come to an arrangement with his colleague and supersede you. A curiate law, he contended, was something a Consul should have, but did not absolutely need. Since he had a province by decree of the

---

258. i.e. Cilicia proper, as distinct from the whole Roman province so called. It has been suggested that Quintus wanted to buy a property adjoining one of his two estates near Arpinum, of which the owner was in Cilicia and so amenable to Lentulus' influence.

259. See Glossary of Terms.

Senate, he would hold military authority under the lex Cornelia[260] until he re-entered the city boundary. What your various friends may write to you I do not know – I understand that opinions differ. Some think you have the right to stay in your province because you are being superseded without a curiate law; others that, if you go, you are entitled to leave a governor in charge. For my part, I am less certain of the legal position (though even that is not so very dubious) than of the advisability of your handing over the province to your successor without delay. Your high standing and prestige, your independence, in which I know you take especial satisfaction, are involved, particularly as you cannot rebuff Appius' exorbitance without incurring some suspicion of a similar fault. I regard myself as no less bound to tell you my sentiments than to defend whatever course you adopt.

After writing the foregoing I received your letter about the tax-farmers. I cannot but commend your sense of justice, but could have wished that you had had the good luck, as it were, to avoid offending the interests or sentiments of that class, which you have always favoured in the past. I shall steadily defend your rulings. But you know their way, you know how strongly hostile they were to the great Q. Scaevola himself. Despite what has happened, I hope you will do everything in your power to reconcile, or at any rate mollify, their feelings towards you. That is difficult I grant, but I think it is what a wise man like yourself ought to do.

39
CICERO TO TIRO

Cumae, 17 April 53

From Tullius to Tiro greetings.

Indeed I want you to join me, but I am afraid of the journey. You have been very seriously ill, you are worn out, what with lack of food and purges and disease itself. Serious illnesses often have serious repercussions, if there is any imprudence. And then, right on top of the two days you will have on the road travelling to Cumae, there will be five

260. Law of Sulla regulating provincial administration.

days for the return journey. I want to be at Formiae on the 28th. Let me find you there, my dear Tiro, well and strong.

My (or *our*) literary brain-children have been drooping their heads missing you, but they looked up a little at the letter which Acastus brought. Pompey is staying with me as I write, enjoying himself in cheerful mood. He wanted to hear my compositions, but I told him that in your absence my tongue of authorship is tied completely. You must get ready to restore your services to my Muses. My promise[261] will be performed on the appointed day (I have taught you the derivation of 'faith').[262] Now mind you get thoroughly well. I shall be with you soon.

Goodbye.

40

Q. CICERO TO M. CICERO

Transalpine Gaul, May (end) or June (beginning) 53

From Quintus to his brother Marcus greetings.

My dear Marcus, as I hope to see you again and my boy and my[263] Tulliola and your son, I am truly grateful at what you have done about Tiro, in judging his former condition to be below his deserts and preferring us to have him as a friend rather than a slave. Believe me, I jumped for joy when I read your letter and his. Thank you, and congratulations!

If Statius' loyalty gives me so much pleasure,[264] how highly you must value the same qualities in Tiro, with the addition of literary accomplishments and conversation and culture, gifts worth even more than they! I have all manner of great reasons to love you, but this is a reason – the very fact that you so properly announced the event to me is a reason. I saw all that is you in your letter.

261. Tiro had been promised his freedom.
262. *fides*, supposed to be derived from *fit* ('is done').
263. Perhaps a mistake for 'your'.
264. Quintus will not have forgotten his brother's annoyance when Statius was freed; Letter 15, p. 55.

I have promised Sabinus'[265] boys all assistance, and shall be as good as my word.

41
CICERO TO ATTICUS

Minturnae, 5 or 6 May 51

Yes indeed, I saw your feelings when we said goodbye[266] and can testify to my own. All the more reason for you to see to it that they don't pass some new decree, so that we may not have to do without one another for more than one year.

With regard to Annius Saturninus, I approve of what you have done. But about guarantees, may I ask you to give them yourself as long as you are in Rome? And there are some guarantees in respect of sale, e.g. for the Mennius and Atilia properties. As for Oppius,[267] the steps taken are what I wished especially in that you have explained about the 800,000. I particularly want this paid, by borrowing if necessary so as not to have to wait for the last penny to come in from my debtors.

I come now to the line in the margin at the end of your letter in which you remind me about your sister. This is how the matter stands. When I got to Arpinum, my brother came over and we talked first and foremost about you, at considerable length. From that I passed to what you and I had said between us at Tusculum anent your sister. I have never seen anything more gentle and pacific than my brother's attitude towards her as I found it. Even if he had taken offence for any reason, there was no sign of it. So much for that day. Next morning we left Arpinum. On account of the holiday[268] Quintus had to stay the night at Arcanum. I stayed at Aquinum, but we lunched at Arcanum – you know the farm. When we arrived there Quintus said in the kindest way 'Pomponia, will

265. Sabinus is very likely Titurius Sabinus, one of Caesar's Legates who had lost his life and his army in the revolt of the Eburones. 'Boys' could mean either 'children' or 'slaves'.

266. Cicero had just set out for his province of Cilicia.

267. This refers to a sum of money borrowed by Cicero from Caesar. Oppius was handling the matter.

268. Probably the festival of the Lares (household gods) on 1 May, when, as here appears, slaves were entertained by their masters.

you ask the women in, and I'll get the boys?'[269] Both what he said and his intention and manner were perfectly pleasant, at least it seemed so to me. Pomponia however answered in our hearing 'I am a guest myself here.' That, I imagine, was because Statius had gone ahead of us to see to our luncheon. Quintus said to me 'There! This is the sort of thing I have to put up with every day.' You'll say 'What was there in that, pray?' A good deal. I myself was quite shocked. Her words and manner were so gratuitously rude. I concealed my feelings, painful as they were, and we all took our places at table except the lady. Quintus however had some food sent to her, which she refused. In a word, I felt my brother could not have been more forbearing nor your sister ruder. And I have left out a number of things that annoyed me at the time more than they did Quintus. I then left for Aquinum, while Quintus stayed behind at Arcanum and came over to see me at Aquinum early the following day. He told me that Pomponia had refused to spend the night with him and that her attitude when she said goodbye was just as I had seen it. Well, you may tell her to her face that in my judgement her manners that day left something to be desired. I have told you about this, perhaps at greater length than was necessary, to show you that lessons and advice are called for from your side as well as from mine.

For the rest, make sure you execute all my commissions before you leave Rome, and write to me about everything, and get behind Pomptinus, and when you have left let me know, and don't ever doubt how much I love and like you.

I parted very amicably from A. Torquatus at Minturnae, an excellent person. You might intimate to him in conversation that I have written something to you.

42

CICERO TO ATTICUS

Tarentum, 22 May 51

Every day, or rather from day to day, my letters to you grow shorter, for every day I suspect more strongly that you have already left for Epirus.

269. Servants and farm-workers.

However, to let you know that I have not forgotten your commission about which I wrote the other day, Pompey says that he is going to appoint five new Prefects in either province to get them exemption from jury service.

As for me, after spending three days in Pompey's company and at Pompey's house I am setting out for Brundisium on 22 May. I leave him in the most patriotic dispositions, fully prepared to be a bulwark against the dangers threatening. I shall expect a letter to tell me how you are and also where you are.

43

CAELIUS RUFUS TO CICERO[270]

Rome, c. 26 May 51

From Caelius to Cicero greetings.

Redeeming the promise I made as I took my leave of you to write you all the news of Rome in the fullest detail, I have been at pains to find a person to cover the whole ground so meticulously that I am afraid you may find the result too wordy. However, I know how curious you are and how much everybody abroad likes to be told of even the most trifling happenings at home. But I do hope you won't find me guilty of uppishness in my performance of this office because I have delegated the work to someone else. It is not that I shouldn't be charmed to give time to remembering you, busy though I am and, as you know, the laziest of letter-writers. But I imagine the volume[271] I am sending you makes my excuses easily enough. I don't know how anyone could have so much time on his hands as to observe all these items, let alone record them. It's all here – the Senate's decrees, the edicts, the gossip, the rumours. If this specimen does not happen to appeal to you, please let me know, so that I don't spend money merely to bore you. If there is any major political event which these hirelings could not cover satisfactorily, I shall

270. The eighth Book of the *Letters to Friends* consists entirely of letters from M. Caelius Rufus. They abound in problems of reading and interpretation.

271. i.e. roll of papyrus.

be careful to write you a full account of the manner of it and of consequent views and expectations.

At the moment we are not looking ahead to anything in particular. Those rumours about elections in Transpadane Gaul[272] were rife only as far as Cumae;[273] when I got back to Rome, I did not hear so much as a whisper on the subject. Moreover, Marcellus[274] has so far not referred the question of appointing new governors in the Gallic provinces to the Senate, and has put it off, so he told me himself, till the Kalends of June. That to be sure has elicited the same sort of talk as was going round about him when we were in Rome.[275]

If you found Pompey, as you wanted to do, be sure to write and tell me what you thought of him, how he talked to you, and what disposition he showed.[276] He is apt to say one thing and think another, but is usually not clever enough to keep his real aims out of view.

As regards Caesar,[277] rumours arrive in plenty about him and they are not pretty – but only of the whispering sort. One says he has lost his cavalry (which I think is certainly a fabrication), another that the Seventh Legion has taken a beating and that Caesar himself is under siege in the country of the Bellovaci, cut off from the rest of his army. But nothing is confirmed as yet, and even these unconfirmed reports are not bandied about generally but retailed as an open secret among a small coterie – you know who. But Domitius claps hand to mouth before he speaks.

On 24 May our pavement gossips[278] had spread it around that you were dead (their funeral, I hope!). All over town and in the Forum there was a great rumour that Q. Pompeius had murdered you on your road. Knowing that Q. Pompeius is operating boats at Bauli with so little to eat that my heart bleeds for him, I was unperturbed, and prayed that if any dangers *are* hanging over you we may be quit of them for the

272. A rumoured move by Caesar to give rights to the Italian Gauls north of the Po.

273. Caelius seems to have accompanied Cicero on his outward journey as far as Pompeii, and is referring to his own return journey to Rome.

274. M. Claudius Marcellus, Consul this year. The date on which Caesar should hand over his province was a main issue in Roman politics during the two years preceding the Civil War. After a vast amount of scholarly debate it is still doubtful when his command legally ended.

275. Perhaps that he was slow and inefficient.

276. cf. Letter 42.

277. Now contending with the aftermath of the great Gallic revolt of 52.

278. More literally 'loungers around the Rostra (in the Forum)'.

price of this lie. Your friend Plancus[279] is at Ravenna. Despite a massive largesse from Caesar, he is the same dismal vulgarian.[280]

Your work on politics[281] is all the rage.

44
CICERO TO ATTICUS

Athens, 27 June (?) 51

After reaching Athens on 24 June I have been here four days waiting for Pomptinus, and have still no definite news of his coming. But my thoughts, believe me, are all with you, and though I have no need of such admonitions the traces of your presence here call you the more vividly to my mind. In fact you are really our single topic of conversation.

But perhaps *you* prefer to hear something about myself. Here is what I have. Up to date no private individual or public body has been put to expense on my account or that of any member of my staff. We take nothing under the lex Julia or as private guests. All my people recognize that they must be careful of my good name. So far, so good. This has not gone unnoticed, and the Greeks are praising it and talking about it at large. As for the future, I am taking great pains over this point, as I saw you wished me to do. But let us save the applause till the end of the speech.

The rest is of such a nature that I often blame my unwisdom in not having found some way of escaping this job. It's so hopelessly uncongenial to me. Indeed and indeed 'let the cobbler ...'.[282] Early days, you may say, and point out that I'm not yet in harness. Too true, and I expect there is worse to come. But even here and now – well, I put up with it, even, as I think and hope, with an excellent grace, but in my heart of hearts I am on thorns. Irritability, rudeness, every sort of stupidity

279. Bursa. Ravenna was in Caesar's province.
280. The word-play is untranslatable. After Caesar's liberality Plancus might be rich (*beatus*) and well provided (*bene instructus*); but he was not happy (*beatus*) and well educated (*bene instructus*).
281. The six Books *On the Republic*.
282. A Greek proverb: 'Let each man practise the craft he knows.'

and bad manners and arrogance both in word and act – one sees examples every day. I won't give you details, not that I want to keep you in the dark but because they are hard to put into words. So you will admire my self-control when we get safely home again. I am getting plenty of practice in that virtue.

So much for this then too. Not that I have anything in mind to write about, for I have not so much as a notion as to what you are doing or where in the world you are. Indeed I have never in my life been so long without knowledge of my affairs, what for example has been done about the money matters relating to Caesar and to Milo.[283] Not only has no one come to me from home, nobody from Rome even has come to tell me what is going on in the political world. So if you have any information on matters which you think would interest me I shall be most grateful if you will get it conveyed to me.

What else is there? Why nothing, except this. I have greatly enjoyed Athens, so far as the city is concerned and its embellishments and the affection the people have for you, the goodwill they seem to have for me. But many things have changed, and philosophy is all at sixes and sevens, anything of value being represented by Aristus,[284] with whom I am staying. I left your friend Xeno (I should say 'our') for Quintus, though as he lives so near by we are together all day. I hope you will write me your plans as soon as you can, so that I know what you are doing and where you will be at any particular time, and above all when you are going to be in Rome.

45

CICERO TO C. MEMMIUS

Athens, June (end) or July (beginning) 51

From M. Cicero to C. Memmius greetings.

I was not quite sure whether it would have been in a way distressing

---

283. Cicero owed Caesar for a loan (see n. 267). He had bought up some of Milo's confiscated property.

284. Brother of Antiochus of Ascalon, whom he succeeded as head of the Academy.

to me to see you in Athens[285] or a pleasure. I should have felt pain in the injustice[286] of which you are the victim, but happiness in the philosophy with which you bear it. However, I would rather I *had* seen you. The measure of distress is not very much diminished when you are out of my sight, and, had I seen you, the pleasure I might have had would assuredly have been greater. So I shall not hesitate to try to see you as soon as I can fairly conveniently do so. In the meanwhile, allow me to raise with you now a matter which can be raised, and I imagine, settled, in correspondence. And first I would ask you not to do anything on my account which you would rather not. I hope you will grant me a favour which, as you will see, matters a good deal to me and not at all to you, but only if you are satisfied beforehand that you will do it gladly.

I have all manner of ties with Patro the Epicurean, except that in philosophy I strongly disagree with him. But in the early days in Rome I was one of those whose acquaintance he particularly cultivated (that was when he was also paying attentions to you and all connected with you). Recently too he gained all he wanted in the way of personal advantages and honoraria with myself as pretty well the chief among his protectors and friends. He was originally recommended to my care and regard by Phaedrus, of whom as a philosopher I had a great opinion when I was a boy, before I knew Philo, and whom even afterwards I respected as a man, honourable, amiable, and obliging.

Well, Patro wrote to me in Rome, asking me to make his peace with you and to beg you to let him have those ruins (or whatever they are) of Epicurus' house. I did not write to you, not wanting your building plans to be interfered with by a vicarious request of mine. When I arrived in Athens he again asked me to write to you to the same effect. This time I consented, because all your friends were agreed that you had given up your building. If that is so, and your interests are now quite unaffected, I hope you will take a lenient view of any little vexation which the untowardness of certain people may have caused you (I know the breed!), out of the great goodness of your heart or even by way of compliment to me. For my part, if you wish to know my personal sentiments, I don't see why he should make such a point of it nor why you should object – except that, after all, it is much less allowable in *you* to make a fuss

285. On his way to his province of Cilicia in 51 Cicero stopped in Athens from 24 June to 6 July.

286. Condemnation for electoral bribery in 52.

about nothing than in him. However, I am sure you know Patro's case and how he puts it. He pleads that he owes a responsibility to his office and duty, to the sanctity of testaments, to the prestige of Epicurus' name, to Phaedrus' adjuration, to the abode, domicile, and memorials of great men. If we wish to find fault with his insistence in this matter, we are at liberty to deride his whole life and philosophical principles. But really, since we have no deadly enmity towards him and others who find these doctrines to their taste, perhaps we ought not to be hard on him for taking it so much to heart. Even if he is wrong, it is silliness rather than wickedness that is leading him astray.

However, to make an end (I must come to it some time), I love Pomponius Atticus like a second brother. Nothing is more precious and delightful to me than to have him as a friend. Nobody is less of a busy-body, less inclined to importune, but I have never known him request anything of me so pressingly as this – not that he is one of the sect,[287] for he is a person of the most comprehensive and refined culture,[288] but he has a great regard for Patro, and had a deep affection for Phaedrus. He is confident that I should only have to signify a wish for you to grant the point, even if you intended to build. But now, if he hears that you have put aside your building project and that I have still not obtained the favour, he is going to think, not that you have been disobliging to me, but that I have not troubled to oblige *him*. May I therefore ask you to write to your people and tell them that the relevant decree of the Areopagus[289] (*hypomnematismos* as they call it) may be rescinded with your blessing?

However, I go back to where I started. Before you decide to comply with my request I want you to be satisfied that you will do so gladly for my sake. None the less, you may be sure that I shall be extremely grateful if you do what I ask.

Goodbye.

287. A notable statement. Atticus' Epicurean leanings were not taken very seriously by those who knew him.

288. The Epicureans by their own profession were not, and Cicero often jeers at their supposed ignorance and stupidity.

289. See n. 57.

CICERO TO ATTICUS

Tralles (?), 27 July 51

Until I get settled somewhere you must not expect my letters to be long or always in my own hand, but when I have the leisure I shall guarantee both. At present we are *en route*, and it is a hot and dusty road. I sent off a letter from Ephesus yesterday and I am sending this from Tralles. I expect to be in my province on the Kalends of August. From that day, if you love me, start moving the calendar. Meanwhile certain welcome reports are coming in, first of quiet from the Parthian quarter, second of the conclusion of the tax-farmers' agreements, lastly of a military mutiny pacified by Appius and arrears of pay discharged up to the Ides of July.

Asia has given me a marvellous reception. No one is a penny the poorer for my coming. I think that all my company are jealous for my good name. None the less I am very apprehensive, but hope for the best. All my party has now arrived with the exception of your friend Tullius. I propose to go straight to the army and devote the remaining summer months to campaigning, the winter ones to administering justice.

Knowing my curiosity about politics to be quite as keen as your own, I hope you will tell me everything, what is going on and what is to come. You can't do me a greater kindness, or rather only one, the greatest of all, and that is to dispatch my commissions, above all that 'domesticity' which you know lies nearest my heart.

Here then is a letter fully of hurry and dust. Those to follow will be more detailed.

CICERO TO ATTICUS

Camp at Pindenissum, 19 December 51

Pindenissum surrendered to me on the Saturnalia,[290] eight weeks after we began the siege. 'Pindenissum?' you'll say. 'And what the deuce may that be? Never heard of it.' Well, that's no fault of mine. I couldn't make Cilicia into Aetolia or Macedonia. You can take it from me here and now: at this time, with this army, and in this place, just so much could be done. Let me give you a *resumé*, as you permit in your last letter.

You know about my arrival in Ephesus, indeed you have congratulated me on the assemblage that day, one of the most flattering experiences of my life. From there, getting wonderful welcomes in such towns as there were, I reached Laodicea on 31 July. There I spent two days with great *réclame*, and by dint of courteous speeches effaced all earlier grievances. I did the same at Apamea, where I spent five days, and at Synnada (three days), at Philomelium (five days), at Iconium (ten). My administration of justice in these places lacked neither impartiality nor mildness nor responsibility.

Thence I arrived in camp on 24 August, and on the 28th reviewed the army near Iconium. As grave reports were coming in about the Parthians, I marched from camp there to Cilicia through that part of Cappadocia which borders Cilicia, so that Artavasdes of Armenia and the Parthians themselves would feel that their way to Cappadocia was blocked. After encamping for five days at Cybistra in Cappadocia I received intelligence that the Parthians were a long way away from that approach to Cappadocia and that the threat was rather to Cilicia. I therefore marched forthwith into Cilicia through the Gates of Taurus.

I reached Tarsus on 5 October and pressed on to the Amanus, which separates Syria from Cilicia at the watershed, a mountain range full of enemies of Rome from time immemorial. Here on 13 October we made a great slaughter of the enemy, carrying and burning places of great strength, Pomptinus coming up at night and myself in the morning. I received the title of general[291] from the army. For a few days we encamped near Issus in the very spot where Alexander, a considerably better general

290. 17 December.
291. *imperator* (see Glossary of Terms).

than either you or I, pitched his camp against Darius. There we stayed five days, plundering and laying waste the Amanus, and then left. Meanwhile – you have heard tell of panics and of nerve-warfare[292] – the rumour of my advent encouraged Cassius, who was shut up in Antioch, and struck terror into the Parthians. Cassius pursued their retreat from the town and gained a success. Osaces, the celebrated Parthian general, died a few days later of a wound received in the flight. My name stood high in Syria.

Bibulus arrived meanwhile. I suppose he wanted to be even with me over this bauble of a title – he started looking for a scrap of laurel in the wedding cake[293] in these same mountains of Amanus. The result was that he lost his entire First Cohort, including a Chief-Centurion, Asinius Dento, a distinguished man in his own class, and the other Centurions of the cohort, also a Military Tribune, Sex. Lucilius, whose father T. Gavius Caepio is a man of wealth and standing. It was certainly a nasty reverse, both in itself and as coming when it did.

For my part I marched on Pindenissum, a strongly fortified town of the Free Cilicians which had been in arms as long as anyone can remember. The inhabitants were wild, fierce folk, fully equipped to defend themselves. We drew a rampart and moat round the town, erected a huge mound with penthouses and a high tower, plenty of siege artillery and a large number of archers. In the end, with a great deal of labour and apparatus and many of our own men wounded but none killed, we finished the job. The Saturnalia was certainly a merry time, for men as well as officers. I gave them the whole of the plunder excepting the captives, who are being sold off today, 19 December. As I write there is about HS 120,000 on the stand. I am handing over the army to my brother Quintus, who will take it into winter quarters in unsettled country. I myself am returning to Laodicea.

So far, so much. But to return to the past. So far as concerns the capital object of your exhortations, the most important point of all, in which you are anxious that I should satisfy even that Ligurian Momus,[294] well, confound me if anything could be more fastidiously correct! But I don't talk of 'restraint' in this connection, a word which suggests virtuous resistance to pleasurable temptation. Never in all my life have I gained

292. A Greek phrase, meaning literally 'the illusions of war'.

293. i.e., to look for glory (the victor's, or Triumphator's, laurel crown) on easy terms. The elder Cato's recipe for a wedding-cake contains laurel bark and the cake was cooked on laurel leaves (De re rustica, 121).

294. The fault-finding god. Perhaps the reference is to an old enemy, Aelius Ligus.

so much pleasure as I do from my integrity here, and it is not so much the *réclame*, which is enormous, as the practice itself that gratifies me. In a word, it has been worth it. I did not know myself, I never quite realized my capabilities in this line. I have a right to a swollen head. It is a fine achievement. Meanwhile here is a scintillation: Ariobarzanes owes his life and throne to me. Just *en passant* I rescued king and kingdom, by good judgement and influence and by showing those who were plotting against him that they could not get near me, much less their money.[295] All the while not a straw was lifted from Cappadocia. I have cheered poor Brutus[296] up as far as I could – I am as fond of him as yourself, I almost said 'as of yourself'. And I hope too that in my entire year of office the province will not be charged a penny.

That is all I have to tell. I am now setting about sending an official letter to Rome. There will be more matter in it than if I had written from the Amanus. But to think that you won't be in Rome! Everything depends however on what happens on the Kalends of March.[297] I am afraid that if Caesar is recalcitrant when the question of his command comes up, I may be kept on. If you were on the spot, I should have no fears.

I come back to the affairs of the town, of which I had for a long while been in ignorance until I learned of them on 16 December from your most agreeable letter. Your freedman Philogenes took great trouble to ensure its safe delivery over a very long and not too safe route. The one you say you gave to Laenius' boys I have not received. The Senate's resolutions on Caesar and your own expectations make pleasant reading. If he yields to them, we are saved. I am the less distressed about Plaetorius' fire because * has been scorched.[298] I'm longing to know why Lucceius took such a strong line about Q. Cassius[299] and what happened.

I am under instructions to give your nephew Quintus his white gown when I get to Laodicea. I shall keep him on a tighter rein. Deiotarus, from whom I have had a large military contingent, has written that he will come to me at Laodicea with the boys. I am looking forward to a

---

295. This incident is fully described in an extant dispatch (*Letters to Friends*, 105).

296. M. Brutus was owed money by the King of Cappadocia, whom Cicero had been charged by the Senate to protect.

297. The question of replacing Caesar in his command was due for debate on the coming I March.

298. The reference is obscure.

299. He had probably been prosecuted or threatened with prosecution for his conduct as Pompey's Quaestor in Spain. Lucceius, Pompey's intimate friend, seems to have been against him; hence, perhaps, his support for Caesar in 49.

letter from Epirus, so that I can keep track of your holidays as well as of your business. Nicanor is doing good work and I am treating him handsomely. I think I shall send him to Rome with my official dispatch; that will ensure careful delivery and at the same time he can bring me back reliable news of and from you. I am obliged to Alexis for so often adding his salutations, but why does he not do it in a letter of his own, as *my* Alexis[300] does to you? We are looking for a *cor* for Phemius.[301] But enough. Look after your health and see that I am told when you mean to return to Rome. Again best wishes for your health.

I was most careful to recommend your affairs and your people to Thermus when I saw him at Ephesus, and I have now done so again by letter; and I found Thermus himself most anxious to oblige you. I wrote to you some time ago about Pammenes' house; please do your best to see that nothing is done to upset the boy's tenure, which he owes to your favour and mine. I think this will be to our joint credit, moreover it will much oblige me.

48

CICERO TO P. SILIUS

Province of Cilicia, 51 or 50

From M. Cicero to P. Silius, Propraetor, greetings.

With P. Terentius Hispo, who works for the Grazing Rents Company[302] as their local manager, I have a great deal of familiar contact, and each of us is indebted to the other for important services, equal and mutual. His reputation very largely depends on his concluding tax agreements with the communes still outstanding. I do not forget that I tried my own hand at the business in Ephesus and was quite unable to get the Ephesians to oblige. However, according to the universal persuasion and my own observation, your complete integrity combined with your remarkable

300. Tiro.

301. A musical slave of Atticus', named no doubt after the minstrel in the *Odyssey*, wanted a local instrument which Cicero calls by the Greek word for 'horn'. It was probably a kind of flute.

302. i.e. a Roman company which bought the right to collect these rents from the provincials.

civility and gentleness have earned you the heartiest compliance of the natives with your every nod. I would therefore particularly request you as a compliment to me to make it your wish that Hispo should get this credit.

Furthermore I am closely connected with the members of the Company, not only because it is under my patronage as a whole but because I am on very close terms with many of them individually. So you will both do my friend Hispo a good turn at my instance and strengthen my relations with the Company. You yourself will reap a rich reward from Hispo's attentiveness (he is very appreciative of a service) and from the influence of the Company members, persons of the highest consequence. You will also do me a great kindness. For you may take it that within the whole sphere of your provincial authority you could do nothing that would oblige me more.

49
CICERO TO APPIUS PULCHER

Laodicea, soon after 11 February 50

From Cicero to Appius Pulcher greetings.

I shall be writing to you at greater length when I get more time. I am writing this in haste, Brutus' boys having met me at Laodicea and told me that they are in a hurry to get back to Rome. So I have given them no letters except this to you and one to Brutus.

Envoys from Appia have handed me a roll from you full of highly unreasonable complaints concerning their building, which is said to have been stopped by a letter of mine. In the same missive you ask me to set them free to proceed with the building as soon as possible before they run into winter, and at the same time you complain with much asperity of my having forbidden them to levy special taxes until I had examined the case and given permission. That, you say, was one way of stopping them, since I could not make any examination until I returned from Cilicia for the winter.

Allow me to answer all these points, and observe the justice of your expostulation. To start with, I had been approached by persons who claimed that they were being subjected to taxation on an intolerable scale. Was it so unfair that I should write instructing them not to proceed until I had investigated the facts of the case? Oh, but I could not do this before winter – that's what you say in your letter. As though it was for me to go to them to investigate, and not for them to come to me! 'At such a distance?' you ask. Come, when you gave them your letter asking me not to stop them building before winter, did you not suppose they would come to me? To be sure they managed this absurdly enough – they did not bring me the letter, which was meant to enable them to do the job during the summer, until after midwinter. But you must understand that the objectors to the taxes are in a large majority over those who want them levied – and that none the less I shall do what I think you wish. So much for the good folk of Appia.

I have heard from my marshal Pausanias, Lentulus' freedman, that you complained to him about my not having gone to meet you. I treated you with contempt, it seems and my arrogance is quite monstrous! The facts are that your boy arrived about the second watch[303] with a message that you would join me before daybreak in Iconium. As there were two roads and he said it was uncertain which of them you were taking, I sent A. Varro, a close friend of yours, by one and my Prefect of Engineers, Q. Lepta, by the other to meet you, instructing both to hasten back from you to me so that I could go to meet you. Lepta came hurrying back to tell me that you had already passed the camp. I went to Iconium immediately. The rest you know.[304] Was it likely that I should not turn out to meet *you* – Appius Claudius, Commander-in-Chief, entitled by traditional practice to the courtesy, and, what is most to the purpose, my friend – I who am in the habit of carrying my desire to please in many such matters further than my own rank and dignity require? But I say no more. Pausanias also told me of the following remark of yours: 'Well, of course! Appius went to meet Lentulus, Lentulus went to meet Ampius;[305] but Cicero go to meet Appius, oh no!' Really! These absurdities from *you* – a man of excellent sound sense, as I judge, much learning also, great knowledge of the world, and, let me add urbanity, which the Stoics very rightly rank as a virtue! Do you suppose that any Appiety

303. About 9 p.m.
304. We do not. But it seems unlikely that a meeting took place.
305. See n. 149.

or Lentulity[306] counts more with me than the ornaments of merit? Even
before I gained the distinctions which the world holds highest, I was never
dazzled by aristocratic names; it was the men who bequeathed them to
you that I admired. But after I won and filled positions of the highest
authority in such a fashion as to let me feel no need of additional rank
or fame, I hoped to have become the equal (never the superior) of you
and your peers. And I may add that I have never observed a different
way of thinking in Cn. Pompeius or P. Lentulus, one of whom I judge
the greatest man that ever lived, the other greater than myself. If *you*
think otherwise, you might do worse than pay rather particular attention
to what Athenodorus, son of Sandon, has to say on these points – in
order to understand the true meaning of *noblesse*.

But to come back to the point. I want you to believe that I am not
only your friend, but your very good friend. Naturally I shall do all I
can in a practical way to enable you to decide that this is really so. As
for yourself, if your object is not to appear bound to work for my interests
while I am away as heartily as I worked for yours, why, I hereby relieve
you of that preoccupation –

> Others stand by me
> to do me grace, and before all wise Zeus.[307]

But if you are a fault-finder by nature, you will not make me any the
less your well-wisher; all you will achieve is to leave me less concerned
about your reactions.

I have written rather frankly, in the consciousness of my own friendli-
ness and goodwill, an attitude which, as I have adopted it out of deliberate
choice, I shall maintain so long as *you* wish.

306. i.e. nobility, as though Appius was the name of a family. In fact it was a personal
name (*praenomen*), but one almost exclusive to the patrician Claudii. Both nouns are, of course,
coined by Cicero.

307. *Iliad*, 1.174 f. 'Wise Zeus' seems to indicate Pompey.

CICERO TO PAPIRIUS PAETUS

Laodicea, mid March (?) 50

From Cicero, Imperator, to Paetus.

Your letter has made a first-rate general out of me. I had no idea you were such a military expert – evidently you have thumbed the treatises of Pyrrhus and Cineas.[308] So I intend to follow your precepts, with one addition – I mean to keep a few boats handy on the coast. They say there's no better weapon against Parthian cavalry! But why this frivolity? You don't know what sort of Commander-in-Chief you have to deal with. In my command here I have put into practice the whole *Education of Cyrus*,[309] a work which I read so often that I wore out the book. But we'll joke another time when we meet, as soon I hope we shall.

Now stand by for orders (or rather to obey them), to use the ancient expression.

I have a great deal to do with M. Fabius, as I think you know, and a great regard for him as a man of the highest integrity and unusual modesty, also because he helps me very effectively in my controversies[310] with your Epicurean boozing-partners. After he joined me at Laodicea and I asked him to stay with me, he received a quite appalling letter, a bolt from the blue, informing him that a farm near Herculaneum, which he owns jointly with his brother, Q. Fabius, had been put up for sale by the latter. M. Fabius has taken this very much to heart. He believed that his brother, who is not remarkable for good sense, had been instigated by his (Marcus') enemies to take this extraordinary step.

Now, my dear Paetus, be a friend and take the whole affair upon yourself, and relieve Fabius of the worry. We need your name and sound judgement, and your personal influence too. Don't let the brothers get into litigation and become embroiled in discreditable lawsuits. Mato and

308. King Pyrrhus of Epirus wrote a treatise on tactics, and his minister Cineas epitomized a work on strategy by one Aelian.

309. Xenophon's work on the Ideal Ruler (cf. *Letters to Atticus* 23 (11.3).2), much of which is concerned with the Ruler as General.

310. Perhaps with reference to the *de Republica*. M. Fabius Gallus was an Epicurean and a *littérateur*.

Pollio[311] are Fabius' enemies. Briefly, I assure you that I cannot write down in full how much you will oblige me if you put Fabius' mind at ease. He thinks, and persuades me, that it all depends on you.

51

CICERO TO CAELIUS RUFUS

Laodicea, 4 April 50

M. Cicero, Imperator, to M. Caelius, Curule Aedile, greetings.

Would you ever have thought that I could find myself short of words – and not only the kind of words you orators use, but even this vernacular small change? The reason is that I am on tenterhooks to hear what is decreed about the provinces. I have a marvellous longing for Rome, and miss my family and friends, you especially, more than you would believe. I am sick and tired of the province. I think I have gained a reputation here such that rather than seek to add to it I should beware of fortune's turns. Besides the whole thing is unworthy of my powers. I am able to bear, am used to bearing, greater loads in the service of the state. Then again, the threat of a great war hangs over us; this I believe I escape if I leave by the appointed day.

About the panthers,[312] the usual hunters are doing their best on my instructions. But the creatures are in remarkably short supply, and those we have are said to be complaining bitterly because they are the only beings in my province who have to fear designs against their safety. Accordingly they are reported to have decided to leave this province and go to Caria. But the matter is receiving close attention, especially from Patiscus. Whatever comes to hand will be yours, but what that amounts to I simply do not know. I do assure you that your career as Aedile is of great concern to me. The date is itself a reminder – I am writing on Great Mother's Day.[313] On your side, please send me an account of the

---

311. Unknowns, unless Pollio is the famous Asinius Pollio.
312. Wanted by Caelius for the show he had to give as Aedile.
313. 4 April, the first day of the festival of Cybele. Her games, as well as the Roman ones, seem to have been the responsibility of the Curule Aediles.

whole political situation as full as you can make it. I shall consider what I hear from you as my most reliable information.

52
CAELIUS RUFUS TO CICERO

Rome, the day after the preceding

From Caelius to Cicero greetings.

How soon you want to leave your present whereabouts I don't know, but for my part, the more successful you have been so far the more I want it. As long as you remain out there, I shall be on thorns about the risk of a Parthian war, for fear some alarm may wipe the grin off my face. This letter will be rather brief – I am giving it without notice to one of the tax-farmers' couriers, who is in a hurry. I gave a longer one to your freedman yesterday.

Nothing new has happened really, unless you want to be told such items as the following – which, of course, you do. Young Cornificius has got himself engaged to Orestilla's daughter. Paula Valeria, Triarius' sister, has divorced her husband for no reason the day he was due to get back from his province. She is to marry D. Brutus. There have been a good many extraordinary incidents of this sort during your absence which I have not yet reported. Servius Ocella would never have got anyone to believe he went in for adultery, if he had not been caught twice in three days. Where? Why, just the last place I should have wished – I leave something for you to find out from other informants! Indeed I rather fancy the idea of a Commander-in-Chief enquiring of this person and that the name of the lady with whom such-and-such a gentleman has been caught napping.

CATO TO CICERO

Rome, latter April 50

From M. Cato to M. Cicero, Imperator, greetings.

Patriotism and friendship alike urge me to rejoice, as I heartily do, that your ability, integrity, and conscientiousness, already proved in great events at home when you wore the gown of peace, are no less actively at work in arms abroad. Accordingly, I did what my judgement allowed me to do: that is to say, I paid you tribute with my voice and vote for defending your province by your integrity and wisdom, for saving Ariobarzanes' throne and person,[314] and for winning back the hearts of our subjects to a loyal support of Roman rule.

As for the decree of a Supplication, if *you* prefer us to render thanks to the Immortal Gods in respect of provision taken for the public good by your own admirable policy and administrative rectitude, not at all the result of chance, rather than to put it down to your own credit – why, I am very glad of it. If, however, you regard a Supplication as an earnest of a Triumph, and on that account prefer the praise to go to accident[315] rather than to yourself, the fact is that a Triumph does not always follow a Supplication. On the other hand, the Senate's judgement that a province has been held and preserved by its governor's mild and upright administration rather than by the swords of an army or the favour of the Gods is a far greater distinction than a Triumph; and that is what I proposed in the House.

I have written to you at some length on this subject (contrary to my normal habit) so that you may realize, as I most earnestly hope you will, my anxiety to convince you of two things: firstly, as touching your prestige, I desired what I conceived to be most complimentary to yourself; secondly, I am very glad that what you preferred has come to pass.

Goodbye, remember me kindly, and follow your chosen course, rendering to our subjects and to the state their due of a strict and conscientious administration.

314. See n. 295.
315. Cato as a Stoic believed in a Providence, but in ordinary language and thought the ideas of fate, providence, gods, and fortune were much confused at this period.

54

CICERO TO CATO

Tarsus, late July 50

From M. Cicero to M. Cato greetings.

I think it is Hector in Naevius who says 'Glad thy praise doth make me, father, praise from one that praised is.'[316] Praise is pleasant, you will agree, when it comes from those who have themselves led honoured lives. Yes, I assure you that the congratulatory terms of your letter and the testimonial you gave me in the House represent to my mind the sum of attainment. I am particularly flattered and gratified to feel that you were glad to accord to friendship what you would have had no hesitation in according to truth. And if many (not to say all) members of our society were Catos (the marvel being that it has produced *one*), how could I think of comparing the triumphal car and crown with an encomium from you? To my way of thinking, and by the unbiased and delicate standards of a philosopher, nothing can be more complimentary than that speech of yours of which my friends have sent me a copy.

But I have explained the reason for my inclination (I will not say 'desire') in my previous letter.[317] Perhaps you did not find it altogether convincing: at any rate it means that I do not regard the honour[318] as something to be unduly coveted, but at the same time that, if proffered by the Senate, I feel I ought by no means to spurn it. I trust, furthermore, that in view of the labours I have undertaken for the public good the House will deem me not unworthy of an honour, especially one so commonly bestowed. If it so turns out, all I ask of you is that (to use your own very kind expressions), having accorded to me what in your judgement is most complimentary to myself, you should be glad if what I prefer comes about. Your actions, your views as expressed in the Senate, your letter, and the very fact that you were present at the drafting of the decree are clear evidence to me that the grant of the Supplication in my honour was agreeable to you. For I am well aware that such decrees are usually drafted by the closest friends of the persons honoured.

316. See n. 168.
317. *Letters to Friends*, 110.
318. A Triumph.

I shall see you soon, as I hope, and only pray we meet in a better political atmosphere than I fear we shall.

55
CICERO TO ATTICUS

Side, c. 3 August 50

Here am I in my province paying Appius all manner of compliments, when out of the blue I find his prosecutor[319] becoming my son-in-law! 'Good luck to that,' say you. So I hope and I am very sure you so desire. But believe me it was the last thing I expected. I had actually sent reliable persons to the ladies in connection with Ti. Nero, who had treated with me. They got to Rome after the *fiançailles*. However I hope this is better. The ladies are evidently quite charmed with the young man's attentiveness and engaging manners. For the rest, no black paint please!

But what's all this? *Panem populo*[320] at Athens? Do you think that is in order? Not that *my* volumes have anything against it, since it was not a largesse to fellow-countrymen but a piece of generosity to foreign hosts. But do you tell *me* to 'think about' the Academy porch, when Appius has already given up *thinking*[321] about Eleusis?

I am sure you will be grieving about Hortensius.[322] For my own part I am deeply distressed. I had made up my mind to live on really close terms with him.

I have put Coelius in charge of the province. You'll say he is a boy, and perhaps a silly boy, without sense of responsibility or self-control. I agree. There was nothing else to be done. The letter I had from you quite a long time ago in which you wrote that you were suspending judgement[323] as to what I ought to do about a deputy struck home. I saw the reasons for your 'suspense of judgement', and they were my

319. Dolabella.
320. Atticus had evidently made a present of grain to the city of Athens.
321. i.e. he had taken action. Cicero had in mind to give a porch (*stoa*) to the Athenian Academy. Appius was making a similar benefaction in Eleusis.
322. Cicero had heard that Hortensius was dying.
323. Atticus had used a Greek term denoting philosophic doubt.

reasons too. Should I hand over to a boy? Contrary to public interest. To my brother then? That was contrary to my own (*except* my brother there was no one whom I could put ahead of the Quaestor, a nobleman too, without insulting him). None the less, so long as the Parthians looked like coming down on us, I had decided to leave my brother, or even for the country's sake to stay on myself in contravention of the Senate's decree. But when by an incredible stroke of luck they disappeared, my doubts were removed. I could hear the talk: 'Aha, left his brother, has he? Hardly what one would call governing for one year only, that! Thought the Senate wanted governors without previous service. This chap's had three years of it.'

So much for the public ear. For your own, I should never have had a minute's peace of mind for fear of some piece of irritability or rudeness or carelessness – these things happen. Then there's his son, a boy, and a boy with a fine conceit of himself – any incident involving him would be *most* distressing. His father was unwilling to send him away and was annoyed at your advising it. But as things are, Coelius – I won't say 'can please himself', but still I am much less concerned. Another point: Pompey, with all his power and backing, chose Q. Cassius without lots cast, similarly Caesar Antony. Was I to offend an officer assigned to me by lot, and have him spying too on the man I appointed? No, this is the better way; there are more precedents for it and for an old man like me it's clearly more appropriate! As for yourself, I have put you in his best books, tremendously so I assure you, and read him your letter or rather your secretary's.

My friend's letters beckon me to a Triumph, something I feel I ought not to neglect in view of this second birth[324] of mine. So you too, my dear fellow, must start wanting it, so that I shan't look so foolish.

324. The return from exile.

56

CAELIUS RUFUS TO CICERO

Rome, c. 8 August 50

From Caelius to Cicero greetings.

What a spectacle you have missed here! If you've made Arsaces[325] prisoner and stormed Seleucia, it wasn't worth the sacrifice. Your eyes would never have been sore again if you'd seen Domitius' face when he heard of his defeat.[326] The polling was heavy, and support for the candidates quite on party lines. Only a tiny minority gave their backing in conformity with personal loyalties. Accordingly Domitius is my bitter enemy. He has not a friend in the world whom he hates more than me![327] – all the more so because he regards himself as having been robbed of the Pontificate[328] and me as the author of the outrage. Now he is furious at the general rejoicing over his discomfiture and at the fact that Antony had only one more ardent supporter (Curio) than myself. As for young Cn. Saturninus, he has been charged by none other than Cn. Domitius.[329] To be sure his past makes him far from popular. We are now waiting for the trial. Actually there is good hope for him after Sex. Peducaeus'[330] acquittal.

On high politics, I have often told you that I do not see peace lasting another year; and the nearer the inevitable struggle approaches, the plainer the danger appears. The question on which the dynasts will join issue is this: Cn. Pompeius is determined not to allow C. Caesar to be elected Consul unless he surrenders his army and provinces; whereas Caesar is persuaded that he cannot survive if he leaves his army. He makes the proposition, however, that both surrender their military forces. So this is what their love-affair, their scandalous union, has come to –

325. i.e. the King of Parthia. The Parthian kings bore the name of the founder of their line in addition to their individual names, like the Ptolemies of Egypt.

326. As a candidate for the vacancy in the Augural College created by the death of Hortensius. He was beaten by Mark Antony.

327. cf. n. 226.

328. The reading is conjectural. If right, it refers to a previous failure of Domitius to gain a place in the College of Pontiffs, of which he later became a member.

329. L. Domitius' son. Cn. (Sentius) Saturninus had no doubt supported Antony.

330. Not Cicero's former Praetor or his son, but perhaps a supporter of Caesar who became governor of Sardinia in 48. The circumstances of his trial are unknown.

not covert backbiting, but outright war! As for my own position, I don't know what course to take; and I don't doubt that the same question is going to trouble you. I have ties of obligation and friendship with these people. On the other side, I love the cause but hate the men.

I expect you are alive to the point that, when parties clash in a community, it behoves a man to take the more respectable side so long as the struggle is political and not by force of arms; but when it comes to actual fighting he should choose the stronger, and reckon the safer course the better. In the present quarrel Cn. Pompeius will evidently have with him the Senate and the people who sit on juries,[331] whereas all who live in present fear and small hope for the future will rally to Caesar. His army is incomparably superior. To be sure there is time enough to consider their respective resources and choose one's side.

I almost forgot the most interesting item of all. Did you know that Appius is performing prodigies of censorial vigour – works of art, size of estates, debt are all grist to his mill. He is convinced that the Censorship is face cream or washing soda, but I fancy he is making a mistake; in trying to scrub out the stains he is laying open all his veins and vitals.[332] Make haste in God's name and man's and get here as soon as you can to laugh at our frolics – at Drusus trying offences under the lex Scantinia,[333] at Appius taking official action about works of art.[334] Believe me, you must hurry. Our friend Curio is considered to have shown good sense in not pressing his point about pay for Pompey's troops.

Well, to sum up: what do I think will happen? If neither of the two goes off to the Parthian war, I see great quarrels ahead in which strength and steel will be the arbiters. Both are well prepared, morally and materially. If it were not for the personal risk involved, Fate is preparing a mighty and fascinating show for your benefit.

331. i.e. the rich and respectable.
332. Or 'flesh'.
333. See Glossary of Terms. Drusus was apparently a notorious offender.
334. Appius had allegedly plundered Greece to assemble his own art collection.

CICERO TO TIRO

Leucas, 7 November 50

From Tullius to his dear Tiro best greetings, also from Marcus and my brother Quintus and Quintus junior.

I read your letter with varying feelings. The first page upset me badly, the second brought me round a little. So now, if not before, I am clear that until your health is quite restored you should not venture upon travel either by land or water. I shall see you soon enough if I see you thoroughly strong again.

You say the doctor has a good reputation, and so I hear myself; but frankly, I don't think much of his treatments. You ought not to have been given soup[335] with a weak stomach. However, I have written to him at some length, and also to Lyso.[336] To Curius, who is a most agreeable fellow, very obliging and good-natured, I have written a great deal, including the suggestion that, if you agree, he should move you over to his house. I am afraid our friend Lyso is a little casual. All Greeks are; also, he has not replied to a letter he received from me. However, you commend him; so you must judge for yourself what is best. One thing, my dear Tiro, I do beg of you: don't consider money at all where the needs of your health are concerned. I have told Curius to advance whatever you say. I imagine the doctor ought to be given something to make him more interested in your case.[337]

Your services to me are beyond count – in my home and out of it, in Rome and abroad, in private affairs and public, in my studies and literary work. You will cap them all if I see you your own man again, as I hope I shall. I think it would be very nice, if all goes well, for you to sail home with Quaestor Mescinius. He is not uncultivated, and he seemed to me to have a regard for you. But when you have given every possible attention to your health, *then* my dear Tiro, attend to sailing

---

335. Or 'gravy' or 'sauce'.
336. Cicero's host at Patrae in whose house Tiro was staying.
337. Apparently the doctor (whose name was Asclapo: see Letter 85) was not charging a special fee. He may have looked after Lyso's household for a regular payment.

arrangements. I don't now want you to hurry in any way. My only concern is for you to get well.

Take my word for it, dear Tiro, that nobody cares for me who does not care for you. Your recovery is most important to you and me, but many others are concerned about it. In the past you have never been able to recruit yourself properly, because you wanted to give me of your best at every turn. Now there is nothing to stand in your way. Put everything else aside, think only of your bodily well-being. I shall believe you care for me in proportion to the care you devote to your health.

Goodbye, my dear Tiro, goodbye and fondest good wishes. Lepta sends you his, so do we all. Goodbye.

7 November, from Leucas.

58

CICERO TO TIRO

Leucas, 7 November 50

From Tullius and Marcus and the Quinti to their nicest and best of Tiros best greetings.

k what a charmer you are! We spent two hours at Thyrreum,[338] and our host Xenomenes is as fond of you as though he had been your bosom companion. He has promised you everything you need, and I believe he will be as good as his word. I think it would be a good plan for him to take you to Leucas when you are stronger, to finish your convalescence there. You must see what Curius and Lyso and the doctor think. I wanted to send Mario back to you for you to send him to me with a letter when you were a little better, but I reflected that Mario could bring me only one letter, and I expect them one after another.

So do what you can, and, if you care for me, see that Acastus goes down to the harbour every day. There will be plenty of folk to whom you can safely give a letter and who will be glad to carry it to me. For my part I shall take advantage of every traveller to Patrae.

I pin all my hope of your getting proper treatment and attention on

338. On the outward journey in 51.

Curius. He has the kindest of hearts and the truest affection for me. Put yourself entirely in his hands. I had rather see you fit and well a little later on than weak straight away. So attend to nothing except getting well – I shall attend to the rest.

Goodbye once again.

Leaving Leucas, 7 November.

59

CICERO TO ATTICUS

Formiae, c. 18 December 50

I have really nothing to write to you about. You know all there is to know, and I on my side have nothing to expect from you. So let me just keep up my old-established habit of not letting anyone go your way without a letter.

The political situation alarms me deeply, and so far I have found scarcely anybody who is not for giving Caesar what he demands rather than fighting it out. The demand is impudent no doubt, but more moderate than was expected (?). And why should we start standing up to him now? 'Sure, 'tis no worse a thing'[339] than when we gave him his five years' extension or when we brought in the law authorizing his candidature *in absentia*. Or did we put these weapons into his hands only to fight him now that he is equipped and ready? You will ask me what line I shall take in the House. Not the same as in my own mind. *There* I shall vote for peace at any price, but in the House I shall echo Pompey, and I shall not do it in a spirit of subservience either. But it is yet another major misfortune for the country that for me especially there is in a way something wrong in dissenting from Pompey on such high matters.[340]

339. From *Odyssey*, XII. 209.
340. Cicero often refers to the debt of gratitude he owed Pompey for coming to his rescue in 57.

CICERO TO ATTICUS

Formiae, 25 or 26 December 50

There is really no need to be so emphatic about Dionysius, as though a nod from you would not satisfy me. Your silence made me the more suspicious because it is a practice of yours to cement friendships by your testimonials and because I am told he has talked about me different ways to different people. But you quite convince me that it is as you say, and so I feel towards him as you wish.

I too had made a note of your day[341] from one of your letters which you wrote me as a touch of fever was coming on and had observed that it would not be inconvenient, relatively speaking, for you to visit me at Alba on 3 January. But don't, I beg you, do anything to the detriment of your health. After all, one or two days are not so important.

I see that Dolabella is down for a third share in Livia's will along with two co-heirs, but is required to change his name. It is a question in political ethics whether it is right for a young man of noble family to change his name under a lady's will. But we shall solve the problem more scientifically when we know approximately how much a third share of a third share amounts to.

Your forecast that I should be seeing Pompey before I came your way has proved correct. On the 25th he overtook me near Lavernium. We went back to Formiae together and talked privately from two o'clock till evening. The answer to your question whether there is any hope of a pacification, so far as I could see from Pompey's talk, which lacked neither length nor detail, is that there isn't even the desire for one. His view is that if Caesar is made Consul, even after giving up his army, it will mean the subversion of the constitution; and he further thinks that when Caesar hears that preparations against him are energetically proceeding he will forgo the Consulate this year and prefer to retain his army and province. But should Caesar take leave of his senses, Pompey is quite contemptuous of anything he can do and confident in his own and the Republic's forces. All in all, though I often thought of 'Mars on both sides',[342] I felt relieved

---

341. i.e., fever-day. Atticus suffered from a quartan fever.
342. i.e., the uncertainties of battle. The phrase is the beginning of a line in the *Iliad*: 'Enyalius (= Ares, Mars) fights on both sides and slays the slayer.'

as I heard such a man, courageous, experienced, and powerful in prestige, discoursing statesmanwise on the dangers of a false peace. We had in front of us a speech made by Antony on 21 December containing a denunciation of Pompey from the day he came of age, a protest on behalf of the persons condemned,[343] and threats of armed force. Talking of which Pompey remarked: 'How do you expect Caesar to behave if he gets control of the state, when his feckless nobody of a Quaestor dares to say this sort of thing?' In short, far from seeking the peaceful settlement you talk of, he seemed to dread it. I think * move him from the idea of abandoning Rome. What irks me the most is that Caesar must be paid his money and the wherewithal for my Triumph diverted to that purpose. It does not look well to be in debt to a political opponent. But of this and much else when we are together.

61

CICERO TO ATTICUS

Near Rome, 18 January 49

I have decided on the spur of the moment to leave before daybreak so as to avoid looks or talk, especially with these laurelled lictors. As for what is to follow, I really don't know what I am doing or going to do, I am so confounded by the rashness of this crazy proceeding of ours. As for yourself, what can I recommend – *I* am expecting advice from *you*. What our Gnaeus has decided or is deciding I don't yet know, cooped up there in the country towns in a daze. If he makes a stand in Italy we shall all be with him, but if he leaves, it's a matter for consideration. So far anyhow, unless I am out of my mind, there has been nothing but folly and recklessness. Pray write to me often, if only just what comes into your head.

343. By the courts set up by Pompey in 52.

CICERO TO TERENTIA AND TULLIA

Formiae, 22 January 49

From Tullius to his dear Terentia, and her father to his darling daughter, and Marcus to his mother and sister best greetings.

My dear hearts, I think you should yet again carefully consider what you are to do – whether you should stay in Rome or with me or in some place of safety. The decision is yours as well as mine.

The points that occur to me are these: Thanks to Dolabella[344] you can stay in Rome safely, and your doing so might help us if there is any outbreak of violence or looting. But on the other hand I am concerned when I observe that all honest men have left Rome and have their womenfolk with them. Moreover, this district where I am is full of towns friendly to me and also of properties of mine, so that you could be with me a good deal, and when we are separated could live comfortably in places of our own. Frankly I have not yet made up my mind which is the better course. You must observe what other ladies of your rank are doing, and take care that when and if you do want to leave you don't find the way barred. Do please consider the matter again together and with our friends. Tell Philotimus to see that the house is barricaded and guarded and please arrange reliable couriers, so that I get some sort of a letter from you every day. But your chief care must be for your health, if you want us[345] to keep ours.

22nd, from Formiae.

344. Now one of Caesar's supporters.
345. Cicero and his son.

63

Q. CICERO TO TIRO

Rome or Campania, January 49

From Q. Cicero to Tiro greetings.

Your health makes us terribly anxious. Travellers report 'no danger, but it will take time', which is a great consolation. Still it's a huge anxiety, if you are going to be away from us for long. Missing you brings home to us how useful and pleasant it is to have you. But though I long to see you with my every thought, I do ask you in all sincerity not to venture upon so long a journey by water and land in winter unless you are thoroughly strong, and not to take ship without careful preliminary enquiries. Cold is hard enough for an invalid to avoid in town houses; how much more difficult to escape the inclemency of the weather at sea or on the road! As Euripides says, 'Cold is a tender skin's worst enemy.'[346] How much trust you put in him I don't know, but *I* look upon every verse he wrote as an affidavit. Mind you get well, if you love me, and come back to us as soon as possible hale and hearty.

Love us and goodbye. Young Quintus sends you his love.

64

CICERO TO ATTICUS

Formiae, 15 or 16 February 49

After I had dispatched a letter to you I received one from Pompey. The bulk of it concerned operations in Picenum as reported by Vibullius and Domitius' levying of troops, things which you in Rome already know. They were not however so cheerful-sounding in this letter as Philotimus had represented them to me in his. I should have sent you the letter itself, but my brother's boy is leaving now suddenly, so I shall send it tomorrow. However in that letter of Pompey's, at the end and in his own hand, are

346. From a lost play.

the words 'As for yourself, I advise you to come to Luceria. You will be as safe there as anywhere.' I took this to mean that he has given up the towns here and the coast for lost, nor am I surprised that having abandoned the head he does not spare the limbs. I am writing back at once and sending a trusty person, one of my staff, to tell him that I am not looking for the safest place I can find. If he wants me to go to Luceria either on his own or the public account, I say I shall go at once. I also urge him to hold on to the sea coast if he wants to be supplied with grain from the provinces. I realize I write this to no purpose, but as formerly on holding the capital so now on not abandoning Italy I am putting my view on record. Clearly the plan is to concentrate all our forces at Luceria and not to make even that a firm point, but to prepare for flight from Luceria itself if we are pressed – so you may be the less surprised if I embark with reluctance in a cause in which there has at no time been any attempt to plan either peace or victory, but always infamous and disastrous flight. I must go, so that rather than appear to be at variance with the honest men I may meet whatever fate fortune brings in company with those who are so called. And yet I can see that Rome will soon be full of honest men, i.e. men of style and substance, full to bursting indeed when the townships here are given up. I should be one of them if I did not have these confounded nuisances of lictors, and I should not be ashamed to be in company with M'. Lepidus, L. Vulcatius and Ser. Sulpicius. None of them is more stupid than L. Domitius or more fickle than Ap. Claudius. Pompey alone counts with me, because of what he did for me, not because of the weight of his name. What weight after all could it carry in this cause? When all of us feared Caesar, Pompey was his friend; now that *he* has started to fear him he expects us all to be Caesar's enemies. However I shall go to Luceria, and it may be that my coming won't make him any happier, for I shall not be able to conceal my disapproval of what has been done so far.

If I could get any sleep I should not bore you with such long letters. If you are in the same case, I very much hope you will repay me in kind.

65
CICERO TO T. FADIUS

Early 49

From M. Cicero to T. Fadius greetings.

I am surprised that you should reproach me, when you have no right to do so; but even, if you *had* the right, it would ill become you. You say you paid me many attentions when I was Consul, and that Caesar will restore you.[347] You say a great deal, but nobody gives you credit.[348] You say you stood for the Tribunate on my account. A pity you are not Tribune all the time, then you would not be looking for an intercessor![349] You say I don't dare to speak my mind – as though my answer to your impudent request smacked of timidity!

The above is just to let you see that even in the style in which you aspire to shine you are a total failure. If you had expostulated with me in civil fashion, I should willingly and easily have cleared myself. I am not ungrateful for what you did, but I *am* vexed at what you wrote. And I am much surprised that you take me, to whom my fellows owe their freedom, for no better than a slave. If the information you say you gave me was false, what do I owe you? If it was true, you are in an excellent position to testify what the Roman People owes *me*.

347. From exile; see *Letters to Friends* 51.
348. Latin *credit* = (a) 'believes', and (b) 'lends money to'. Fadius had apparently asked Cicero to stand surety and, on receiving a negative answer, written again in terms which put Cicero in a rage. The harsh, offensive tone of this letter is unique in his correspondence.
349. *intercessor* = (a) 'one who (as Tribune) casts a veto', and (b) 'surety'.

Cales,[350] *night of 18–19 February 49*

Troubled as I am by matters of the gravest and saddest consequence and lacking the opportunity of consulting with you in person, I still want the benefit of your advice. The whole question at issue is this: if Pompey leaves Italy, as I suspect he will, what do you think I ought to do? It may help you to advise me if I set out briefly the points which occur to my mind in favour of either course.

Besides the signal obligations to Pompey under which I lie in the matter of my restoration and my personal friendship with him, the public cause itself leads me to feel that my course and my fortunes should be linked with his. There is a further point. If I stay and desert that company of right-minded and illustrious Romans, I must needs fall into the hands of one man. That man, it is true, lets it appear in many ways that he is my friend, and, as you know, I set myself long ago to make him such because of my premonition of the storm that was brewing, but two things are to be considered: first, how far he is to be trusted, second, no matter how definitely his amity is assured, whether it is the part of a brave man and a patriot to remain in a city in which he has held the highest offices and commands, has done great things, and been invested with an exalted priestly function, in a reduced status and in prospect of danger along perhaps with some discredit (?) should Pompey ever restore the constitution. So much on one side.

Now look at what can be said on the other. Our friend Pompey's proceedings have throughout been destitute alike of wisdom and of courage; and, I may add, contrary throughout to my advice and influence. I say nothing of ancient history – his building up and aggrandizing and arming Caesar against the state, his backing the violent and unconstitutional passage of Caesar's laws, his addition of Transalpine Gaul to Caesar's command, his marriage to Caesar's daughter, his appearance as Augur at P. Clodius' adoption, his greater concern for my restoration than for the prevention of my banishment, his prolongation of Caesar's tenure, his consistent support during Caesar's absence, his pressure (even during his

---

350. Cicero stopped here on his way to join Pompey, but returned to Formiae the next day on receiving the news about Corfinium (see next letter).

third Consulship, after he had taken up the role of champion of the constitution) on the ten Tribunes to propose their law enabling Caesar to stand *in absentia*, a privilege which he confirmed after a fashion by a law of his own, his opposition to Consul M. Marcellus when he tried to fix the Kalends of March as the term of Caesar's command in Gaul – to say nothing of all this, what could be more undignified or more disorderly than this withdrawal from the capital or rather this disgraceful flight in which we are now involved? Would not *any* peace terms have been preferable to the abandonment of the mother city? The terms were bad I grant, but was anything worse than this?

You may say that he will restore the constitution. When? What provision is there for implementing such hopes? Picenum has been lost, the road to the capital left open, its entire wealth, public and private, handed over to the enemy. To cap all, there is no organization, no power, no rallying-point for would-be defenders of the constitution. Apulia was selected, the most sparsely populated area in Italy and the most remote from the onset of this war, apparently in despair as a coastal region convenient for flight. I declined (?) Capua,[351] not that I shirked the post, but I did not want to be a leader without a force (?) in a cause which aroused no passion either in any order or, overtly, among private individuals, and in which the feelings of the honest men, though not wholly inactive, were as usual far from keen, whereas the populace and the lower orders sympathized, as I myself observed, with the other side and many were eager for revolution. I told Pompey to his face that I would undertake nothing without troops and money. Accordingly I have had nothing whatever to do, because I saw from the start that flight pure and simple was intended. If I now follow it, what is to be my route? I cannot go with Pompey. When I set out to join him I learned that Caesar's whereabouts made it unsafe for me to go to Luceria. I must take ship by the Western Sea to an uncertain destination in the depths of winter. Then again, am I to go with my brother or without him with my son, or how? Either way will involve the greatest embarrassment and distress of mind. And imagine Caesar's fury against me and my possessions when I am away. It will be more bitter than in other cases because he will perhaps reckon that an attack on me will bring him a measure of popularity. Then look at the awkwardness of taking these shackles of mine, I mean these laurelled *fasces*, overseas. And what place will be safe for us, even supposing we

351. Reading and interpretation controversial. See my edition. Vol. IV, appendix II.

have calm seas, until we reach Pompey? – and we know neither route nor destination.

Supposing on the other hand I stay behind and find a place in Caesar's party, I shall be doing what L. Philippus and L. Flaccus and Q. Mucius[352] did during Cinna's régime – however it turned out for the last named. And yet Mucius used to say that he saw his fate would be what it actually was but preferred it to marching in arms against the walls of his native city. Thrasybulus chose otherwise and perhaps better. Still there is something to be said for Mucius' line and point of view, something too for Philippus' – trimming one's sails when necessary, but taking one's opportunity when it comes. But there too these same *fasces* get in my way. Supposing Caesar is friendly to me, which is not certain, but suppose it: he will offer me my Triumph. To refuse may be dangerous, to accept will damage me with the honest men. 'A difficult, an insoluble problem', you may say. Yet solved it has to be. What alternative is there? And in case you think I am more inclined towards staying because I have argued at greater length that way, it may be, as is often the case in controversies, that there are more words on one side but more truth on the other. Therefore, as a man calmly weighing in his mind a matter of the greatest importance, I ask your advice. I have a ship in readiness at Caieta and another at Brundisium.

But lo and behold! As I write this very letter at night in my lodge at Cales, here come messengers and a letter to announce that Caesar is before Corfinium and Domitius inside the town, with a powerful army eager for battle. I don't believe that Gnaeus will crown all by leaving Domitius in the lurch – though he *had* sent Scipio with two cohorts to Brundisium and written to the Consuls that he wished one of them to take the legion raised by Faustus to Sicily. But it will be a disgraceful thing to desert Domitius when he is begging for help. There is a hope of sorts, not much so far as I am concerned but strongly held hereabouts, that Afranius has engaged and beaten Trebonius in the Pyrenees, further that your friend Fabius has changed sides with * cohorts; and the long and short of it is that Afranius is on his way here with a large force. If that is true perhaps there will be no evacuation of Italy after all. As for me, since Caesar's movements are uncertain – it is thought he may march either on Capua or on Luceria –

352. Scaevola the Pontifex. These three leading Roman nobles remained in Rome during the Marian domination (87–83). The third was killed by the Marians, the two former went over to Sulla when he returned to Italy.

I have sent Lepta to Pompey with a letter. I myself am returning to Formiae to avoid falling into a trap.

I desired you to know this. I have written in a more composed frame of mind than when I last wrote, not intruding any opinion of my own but seeking yours.

67

CICERO TO ATTICUS

Formiae, 1 March 49

My clerk's hand will serve as an indication of my ophthalmia and likewise as an excuse for brevity, not that there is anything to say *now*. My whole mind is fixed in expectation of news from Brundisium. If Caesar has found our Gnaeus there, there is a faint hope of peace, but if he has crossed over beforehand, there is the fear of a deadly war.

But do you see what sort of man this is into whose hands the state has fallen, how clever, alert, well prepared? I verily believe that if he takes no lives and touches no man's property those who dreaded him most will become his warmest admirers. Both town and country people talk to me a great deal. They really think of nothing except their fields and their bits of farms and investments. And look how the tables are turned! They fear the man they used to trust and love the man they used to dread. I cannot think without distress of the blunders and faults on our side which have led to this result. My forecast of what impends I have already given you and I am now waiting to hear from you.

68

CAESAR TO OPPIUS AND BALBUS[353]

On the march, c. 5 March 49

I am indeed glad that you express in your letter such hearty approval of the proceedings at Corfinium. I shall willingly follow your advice, all the more willingly because I had of my own accord decided to show all possible clemency and to do my best to reconcile Pompey. Let us try whether by this means we can win back the goodwill of all and enjoy a lasting victory, seeing that others have not managed by cruelty to escape hatred or to make their victories endure, except only L. Sulla, whom I do not propose to imitate. Let this be the new style of conquest, to make mercy and generosity our shield. As to how that is to be done, certain possibilities occur to me and many more can be found. I request you to apply your thoughts to these matters.

I captured N. Magius, Pompey's Prefect. Naturally I followed my set practice and immediately discharged him.[354] Two Prefects of Engineers of Pompey's have now fallen into my hands and been released by me. If they wish to show themselves grateful they should urge Pompey to prefer my friendship to that of those who have always been his and my bitter enemies, by whose machinations the country has been brought to its present pass.

69

CICERO TO CAESAR

Formiae, 19 or 20 March 49

When I read your letter received from our friend Furnius in which you urge me to come to Rome, I was not so much surprised by your wish to 'avail yourself of my advice and standing', but I did ask myself what you meant by 'influence' and 'help'. However, hope led me towards the notion

353. The addressees sent a copy of this letter to Cicero, who passed it on to Atticus.
354. Actually Caesar sent Magius to Pompey with a request for a conference.

that, as suits the wisdom which you possess in so admirable and exceptional a degree, you might be desirous of instituting negotiations for peace,
tranquillity, and civic harmony; and I conceived myself to be by nature and
public image not ill fitted to help in such an undertaking. If I am correct,
and if you are at all concerned to maintain our friend Pompey and win
him back to yourself and the Republic, you will surely find no more
suitable person than myself for that purpose. I advocated peace to him
always, and to the Senate as soon as I had opportunity. When arms were
taken up, I had nothing to do with the war, and I judged you therein to
be an injured party in that your enemies and those jealous of your success
were striving to deprive you of a mark of favour[355] accorded by the Roman
people. But as then I not only gave my own support to your position but
also urged others to come to your assistance, so now I am deeply concerned
for Pompey's. It is some years since I chose you and him as two men to
cultivate above all others and as, what you are, my very dear friends.

Accordingly I ask you, or rather I beg and implore you with all my heart,
to spare amid your grave preoccupations some time to consider how by
your kindness I may meet the claims of honour, gratitude, and loyalty in
the remembrance of a signal obligation. Even if my request concerned only
myself I should hope that from you I should obtain it; but I believe it affects
both your honour and the public welfare that I, as a friend of peace and
of you both, should through you be preserved as the most appropriate
agent for restoring harmony between yourself and Pompey and between
Romans in general.

I have already thanked you concerning Lentulus,[356] for saving as a
citizen one who once saved me. But now that I have read the letter which
he has sent me full of gratitude for your kindness and generosity * * * that
in saving him you have saved me too. If my gratitude to Lentulus is
apparent to you, then I beg you to let me show the like to Pompey.[357]

355. The privilege of standing for the Consulship *in absentia*.
356. Lentulus Spinther was captured by Caesar at Corfinium and released.
357. This letter was widely circulated, presumably by Caesar, and aroused some adverse
comment. Cicero defends it in *Letters to Atticus*, 188.

70

CICERO TO ATTICUS

Formiae, 26 March 49

Though I have nothing to say to you I am sending this letter in order not to miss a day. They tell me that Caesar will stay the night of the 27th at Sinuessa. A letter from him was delivered to me on the 26th in which he now counts on my 'resources', not, as in his former letter, on my 'help'. I had written applauding his clemency at Corfinium and he had replied as follows:

CAESAR IMPERATOR TO CICERO IMPERATOR

You rightly surmise of me (you know me well) that of all things I abhor cruelty. The incident gives me great pleasure in itself, and your approval of my action elates me beyond words. I am not disturbed by the fact that those whom I have released are said to have left the country in order to make war against me once more. Nothing pleases me better than that I should be true to my nature and they to theirs.

As for yourself, I hope I shall find you at Rome so that I can avail myself as usual of your advice and resources in all things. Let me add that I find your son-in-law Dolabella the most delightful of company. I shall owe him the more on this account – he will not be able to do otherwise;[358] his kindness of heart, his good feeling, and his goodwill towards me guarantee it.

71

CICERO TO ATTICUS

Formiae, 28 March 49

In both particulars I followed your advice. My language was such as to earn his respect rather than his thanks and I stood firm against going to Rome. But we were wrong in thinking him accommodating; I have never found anybody less so. He said I was passing judgement against him, that the rest would be slower to come if I did not. I replied that their position was different. After a long discussion: 'Come along then and work for

358. i.e., 'than persuade you to return to Rome'.

peace.' 'At my own discretion?' I asked. 'Naturally,' he answered. 'Who am I to lay down rules for you?' 'Well,' I said, 'I shall take the line that the Senate does not approve of an expedition to Spain or of the transport of armies into Greece, and,' I added, 'I shall have much to say in commiseration of Pompey.' At that he protested that this was not the sort of thing he wanted said. 'So I supposed,' I rejoined, 'but that is just why I don't want to be present. Either I must speak in that strain or stay away – and much besides which I could not possibly suppress if I were there.' The upshot was that he asked me to think the matter over, as though seeking a way to end the talk. I could not refuse. On that note we parted. So I imagine Caesar is not pleased with me. But I was pleased with myself, an experience I have not had for quite a long time.

For the rest, gods! What an *entourage*, what an underworld,[359] to use your favourite expression! Celer was there, as one of the Heroes.[360] What an unprincipled adventure! What a gang of desperadoes! And then to think that Servius' son and Titinius' were in the army beleaguering Pompey! Six legions! He is alert and audacious. I see no end to the mischief. Now is the time for you to produce your advice. This was to have been the end.

But I nearly forgot to mention Caesar's disagreeable Parthian shot. If, he said, he could not avail himself of my counsels, he would take those he could get and stop at nothing. Well, have you 'seen the great man'?[361] At any rate you must have groaned as you read. You ask for the rest of the story. Why, he left straight away for *, and I am leaving for Arpinum. From there I await that 'harbinger'[362] of yours. You will say 'Can't you let bygones be bygones? Even our leader's forecasts were not always correct.'[363]

But I am waiting to hear from you. It is no longer possible to say now, as formerly, 'see how this turns out'. Our meeting was to be the end. I don't doubt that it has put him out of humour with me. All the more

359. Atticus' name for Caesar's *entourage*. The Greek word, meaning 'summoning of the dead', is the title of the eleventh Book of the *Odyssey*, in which Odysseus calls up the ghosts from Hades. Many of Caesar's followers were disgraced or bankrupt outcasts from respectable society, who had emerged like ghosts at the summons of Odysseus-Caesar.

360. Like the 'heroes' of *Odyssey*, XI, whose shades were summoned from Hades (see n. 359).

361. Apparently a quotation from Atticus' letter asking Cicero to describe the interview.

362. Literally 'the twitterer', i.e., the spring swallow, from Leonidas of Tarentum's epigram, which starts: "Tis the season for sailing; for the twittering swallow is here already, and the delightful Zephyr.'

363. Mention of the swallow seems to have recalled to Cicero's mind Atticus' optimistic forecast of Caesar's attitude; Cicero, he may have written, could settle matters comfortably with Caesar and then sit back and wait for the 'twitterer'. 'Our leader' is Pompey.

reason for rapid action. Do let me have a letter, a political letter. I am
eagerly waiting to hear from you now.

72
CICERO TO ATTICUS

Cumae, 5 May 49

What is to become of me? Who is in a more unhappy, and not only that
but by now in a more discreditable position than I? Antony[364] says he has
received specific orders about me – he has not yet seen me himself
however, but so informed Trebatius. What am I to do now? Nothing goes
right for me, and the most carefully laid plans turn out abominably. I
thought that having gained Curio I had won the whole battle. He had
written about me to Hortensius[365] and I can depend upon Reginus
absolutely. I had no idea that this fellow would have anything to do with
this sea. Where shall I turn now? I am watched on all sides.

But that's enough moaning. I must sail off on the sly then, and creep
secretly on board some freighter. I must not let it appear that the prohibi-
tion is collusive. I must make for Sicily. Once I make Sicily bigger things
will be in my grasp.[366] If only things go right in Spain! Though as regards
Sicily too I only hope it may be true, but so far we have had no luck –
there's a report that the people have rallied to Cato, begged him to put up
a fight, promised everything, and that he was sufficiently impressed to
start raising troops. I don't believe it. Still the source is respectable. I know
the province *could* have been held. From Spain we shall soon have news.

We have C. Marcellus[367] here, who intends, or makes a good show of
intending, pretty much the same as myself. Not that I have seen him in
person, but I hear this from a close friend of his. Write, pray, if you have
any news, and I shall write to you immediately if I put anything in hand.
I shall handle young Quintus pretty strictly. I wish I was in a position to
do good. But please tear up sometime the letters in which I have written

364. Governing Italy in Caesar's absence.
365. Commanding a Caesarian naval squadron in the Tyrrhene (Tuscan) sea.
366. On this cryptic remark see my edition, Vol. IV, appendix VI.
367. Consul in 50.

sharply about him for fear something may some day leak out. I'll do the same with yours.

I am awaiting Servius,[368] but don't expect anything good from him. You shall know whatever there may be to know.

73
CICERO TO TERENTIA

Aboard ship, Caieta, 7 June 49

From Tullius to his dear Terentia best greetings.

All the miseries and cares with which I plagued you to desperation (and very sorry I am for it) and Tulliola too, who is sweeter to me than my life, are dismissed and ejected. I understood what lay behind them the day after our parting. I threw up pure bile during the night, and felt an instantaneous relief as though a God has cured me. To that God you will make due acknowledgement in piety and purity after your custom.

I trust we have a very good ship – I am writing this directly after coming aboard. I shall next write many letters to our friends, commending you and our Tulliola most earnestly to their care. I should give you words of encouragement to make you both braver if I had not found you braver than any man. And after all, I trust things are now in better train. You, I hope, will be as well off as possible where you are, and I shall at last be fighting for the commonwealth alongside my peers. First and foremost, I want you to take care of your health. Second, if you agree, please use the country houses which will be farthest away from army units. The farm at Arpinum with the servants we have in town will be a good place for you if food prices go up.

Darling Marcus sends you his best love. Once again take care of yourself and goodbye.

Dispatched 7 June.

368. Sulpicius Rufus.

DOLABELLA TO CICERO

Caesar's camp near Dyrrachium, May 48

From Dolabella to Cicero greetings.

If you are well I am glad. I myself am well and so is our Tullia. Terentia has been rather out of sorts, but I know for certain that she has now recovered. Otherwise all your domestic affairs are in excellent shape.

You did me an injustice if at any time you suspected that in advising you to throw in your lot with Caesar and with me, or at least to retire into private life, I was thinking of party interests rather than of yours. But now, when the scales are coming down on our side, I imagine that only one thing can possibly be thought of me, namely, that I am proffering advice to you which it would be contrary to my duty as your son-in-law to withhold. On your side, my dear Cicero, you must take what follows, whether it meets with your approval or not, in the persuasion that I have thought and written it out of the most sincere loyalty and devotion to yourself.

You see Cn. Pompeius' situation. Neither the glory of his name and past nor yet the kings and nations of whose dependence he used so often to boast can protect him. Even the door of an honourable retreat, which humble folk find open, is closed to him. Driven out of Italy, Spain lost, his veteran army taken prisoner, he is now to crown all blockaded in his camp, a humiliation which I fancy has never previously befallen a Roman general. Do therefore, as a man of sense, consider what he can have to hope or we to fear; so you will find it easier to take the decision most expedient for you. One thing I beg of you: if he does manage to escape from his present dangerous position and takes refuge with his fleet, consult your own best interests and at long last be your own friend rather than anybody else's. You have done enough for obligation and friendship; you have done enough for your party too and the form of commonwealth of which you approved. It is time now to take our stand where the commonwealth is actually in being rather than, in following after its old image, to find ourselves in a political vacuum.

Therefore, dearest Cicero, if it turns out that Pompey is driven from this area too and forced to seek yet other regions of the earth, I hope you will retire to Athens or to any peaceful community you please. If you decide to do that, please write and tell me, so that if I possibly can I may hasten to your side. Any concessions that you need from the Commander-in-Chief to safeguard your dignity you will yourself obtain with the greatest ease from so kindly a man as Caesar; but I believe that *my* petitions will carry more than negligible weight with him.

I trust to *your* honour and kindness to see that the courier I am sending you is able to return to me and brings a letter from you.

75
CICERO TO ATTICUS

Pompey's camp, 15 July 48

I have received your letter from Isidorus and two others dispatched subsequently. From the most recent I learned that the properties have not sold. So please arrange for her[369] needs to be met through you. I shall find the Frusino place a convenient acquisition, if it is given me to enjoy it. You wonder why I do not write. I am deterred by lack of matter; I have nothing worth a letter, finding as I do no sort of satisfaction either in the happenings or the doings here. If only I had *talked* to you in days gone by instead of writing! I am looking after your interests with those here as best I can. Celer will tell you the rest. I myself have so far avoided any responsibility, the more so as nothing could be done in a manner appropriate to me and my past career.

369. Tullia's.

CICERO TO ATTICUS

Brundisium, 4 November 48

It would be intensely painful for me to tell you in writing of the causes – bitter, grave, and strange as they are – which have influenced me, driving me to follow impulse rather than reflection. They were powerful enough at any rate to bring about the result you see. So what am I to write to you about my situation or what I should ask of you I cannot tell. The facts, the main state of the case, are before you.

For my part I perceived from your letters, both those you have written jointly with other people and those in your own name, what I had already guessed would be the case, that you are as it were unnerved by the unexpectedness of what has happened and are casting around for new ways of protecting me.

You say you think I ought to draw nearer, travelling through the towns at night. I don't quite see how that is to be done. I don't have stopping places so suitably spaced that I can spend all the daylight hours in them; and so far as your object[370] is concerned, it doesn't make much difference whether people see me in a town or on the road. However I shall think over this point, like others, and try to see how it can best be managed.

Mental and physical discomfort passing belief have made it impossible for me to compose many letters. I have only answered those from whom I have received them. I should be glad if you would write to Basilus and anyone else you think fit, including Servilius, as you think fit, in my name. I know it is a long while since I sent so much as a line to you people, but you will understand from this present letter that it is matter I lack, not will.

You ask about Vatinius. Neither he nor anyone else is lacking in friendly offices, if they could find any way to help me. Quintus was most unamiably disposed towards me at Patrae. His son joined him there from Corcyra. I imagine they left with the rest.

370. Secrecy.

CICERO TO ATTICUS

Brundisium, 23 (?) December 48

Of the worries which harass me you will learn from Lepta and Trebatius,
though no doubt you see them for yourself. I am paying a heavy penalty
for my rashness, which you would have me think prudence. Not that I
want to discourage you from arguing in that strain and writing to me as
often as you can. Your letters do bring me some relief at this time. Your
most zealous endeavours are needed with those who wish me well and
have influence with Caesar, especially Balbus and Oppius, to get them to
write on my behalf as zealously as may be. I am being attacked, so I hear,
both by certain persons on the spot and in letters. These must be counter-
acted, as the importance of the matter requires. *[371] is there, my bitter
enemy. Quintus has sent his son not only to make his own peace but to
accuse me as well. He is going about saying that I am traducing him to
Caesar, which Caesar himself and all his friends contradict. And wherever
he is he never stops heaping all manner of abuse upon me. It is the most
unbelievable thing that has ever happened to me, and the bitterest of my
present woes. Persons who professed to have heard him at Sicyon with
their own ears using scandalous language about me before a large company have repeated it to me. You know the style, you may even have
experienced it. It has all been turned on me. But I make the pain worse
by dwelling on it, and give you pain also. So I return to my point: see to it
that Balbus sends someone especially for this purpose. Please send letters
in my name to those to whom you think proper. Goodbye.

23 (?) December.

---

371. The manuscripts read 'Furnius', which can hardly be right since both before and
afterwards Cicero and C. Furnius were on very friendly terms. 'There' is Alexandria, where
Caesar spent October 48–June 47.

CICERO TO TERENTIA

Brundisium, 14 June 47

From Tullius to his dear Terentia greetings.

I hope you are well, as I am.

Tullia joined me on 12 June. She is so wonderfully brave and kind that it gives me even greater pain to think that through my carelessness she is placed far otherwise than befitted a girl of her station and so good a daughter.

I am thinking of sending Marcus to Caesar, and Cn. Sallustius with him. I shall send you word when he leaves. Take good care of your health.

Goodbye.

14 June.

CICERO TO TERENTIA

Brundisium, 19 June 47

Tullius to Terentia greetings.

I hope you are well.

As I wrote to you earlier, I had decided to send Marcus to Caesar, but changed my mind because there are no reports of his coming home. On other matters there is nothing new, but Sicca will tell you what I wish and think expedient at this time. I still have Tullia with me. Take good care of your health.

Goodbye.

19 June.

CICERO TO ATTICUS

Brundisium, 5 July 47

I readily agree with your letter in which you demonstrate at some length that there is no advice by which you could help me. Comfort assuredly there is none which could alleviate my distress. Nothing has come about by chance (that would be bearable), it is all my own doing, through errors and sufferings of mind and body which the persons nearest to me unfortunately did not choose to counteract. Therefore, since no hope is offered me either of your advice or of any comfort whatsoever, I shall not look for these things from you henceforth. I only ask you not to make any break, to write to me whatever comes to your mind whenever you have a bearer and as long as there is a recipient. That will be no long time.

There is an unauthoritative report that Caesar has left Alexandria. It arose from a letter of Sulpicius', which all subsequent advices have gone to confirm. As its truth or falsity does not make any personal difference to me, I cannot say which I should prefer.

I wrote to you some time back about the will.[372] I wish * * *. This poor child's long-suffering affects me quite beyond bearing. I believe her like on earth has never been seen. If there is any step in my power which might protect her in any way, I earnestly desire you to suggest it. I realize that there is the same difficulty as formerly in giving advice (?). Still, this causes me more anxiety than everything else put together. We were blind about the second instalment. I wish I had acted differently, but it's too late now. I beg you, if anything in my desperate situation can be scraped together, any sum raised and put away in safety, from plate or fabrics (I have plenty of them) or furniture, you will attend to it. The final crisis seems to me to be upon us. There is no likelihood of peace terms, and the present régime seems ready to collapse even without external pressure. This too, if you think fit, please discuss with Terentia at a suitable moment. I cannot write all that is in my mind. Goodbye.

5 July.

372. Cicero was afraid that Terentia might make a will which would be unfair to their children. He also wanted her to forestall the threat of confiscation which hung over them both.

Brundisium, August 47

M. Cicero to C. Cassius greetings.

Both of us, hoping for peace and hating civil bloodshed, decided to hold aloof from persistence in an unnecessary war. But as I am regarded as having taken the lead in that course, perhaps my feeling towards you in this context should hold more of responsibility than of expectation. And yet I often recall how in talking familiarly to each other, you to me no less than I to you, we were both led to the persuasion that our verdict, if not the entire issue, might properly be decided by the result of a single battle. Nor has anyone ever fairly blamed us for taking this view, excepting those who think the commonwealth had better be wiped out altogether than survive in an enfeebled and attenuated form. For my part I saw no hope (obviously) from its destruction, but great hope from its remnants.

The sequel, however, was unexpected – the wonder is that such events could happen rather than that we did not see them coming and, being but human, could not divine them. For my part, I confess my forecast was that, once the fated and fatal battle, so to speak, had been fought, the victors would turn their attention to the general survival and the vanquished to their own. At the same time I thought that both the one and the other depended upon swift action by the victorious leader. Had that been forthcoming, Africa would have experienced the clemency which Asia came to know, as did Achaia also, whose ambassador and intercessor was, I believe, none other than yourself. But the crucial moments were lost, the moments which matter most, especially in civil warfare. A year intervened, leading some to hope for victory and others to care nothing even for defeat. The blame for all these calamities lies at fortune's door. Who could have expected that the main hostilities would have been so long held up by the fighting at Alexandria, or that this what's-his-name, Pharnaces, would menace Asia so formidably?

We thought alike, but we fared differently. *You* made for a quarter[373] where you would be present at the making of decisions and able to foresee events to come, the best comfort for an anxious mind. *I* made haste to meet

---

373. Cassius had joined Caesar in the East.

Caesar in Italy (so we thought), on his way home after sparing many valuable lives, and to urge him to peace – spurring a willing horse, as they say. The consequence was that I have been, and still am, at a vast distance away from him. I am living amidst the groans of Italy and the pitiful plaints of Rome. Perhaps I and you and every man, each according to his powers, might have done something to help, if authoritative backing had been available.

So I would ask you, in virtue of your unfailing kindliness towards me, to write to me and tell me what you see and feel, what you think I have to expect and ought to do. A letter from you will mean a great deal to me. I only wish I had followed the advice in that first letter of yours from Luceria.[374] I should have kept my standing and avoided all unpleasantness.

82
CICERO TO TERENTIA

Near Venusia, 1 October 47 [375]

From Tullius to his dear Terentia greetings.

I think I shall get to Tusculum either on the Nones or on the following day. Kindly see that everything there is ready. I may have a number of people with me, and shall probably make a fairly long stay there. If there is no tub in the bathroom, get one put in; likewise whatever else is necessary for health and subsistence.

Goodbye.

Kalends of October, from the district of Venusia.

---

374. The letter here referred to must have advised Cicero to stay out of the war. It was probably written in February 49, just before the fall of Corfinium. Pompey set up his headquarters at Luceria about 25 January.

375. The last extant letter to Terentia, written on Cicero's way back from Brundisium to Rome.

83

Rome, 47 (late) or 46 (early)

From Cicero to M. Varro greetings.

The letter which you sent to Atticus and which he read to me informed me of your doings and whereabouts, but as to when we are to see you, I could not so much as make a guess from that letter. However, I am coming to hope that your advent is not far away.[376] I wish I may find some comfort in it, though our afflictions are so many and so grievous that nobody but an arrant fool ought to hope for any relief. And yet either you may be able to help me or perhaps I may in some way be able to help you. For I should tell you that since my return I have restored my relations with my old friends, that is to say my books. Not that I had renounced their companionship because I was annoyed with them – it was because they gave me a sense of shame. I felt that in casting myself into a turmoil of events with altogether untrustworthy associates I had failed in obedience to their precepts. They forgive me. They call me back to the old intercourse and tell me that you in staying faithful to it were wiser than I. And so I have made my peace with them and we are together again. That is why I think I may properly hope that once I see you I shall find both present and impending troubles easy to bear.

So whatever rendezvous you favour, be it Tusculum or Cumae,[377] or my house or yours, or (what would be my last choice) Rome, you may be sure I shall make it appear the most convenient for both of us, only provided we are together.

376. Varro may not yet have returned to Italy.
377. Both Cicero and Varro had villas in both areas.

CICERO TO M. BRUTUS

Rome, 46

From Cicero to Brutus greetings.

I have always noticed the particular care you take to inform yourself of all that concerns me, so I do not doubt that you not only know which township I hail from but also know how attentively I look after the interests of my fellow-townsmen of Arpinum. All their corporate income, including the means out of which they keep up religious worship and maintain their temples and public places in repair, consists in rents from property in Gaul.[378] We have dispatched the following gentlemen, Roman Knights, as our representatives to inspect the properties, collect sums due from the tenants, and take general cognizance and charge: Q. Fufidius, son of Quintus; M. Faucius, son of Marcus; Q. Mamercius, son of Quintus.

May I particularly request of you in virtue of our friendship to give your attention to the matter, and to do your best to see that the business of the municipality goes through as smoothly and rapidly as possible with your assistance. As for the persons named, let me ask you to extend them, as you naturally would, all possible courtesy and consideration. You will attach some worthy gentlemen to your connection and your favour will bind a township which never forgets an obligation. As for myself, I shall be even more beholden than I should otherwise have been, because, while it is my habit to look after my fellow-townsmen, I have a particular concern and responsibility towards them this year. It was my wish that my son, my nephew, and a very close friend of mine, M. Caesius, should be appointed Aediles this year to set the affairs of the municipality in order – in our town it is the custom to elect magistrates with that title and no other. You will have done honour to them, and above all to me, if the corporate property of the municipality is well managed thanks to your goodwill and attention. May I again ask you this favour most earnestly?

---

378. Cisalpine. Brutus was governor.

85

CICERO TO SERVIUS SULPICIUS RUFUS

Rome, 46

From Cicero to Servius greetings.

Asclapo, a physician of Patrae, is on familiar terms with me. I liked his company, and had favourable experience of his professional skill when members of my household were taken sick. He gave me satisfaction in this connection as a knowledgeable doctor, and also a conscientious and kindly one. Accordingly I am recommending him to you, and would request you to let him understand that I have written about him with some particularity, and that my recommendation has been to his no small advantage. I shall be truly obliged.

86

CICERO TO VARRO

Rome, May (late) 46

I was at dinner with Seius when a letter from you was delivered to each of us. Yes, I think it's seasonable now.[379] As for the difficulties I put up previously, I'll confess my craftiness. I wanted to have you near by in case some chance of good turned up. 'Two heads',[380] you know. Now, since all is settled, we must hesitate no longer – full speed ahead.[381] When I heard about L. Caesar junior,[382] I said to myself 'What can I, his father, look

---

379. To go to Campania.
380. *Iliad* x. 224: 'When two go together, one notices before the other.'
381. Literally 'with horse and foot', i.e. without any holding back. 'We must make friends with the winning party' is implied.
382. i.e. about his death in Africa. Cicero, perhaps mistakenly, implies that this took place by Caesar's orders.

for?'[383] So I go dining every night with our present rulers. What am I to do? One must go with the times.

But joking aside (especially as we have nothing to laugh about), 'Africa, grim land's a-tremble in terrific tumult tossed.'[384] There is nothing 'negative'[385] that I don't apprehend. In answer to your questions as to date, route, and destination, we know nothing yet. Even as to Baiae, some think he may come by way of Sardinia. That is one of his properties that he has not yet inspected. It's the worst he owns, but he doesn't despise it. I myself, to be sure, think he's more likely to travel by way of Sicily. But we shall soon know. Dolabella is coming, and I expect he will be our schoolmaster. 'The teacher's oft inferior to the taught.' However, if I know what you have decided, I shall try to accommodate my plans to yours. So I expect to hear from you.

87

CICERO TO VARRO

Rome, June (latter half) 46

From Cicero to Varro.

Our friend Caninius told me from you to write if there should be anything which I thought you ought to know. Well, the arrival is awaited – that is no news to you. But when he wrote, as I suppose, that he would be coming to his place at Alsium,[386] his friends wrote to dissuade him, telling him that there were many people thereabouts whose presence would be annoying to him, and many whom *his* presence would annoy; Ostia, in their opinion, would make a more convenient landing-place. I do not myself see what odds it makes, but Hirtius told me that both he and

383. i.e. 'what have I got to expect?' Cicero recalls this scrap of Terence's *Girl from Andros* (112) (probably without remembering its dramatic context, which is foreign to his point) because 'father' suggests an older man as compared to a young one.

384. From Ennius' *Annals*.

385. A Greek term from Stoic philosophy, which recognized virtue as the only good but allowed that other things (e.g. health, wealth, and their opposites) were on one side or other of complete indifference. Varro was an expert on Greek philosophy.

386. Or 'the district of Alsium'.

Balbus and Oppius wrote advising him in this sense – persons whom I know to be fond of you.

I wanted you to hear of this so you should know where to arrange to stay, or rather so you should make arrangements in both localities, since what *he* will do is uncertain. At the same time I have shown off to you the familiar footing on which I stand with these gentry, and how I am taken into their counsels. I see no reason why I should object to that. It is one thing to put up with what has to be put up with, another to approve what ought to be disapproved – though for my part I don't any longer know what to disapprove of, except the beginnings of it all, which were a matter of volition. I saw (you were away) that our friends were desirous of war, whereas the person we are expecting was not so much desirous as unafraid of it. That then came within the scope of design, all else followed inevitably. And victory had to fall to one or the other.

I know that your heart was always as heavy as mine. Not only did we foresee the destruction of one of the two armies and its leader, a vast disaster, but we realized that victory in civil war is the worst of all calamities. I dreaded the prospect, even if victory should fall to those we had joined. They were making savage threats against the do-nothings, and your sentiments and my words were alike abhorrent to them. As for the present time, if our friends had gained the mastery, they would have used it very immoderately. They were infuriated with us. One might have supposed that we had taken some resolution for our own safety which we had not advised them to take for theirs, or that it was to the advantage of the state that they should go to brute beasts[387] for help rather than die outright or live in hope – admittedly no very bright hope, but still hope.

We live, it may be said, in a state that has been turned upside down. Undeniably true. But that bears hard on persons who have not prepared resources for themselves against all life's contingencies. Here is the point to which the flow of these remarks, more prolix than I wished, had been tending. I have always thought you a great man and I think you so now, because in this stormy weather you almost alone are safe in harbour. You reap the most precious fruits of learning, devoting your thoughts and energies to pursuits which yield a profit and a delight far transcending the exploits and pleasures of these worldlings. These days you are now spending down at Tusculum are worth a lifetime by my reckoning. Gladly would I leave all earthly wealth and powers to others, and take in exchange a licence to live thus, free from interruption by any outside force.

387. The elephants of King Juba of Numidia, an ally of the republicans.

I am following your example as best I can, and most gladly find repose in literary studies. Surely nobody would begrudge us this. Our country will not or cannot use our services, so we return to a mode of life which many philosophers (mistakenly perhaps, but many) have considered actually to be preferred to the political. The state now grants its permission. Are we not then at liberty to give full rein to pursuits which in the judgement of great thinkers carry a sort of exemption from public employment?

However, I am going beyond Caninius' commission. *He* asked me to write if anything came to my knowledge of which you were unaware; and here am I telling you what you know better than I, your informant. So I shall do what I was asked, and see that you are not left in ignorance of any items relevant to the present situation that may come my way.

88

CICERO TO PAPIRIUS PAETUS

Tusculum, c. 23 July 46

Cicero to Paetus greetings.

While I was at a loose end at Tusculum, having sent my pupils to meet their friend[388] with the idea that they should at the same time put me in the best possible odour with him, I received your most charming letter. It appears then that my plan meets with your approbation: like Dionysius the tyrant,[389] who is said to have opened a school at Corinth after his expulsion from Syracuse, I have set up as a schoolmaster, as it were, now that the courts are abolished and my forensic kingdom lost. Well, I too am pleased with my plan, which brings me many advantages. To begin with, I gain some protection against the hazards of these times, which is what is most needed just now. What that amounts to I don't know; all I can see is that nobody else has yet produced a plan which I consider superior to mine – unless perhaps it would have been better to die. Better to die in one's bed, I admit it; but that did not happen. At the battle I was not

---

388. i.e. Hirtius and Dolabella to meet Caesar on his return from Africa. When he says he sent them Cicero is probably joking – they would naturally go anyway.

389. Dionysius II of Syracuse.

present. The others – Pompey, your friend Lentulus,[390] Scipio, Afranius –
came to miserable ends. But Cato's, you say, was splendid. Well, that will
be open to me any time I choose. I have only to see that it does not become
so much a matter of necessity for me as it was for him. I am doing just
that. This then to begin with.

Next, I benefit directly, first in health, which I lost when I gave up my
exercises; and then my oratorical faculty, if I had any, would have dried
up had I not gone back to these exercises. There is a final point, which *you*
might perhaps put first: I have already polished off more peacocks than
you young pigeons. While you enjoy Haterius' legal gravity[391] in Naples,
I regale myself with Hirtius' gravy here. Be a man then, and come along!
Let me teach you the principia you want to learn – though it will be a case
of teaching my grandmother.[392] But, as I see the situation, if you can't sell
your valuations[393] or fill a pot with sixpences,[394] you have got to move back
to Rome. Better die of stomach-ache here than starvation down there. I
see you have lost your money, and I expect it is just the same with your
friends. So if you don't look ahead, it's all up with you. You can get up on
that mule, which you say you still have left after spending your gelding
on food, and ride to Rome. There will be a chair for you in school as
assistant-master next to mine, and a cushion will follow.

---

390. L. Lentulus Crus, Consul in 49.
391. Literally 'Haterian law', Haterius being presumably a jurist. There is a play on two
senses of *ius*, 'law' and 'sauce'.
392. Literally 'of the pig teaching Minerva' – a proverbial saying. The pig was regarded as
the most stupid of animals.
393. i.e. properties compulsorily accepted in lieu of debts.
394. i.e. 'if you don't have enough money to fill a pot with silver coins (*denarii*)'.

CICERO TO PAPIRIUS PAETUS

Rome, early August 46

From Cicero to Paetus.

I was doubly delighted with your letter – laughed myself, and saw that you are now capable of laughing. As a light-armed buffoon,[395] I did not object to your pelting me with insults.[396] What does vex me is that I have not been able to get down to your part of the world as I had arranged. You would have found me a comrade[397] in arms rather than a guest. And what a warrior! Not the man you used to lay low with your *hors d'œuvres*. I bring an appetite unimpaired to the eggs,[398] and so carry on the good work down to the roast veal. 'What an accommodating fellow!' you used to say of me. 'What an easy man to entertain!' Not any more! I have dropped all my concern for public affairs, all preoccupation with what to say in the Senate, all study of briefs, and flung myself into the camp of my old enemy Epicurus. I don't aim at the excesses of Rome, however, but at *your* elegance – your former elegance, I mean, when you had money to spend (though, to be sure, you never owned more real estate[399] in your life).

So be prepared! You are dealing with a hearty eater, no longer wholly ignorant of what's what; and you know how opsimaths assert themselves. You had best forget about your little baskets[400] and your scones. I have acquired enough of the art by now to dare invite your friend Verrius and Camillus (the very acme of refinement and elegance!) on several occasions. More, I even had the audacity to give a dinner to Hirtius (think of it!) – no peacock, though. At that meal nothing proved beyond my cook's powers of imitation except the hot sauce.

395. Paetus had apparently called Cicero *scurra veles* ('skirmisher jester'), perhaps because he had begun the fight. The verb *velitari* is used elsewhere of verbal skirmishing.

396. Untranslatable pun on *malis* (with a short 'a') = 'abuse' and *malis* (with a long 'a') = 'apples' (which might be thrown at a buffoon).

397. Literally 'tent-mate'. The military metaphor continues, but the word may imply a longer stay than would be normal for a guest.

398. Here regarded as beginning the main meal, as opposed to the *hors d'œuvres*. The roast veal would be the last course, followed by dessert (*mensae secundae*).

399. Which Paetus had been forced to take from his debtors.

400. Containing dates, as at Trimalchio's feast (Petronius, 40.3), or something of the kind. The meaning of the word translated 'scones' is doubtful.

So this is the way I live nowadays. In the morning I receive callers – both honest men (numerous, but depressed) and these jubilant victors, who, I must say, are most obliging and friendly in their attentions to me. When the stream has ceased to flow, I absorb myself in literary work, writing or reading. Some of my visitors listen to me as a man of learning, because I know a little more than themselves. All the rest of the time is given to the claims of the body. As for my country, I have already mourned her longer and more deeply than any mother ever mourned her only son.

But if you are my friend, take care of your health, or I shall be consuming your substance while you lie flat on your back. For I have made up my mind not to spare you, well or sick.

90

CICERO TO PAPIRIUS PAETUS

Rome, shortly before 17 November (true calendar) 46

From Cicero to Paetus greetings.

I am scribbling the lines of which you are reading a copy on my tablets after taking my place at dinner at two-thirty of the afternoon. If you wish to know where, my host is Volumnius Eutrapelus. Your friend Atticus and Verrius are on either side of me. Does it surprise you that we have become such a merry lot of slaves? Well, what am I to do? I ask *you*, since you are going to philosophy lectures. Am I to torture and torment myself? What should I gain? And how long should I keep it up? You may advise me to spend my life in literary work. Surely you realize that this *is* my only occupation, that if I did not spend my life in that way I could not live at all. But even literary work has, I won't say its saturation-point, but its due limit. When I leave it, little as I care about dinner (the one problem *you* put to philosopher Dio),[401] I really do not see anything better to do with the time before I go to bed.

Well, to the rest of my tale. Cytheris lay down next Eutrapelus. 'So?' I hear you say, '*Cicero* at such a party,

---

401. Otherwise unknown; but see below.

'He the admired, upon whose countenance
The Greeks all turned their eyes?'[402]

I assure you I had no idea *she* would be there. But after all, even Aristippus
the Socratic did not blush when someone twitted him with keeping Lais
as his mistress. 'Lais is my mistress,' said he, 'but I'm my own master' (it's
better in the Greek;[403] make your own rendering, if you care to). As for
me, even when I was young I was never attracted by anything of that sort,
much less now that I'm old. It's the party I enjoy. I talk about whatever
comes uppermost, as they say, and transform sighs into shouts of laughter.
Do you manage matters better, actually making mock of a philosopher?
When he put his question whether anybody had anything to ask, you
called out 'Who's going to ask me to dinner? Been wondering all day.'[404]
The poor dunderhead[405] thought you would be enquiring whether there
is one sky or an infinite number. What business is that of yours? But,
confound it, is a dinner any business of yours, especially one in *this*
house?[406]

Well, so life passes. Every day a bit of reading, or a bit of writing. Then,
since something is due to my friends, I dine with them. We don't go beyond
the law, if there is such a thing nowadays, we even stop short of it, and
that by a considerable margin. So you don't have to dread my arrival.
You'll receive a guest with a small appetite for food, but a large one for
frolic.

402. Source unknown.

403. The Latin means literally 'I possess Lais but am not possessed by her'. In the Greek
ekhomai has a double sense, 'I am possessed by' and 'I cling to'.

404. The lecturer asked *'numquis quid quaerit?'* ('any questions'). Paetus replied *'cenam
quaero'*, 'I'm looking for a dinner'.

405. Cicero was fond of so referring to Epicurean philosophers because of their professed
hostility to culture; cf. n. 288.

406. The house of such a person as Eutrapelus.

CICERO TO PAPIRIUS PAETUS

Cumae, 22 November (true calendar) 46

From Cicero to Paetus.

I arrived at Cumae yesterday and shall perhaps be with you tomorrow. But when I know for certain, I shall send you word a little beforehand. To be sure, when M. Caeparius met me in Poultry Wood[407] and I asked after you, he told me you were in bed with the gout in your feet. I was properly sorry of course, but decided to come all the same – to see you, visit you, and even dine, for I don't suppose your cook is a fellow-sufferer. Expect a guest then – a small eater and a foe to sumptuous banquets.

92
CICERO TO M. MARIUS

Cumae, 21 or 22 November (true calendar) 46

From M. Cicero to M. Marius greetings.

On 21 November I arrived at my place near Cumae with your, or rather our, friend Libo. I mean to go on to Pompeii straight away, but shall send you word in advance. I always wish you to keep well, but particularly during my visit; for you see what a long time it is since we were last in one another's company. So if you have an appointment with the gout, please put it off for another day. Take care of yourself then, and expect me in two or three days' time.

---

407. Silva Gallinaria, a pine forest on the coast north of Cumae.

CICERO TO M. FABIUS GALLUS

Rome, December 46

From Cicero to M. Fabius Gallus greetings.

I had just got in from Arpinum when I was handed a letter from you. By the same bearer I received a letter from Avianius,[408] containing a very handsome offer to debit me after he arrives from any date I please. Now pray put yourself in my shoes. Can you reconcile it with your sense of decency or with mine to ask for credit in the first place, and in the second for more than a year's credit? But everything would be straightforward, my dear Gallus, if you had bought what I needed and within the price I had wished to pay. Not but what I stand by these purchases you say you have made, indeed I am grateful. I fully understand that you acted out of goodwill, affection indeed, in buying the pieces which pleased you (I have always regarded you as a very fine judge in any matter of taste), and which you considered worthy of me. But I hope Damasippus doesn't change his mind, for, frankly, I don't need any of these purchases of yours. Not being acquainted with my regular practice you have taken these four or five pieces at a price I should consider excessive for all the statuary in creation. You compare these Bacchantes with Metellus'[409] Muses. Where's the likeness? To begin with, I should never have reckoned the Muses themselves worth such a sum – and all Nine would have approved my judgement! Still, that would have made a suitable acquisition for a library, and one appropriate to my interests. But where am I going to put Bacchantes? Pretty little things, you may say. I know them well, I've seen them often. I should have given you a specific commission about statues which I know, if I had cared for them. My habit is to buy pieces which I can use to decorate a place in my palaestra,[410] in imitation of lecture-halls. But a statue of Mars! What can I, as an advocate of peace, do with that? I'm glad there was none of Saturn – I should have thought those two between them had

---

408. Doubtless the sculptor, C. Avianius Evander. Gallus had bought some statues from him on Cicero's behalf.
409. Probably Metellus Scipio.
410. Probably in his house on the Palatine.

brought me debt! I had sooner have had one of Mercury[411] – we might fare better in our transactions with Avianius!

As for that table-rest which you had earmarked for yourself, if you like it, you shall have it; but if you have altered your mind, I'll keep it of course. For the sum you have spent I should really have much preferred to buy a lodge at Tarracina,[412] so as not to be continually imposing on hospitality. To be sure, I realize that my freedman is to blame (I had given him quite definite commissions), and Junius too – I think you know him, Avianius' friend. I am making some new alcoves in the little gallery of my house at Tusculum, and I wanted some pictures for their decoration – indeed, if anything in this way appeals to me, it is painting. However, if I have to keep these things of yours, please let me know where they are, and when they are sent for, and what mode of transport. If Damasippus changes his mind, I shall find some Damasippus *manqué*, even if it means taking a loss.

You write again about the house. I had already given directions on this head to my girl Tullia as I was leaving – I got your letter that same hour. I had also taken it up with your friend Nicias, since he is on familiar terms with Cassius,[413] as you know. On my return, before I read this last letter of yours, I asked Tullia how she had got on. She said she had gone to work through Licinia (I have an impression, though, that Cassius does not have a great deal to do with his sister), and that Licinia in her turn said that while her husband was away (Dexius has left for Spain) she did not venture to move house in his absence and without his knowledge. I take it very kindly that you set so much store on our friendly day-to-day intercourse that you took a house so as to live not only in my neighbourhood but in my actual company, and that you are in such a hurry to move. But on my life I won't admit that you are any more eager for that arrangement than myself. So I shall try every way, conscious as I am of what it means to me and to both of us. If I have any success, I'll let you know. Write back on all points and inform me, if you will, when I am to expect you.

411. The god of gain. In astrology Saturn and Mars generally bring the opposite.

412. Cicero had recently visited his Campanian villas and will have stayed at Tarracina *en route*; perhaps Gallus was his host.

413. Probably not C. Cassius, but perhaps his younger brother Lucius. Or 'Cassius' may be a scribal error for 'Crassus', as Manutius conjectured.

CICERO TO M. FABIUS GALLUS

Tusculum, late 46 or early 45

From Cicero to Gallus greetings.

For ten days my stomach had been seriously out of order, but as I did not have a fever I could not convince the folk who wanted my services that I was really sick. So I took refuge here at Tusculum, after two days of strict fasting – not so much as a drop of water! Famished and exhausted, I was craving your good offices rather than expecting you to demand mine. I am terrified of all forms of illness, but especially of dysentery – your master Epicurus gets a rough handling from the Stoics for complaining of trouble with his bladder and his bowels, the latter being according to them a consequence of over-eating and the former of an even more discreditable indulgence! Well, I was really afraid of dysentery. However, I think I am better for the change, or maybe the mental relaxation; or perhaps the malady is simply wearing itself into abatement.

But in case you wonder how this happened or what I did to deserve it, the Sumptuary Law, supposed to have brought plain living, has been my downfall. Our *bons vivants*, in their efforts to bring into fashion products of the soil exempted under the statute, make the most appetizing dishes out of fungi, potherbs, and grasses of all sorts. Happening on some of these at an augural dinner at Lentulus'[414] house, I was seized with a violent diarrhoea, which has only today begun (I think) to check its flow. So: oysters and eels I used to resist well enough, but here I lie, caught in the toils of Mesdames Beet and Mallow! Well, I shall be more careful in future. As for you, you heard of it from Anicius (he saw me in the qualms), and that should have been reason enough for a visit, let alone a letter.

I intend to stay here until I have convalesced, having lost strength and weight. But I expect I shall recover both easily enough, once I have thrown off the attack.

414. The younger Lentulus Spinther.

CICERO TO CASSIUS

Rome, January (beginning) 45

M. Cicero to C. Cassius greetings.

Your couriers are a queer set – not that *I* mind; but when they go away they demand a letter, while when they arrive they bring none. Even so, it would be more convenient if they gave me a little time to write, but they arrive with their travelling caps on and say their party is waiting for them at the city gate. So you must forgive me. You are going to get a second short letter. But you may look forward to full amends. Though I can't think why *I* am apologizing to *you*, when your people come to my house empty-handed and go back with letters.

Here in Rome (just to write you something after all) we have a death to talk about – P. Sulla senior. Some say it was bandits, others overeating. The public doesn't care which, as there's no doubt that he's ashes. You will bear the news like the philosopher you are. Still, the town has lost a *personnage*. They think Caesar will take it hard – he'll be afraid the public auctions[415] may go with less of a swing. Mindius Marcellus[416] and Attius the perfumer are delighted to have shed a competitor.

From Spain nothing new, but keen expectancy of news. Rumours tending to gloom, but nobody to vouch for them. Our friend Pansa left Rome[417] in uniform[418] on 30 December, an unmistakable illustration of what you have latterly begun to question – that Right is to be chosen *per se*. He has given a helping hand to many persons in distress and behaved like a human being in these bad times; accordingly he went off in astonishingly good odour with honest men.

So you are still at Brundisium. I heartily approve and rejoice. Upon my word, I think you will do wisely to avoid worry to no purpose. We who care for you will be glad if you do. And in future, when you send a line

415. Sales of confiscated property.
416. Later a naval commander in the service of his friend and fellow-townsman, Octavian. Nothing further is known of Attius.
417. We do not know where he was going.
418. See Glossary of Terms.

home, be a good fellow and remember me. I shall never knowingly let anybody go to you without a letter from me.

Goodbye.

96

CASSIUS TO CICERO

Brundisium, January (last half) 45

From C. Cassius to M. Cicero greetings.

I trust you are well.

You may be sure that nothing I do in this sojourn of mine abroad is done more willingly than writing to you. It is as though I was chatting and joking with you in the flesh. That does not, however, come about because of Catius' 'spectres' – in return for him I'll throw so many clodhopping Stoics back at you in my next letter that you'll declare Catius Athenian born![419]

I am glad that our friend Pansa left Rome in uniform amid general goodwill, both for his own sake and, let me add, for all our sakes. For I trust people will realize how intense and universal is hatred for cruelty and love for worth and clemency, so that they will see how the prizes most sought and coveted by the wicked come to the good. It is hard to persuade men that Right[420] is to be chosen *per se*; but that Pleasure and Peace of Mind are won by virtue, justice, and Right is both true and easily argued. Epicurus himself, from whom all these sorry translators of terms, Catius, Amafinius, etc., derive, says: 'To live pleasurably is not possible without living rightly and justly.' Thus it is that Pansa, whose goal is Pleasure, retains Virtue; and those whom you and your friends call Pleasure-lovers are Right-lovers and Justice-lovers, practising and retaining all the virtues. And so Sulla[421] (whose judgement[422] we must respect) saw that the

419. A rejoinder to a joke of Cicero's (*Letters to Friends* 215) about the Epicurean theory of perception through images ('spectres') given off by sensory objects. Cassius was a convert to Epicureanism.

420. Initial capitals indicate Greek terms.

421. See previous letter.

422. Perhaps in allusion to Sulla's conviction on charges of electoral malpractice in 66.

philosophers were at loggerheads: instead of trying to discover *what* was good, he went and bought up all the goods he could find! Indeed I have borne his death with fortitude. However, Caesar will not let us miss him long – he has other victims of justice to offer us in his place. Nor will *he* miss Sulla's activity in the auction rooms – he will only have to look at Sulla junior.

Now to get back to public affairs, let me know in your reply how things are going in Spain. I'm devilish worried, and I'd rather have the old easy-going master than try a cruel new one. You know what a fool Gnaeus[423] is, how he takes cruelty for courage, how he thinks we always made fun of him. I'm afraid he may answer our persiflage with his sword, hobbledehoy-fashion. If you love me, tell me what is going on. Ah, how I should like to know your frame of mind as you read this! Anxious or easy? I should know by the same token what I ought to do.

Not to be too prolix, goodbye. Go on caring for me. If Caesar has won, expect me quickly back.

97

CICERO TO TIRO

Rome (?), 46 or 45 (?)

From Tullius to Tiro greetings.

Well then! Isn't that as it should be? *I* think so, and should like to make it 'to his dear Tiro'.[424] However, let us beware of jealous malice, if you wish – the malice I have often despised.

I am glad your perspiration has done you good. If my place at Tusculum has done you good too, heavens, how much better I shall love it! But if you love me, and if you don't you make a very pretty pretence of it, which after all answers nicely – well, however that stands, humour your health.

423. Pompey's elder son.

424. Tiro seems to have suggested that the heading of Cicero's previous letter, 'Tullius to Tiro greetings', was too familiar. To all other correspondents except his wife and brother Cicero uses his *cognomen*. Yet earlier letters to Tiro were similarly headed, and most of those after his manumission add *suo* ('his dear'). Perhaps the letter to which Tiro referred had to be shown to a third party.

In your devotion to me you have not hitherto devoted yourself enough to that. You know what it requires – digestion, no fatigue, a short walk, massage, proper evacuation. Mind you come back in good shape. I should love not only you but my house at Tusculum the more.

Prod Parhedrus to hire the garden himself. That will give the gardener a jolt. That rascal Helico used to pay HS 1,000 when there was no sun-trap, no drain, no wall, no shed. After all my expense is this fellow going to make fools of us? Give him a hot time, as I did Motho[425] and in consequence have more flowers than I can well use.

I should like to know what is happening about Crabra,[426] even though nowadays water is really too plentiful. I shall send the sundial and the books when the weather is clear. But have you no books with you? Or are you composing something Sophoclean? Mind you have results to show.

Caesar's familiar A. Ligurius is dead, a good fellow and a friend of mine. Let me know when we are to expect you. Look after yourself carefully.

Goodbye.

98

CICERO TO CAESAR

Rome (?), winter of 46–45

From Cicero to Caesar greetings.

Young P. Crassus was my favourite among the whole range of our aristocracy. From his earliest youth I had good hopes of him, but he rose really high in my estimation when I saw how well you thought of him. Even during his lifetime I had a great regard and liking for his freedman Apollonius. He was warmly attached to Crassus, and admirably fitted to join him in his liberal interests, so naturally Crassus was very fond of him. After Crassus' death I thought him all the worthier of admission to my patronage and friendship because he felt it proper to pay respect and attention to those whom Crassus had loved and who had loved him in

---

425. Perhaps gardener at the house on the Palatine.
426. The Aqua Crabra, an aqueduct running into Rome, supplied water to the villa, for which Cicero paid.

return. Accordingly he joined me in Cilicia, where his loyalty and good sense proved very useful to me in many connections. And I believe that in the Alexandrian War such service as his zeal and fidelity could render you was not lacking.

Hoping that you are of the same opinion, he is leaving to join you in Spain, mainly on his own initiative, but not without encouragement from me. I did not promise him a recommendation, not that I did not think it would carry weight with you, but because a man who had seen military service at your side and whom Crassus' memory made one of your circle did not seem to me to need one. And if he did wish to make use of recommendations, I knew he could obtain them elsewhere. But I am glad to give him a testimonial of what I think of him, since he makes a point of it and my experience has shown me that you pay attention to such.

I know him to be a scholar, devoted to liberal studies from boyhood. For he was much in my house from an early age with Diodotus the Stoic, a most erudite person in my opinion. Now his imagination has been captured by your career, and he wants to write an account of it in Greek. I think he can do it. He has a strong natural talent cultivated by practice, and has for a long time been engaged in this type of literary work. To do justice to your immortal fame is his passionate ambition.

Well, there you have my considered testimony, but your own keen discernment will provide you with a much easier means of assessing the matter. And after all, I do recommend him to you, having said I should do no such thing. Any kindness you do him will particularly oblige me.

99
CICERO TO ATTICUS

Astura, 9 March 45[427]

Please see that my excuses are made to Appuleius from day to day, since a once for all excuse does not seem advisable. In this lonely place I do not talk to a soul. Early in the day I hide myself in a thick, thorny wood, and don't emerge till evening. Next to yourself solitude is my best friend. When I am alone all my conversation is with books, but it is interrupted

427. About a month after Tullia's death.

by fits of weeping, against which I struggle as best I can. But so far it is an unequal fight. I shall answer Brutus as you recommend. You shall have the letter tomorrow. Forward it when you have the opportunity.

100
CICERO TO ATTICUS

Astura, 10 March 45

I wouldn't have you leave your affairs to visit me; better for me to come to you if you are going to be held up for some considerable time. I would never have gone out of your sight if it had not been that nothing, *nothing* was any use to me. But if any relief were possible it would be in you and you only; and as soon as anyone can give it, that person will be you. And yet at this moment I cannot bear to be away from you. But we agreed that your house was not suitable, and I cannot stay in mine; and even if I were somewhere closer by, I should still not be in your company. The same thing that is holding you up now would still hold you up and prevent you from spending much time with me. Thus far the loneliness here suits me as well as anything. I am afraid Philippus may break it. He arrived yesterday evening. Reading and writing bring me, not solace indeed, but distraction.

101
CICERO TO ATTICUS

Astura, 28 March 45

I write this in my own hand. Pray see what is to be done. Publilia wrote to me that her mother had talked to Publilius and would come over with him for a talk with me, and that she would accompany them if I would allow it. She begs me beseechingly and at some length to permit this and to send her a reply. You see what a tiresome business this is. I wrote back that I was in an even poorer way than when I told her I wanted to be alone, so I should prefer her not to come at present. I thought that if I did not reply at all she would come with her mama. Now I don't think she will, as the letter was obviously not her own composition. But I also want to avoid what clearly *is* impending, a visit from the other two;[428] and the only way to avoid it is to make myself scarce. A nuisance, but it has to be. Now I want you to find out just how long I can stay here without getting caught. You'll go about it, to use your own word, gently.

Would you please propose to Marcus, that is if you think it not unreasonable, that he should balance his expenses abroad with my rents from the Argiletum and the Aventine, which would easily have been enough to content him if he had taken a house in Rome, as he had in mind; and having made that proposal, would you please yourself make all necessary arrangements as to how we are to supply him with the money he needs from these rents. I'll guarantee that Bibulus or Acidinus or Messalla,[429] who I hear are going to be in Athens, will not spend more than the proceeds of these rents. So would you kindly see who are the tenants and what they pay, and further that they are the kind of people to pay punctually, and what should be allowed in the way of travel expenses and outfit. There would certainly be no need for a pack-animal in Athens, while for his use on the journey there are more in my stables than will be needed, as you too observe.

102
SERVIUS SULPICIUS RUFUS TO CICERO

Athens, mid March 45

From Servius to Cicero greetings.

When the report reached me of the death of your daughter Tullia, I was indeed duly and deeply and grievously sorry, and I felt that the blow had struck us both. Had I been in Rome, I should have been with you and shown you my grief in person. And yet that is a melancholy and bitter sort

428. Publilia's mother and her brother (?) Publilius.
429. All three were young men of noble family.

of comfort. Those who should offer it, relations and friends, are themselves no less afflicted. They cannot make the attempt without many tears, and rather seem themselves to stand in need of comfort *from* others than to be capable of doing their friendly office *for* others. None the less, I have resolved to set briefly before you the reflections that come to my mind in this hour, not that I suppose you are unaware of them, but perhaps your grief makes them harder for you to perceive.

What reason is there why your domestic sorrow should affect you so sorely? Think how fortune has dealt with us up to now. All that man should hold no less dear than children – country, dignity, standing, distinctions – has been snatched away from us. Could this one further mishap add appreciably to your grief? How should not any heart practised in such experience have grown less sensitive and count all else as of relatively little consequence?

But I suppose you grieve for *her*. How often must you have thought, and how often has it occurred to me, that in this day and age they are not most to be pitied who have been granted a painless exchange of life for death! What was there after all to make life so sweet a prospect for her at this time? What did she have or hope? What comfort for her spirit? The thought perhaps of spending her life wedded to some young man of distinction? Do you suppose it was possible for you to choose from this modern generation a son-in-law suitable to your standing, to whose protection you could feel safe in confiding your child? Or the thought of bearing children herself, whose bloom would cheer her eyes, sons who could maintain their patrimony, would seek public office in due course, and act in public affairs and in their friends' concerns like free men? Was not all this taken away before it was granted? The loss of children is a calamity, sure enough – except that it is a worse calamity to bear our present lot and endure.

I want to tell you of something which has brought *me* no slight comfort,[430] in the hope that perhaps it may have some power to lighten your sorrow too. As I was on my way back from Asia,[431] sailing from Aegina towards Megara, I began to gaze at the landscape around me. There behind me was Aegina, in front of me Megara, to the right Piraeus, to the left Corinth; once flourishing towns, now lying low in ruins before one's eyes. I began to think to myself: 'Ah! How can we manikins wax indignant if one of us dies or is killed, ephemeral creatures as we are, when the corpses of so many towns lie abandoned in a single spot? Check yourself,

430. If Sulpicius had suffered a bereavement we do not know what it was.
431. i.e. from Samos. Sulpicius will have been returning to Rome in the autumn of 47.

Servius, and remember that you were born a mortal man.' That thought, I do assure you, strengthened me not a little.[432] If I may suggest it, picture the same spectacle to yourself. Not long ago so many great men died at one time, the Roman Empire was so gravely impaired, all its provinces shaken to pieces; can you be so greatly moved by the loss of one poor little woman's frail spirit? If her end had not come now, she must none the less have died in a few years' time, for she was mortal. You too must take your mind and thoughts away from such things, and dwell instead on recollections worthy of the character you hold. Tell yourself that she lived as long as it was well for her to live, and that she and freedom existed together. She saw you, her father, Praetor, Consul, and Augur. She was married to young men of distinction. Almost all that life can give, she enjoyed; and she left life when freedom died. How can you or she quarrel with fortune on that account?

And then, do not forget that you are Cicero, a man accustomed to give rules and advice to others. Do not be like a bad physician, who professes medical knowledge to his patients but does not know how to treat himself. Rather lay to your heart and place before your mind the precepts you are wont to offer others. There is no grief that is not lessened or softened by the passage of time. For *you* to wait for this time to pass, instead of anticipating the result by your own good sense, does you discredit. And if consciousness remains to those below, loving you as she did, dutifully fond as she was of all her family, *she* assuredly does not wish you to act so. Listen then for her dead sake, for the sake of others, your well-wishers and friends who are sad for your grief, and for your country's sake, so that if need arise she may have the benefit of your service and counsel. And then, since in the pass to which we have come we must not disregard even *this* aspect, do not let anyone suppose that it is not so much a daughter you are mourning as the public predicament and the victory of others.

I am ashamed to write at greater length to you on this matter, lest I seem to doubt your good sense, and so I shall end my letter with one final observation. We have seen more than once how notably you sustain prosperity, and how great the glory you gain thereby. Let us recognize at last that you are no less able to bear adversity, and that you count it no heavier load than you should, lest of all fine qualities you may seem to lack this only.[433]

432. Byron refers to this passage in *Childe Harold* (Canto V, stanza 4), as does Sterne, *Tristram Shandy*, V, 3, who probably got it from Burton.
433. Livy wrote of Cicero that he bore none of his misfortunes like a man except death.

As for me, I shall inform you of what is going on here and of the state of the province when I hear that your mood is calmer.

Goodbye.

103
CICERO TO SERVIUS SULPICIUS RUFUS

Atticus' villa near Nomentum, mid April 45

From M. Cicero to Ser. Sulpicius greetings.

Yes, my friend, I wish you had been with me, as you say, in my most grievous affliction. How much your presence would have helped me by consolation and by sorrow well-nigh equal to my own I readily recognize from the measure of easement I felt when I read your letter. You have written the words that could alleviate mourning and your own no small distress has given you the means of comforting mine. But your son Servius has shown by every friendly attention that could be rendered at such a time how much he thinks of me and how welcome he believes such a disposition on his part will be to you. I have often felt more pleasure in his attentions than I feel now (as you may imagine), but never more grateful.

Not only am I comforted by your words and (I might almost say) your fellowship in sorrow, but by your counsel as well. I feel it discreditable in me not to bear my bereavement as so wise a man as you considers it should be borne. But sometimes I am overwhelmed, and scarcely offer any resistance to grief, because I have no such solaces as others in similar plight, whose examples I set before my mind, did not lack. Q. Maximus[434] lost a son of consular rank, high reputation, and splendid record. L. Paulus[435] lost two in a single week. Then there was Galus in your own family[436] and M. Cato,[437] who lost a son of the highest intellectual and moral qualities. But they lived in periods when the honourable standing

---

434. Q. Fabius Maximus 'Cunctator'.

435. L. Aemilius Paulus, victor of Pydna.

436. i.e. *gens*. C. Sulpicius Galus was Consul in 166.

437. The Censor. Cicero had collected many such examples in his lost 'Consolation', addressed to himself.

they enjoyed in public life assuaged their mourning. *I* had already lost those distinctions which you yourself mention and which I had gained by dint of great exertions. The one comfort still left to me was that which has now been snatched away. Neither my friends' concerns nor the administration of the state detained my thoughts. I had no wish to appear in the courts, I could not endure the sight of the Senate-House. I considered, as was the fact, that I had lost all the fruits of my work and success. However, I reflected that I shared this situation with yourself and certain others; I conquered my feelings and forced myself to bear it all patiently. But while I did so, I had a haven of refuge and repose, one in whose conversation and sweet ways I put aside all cares and sorrows.

Now this grievous blow has again inflamed the wounds I thought healed. When in the past I withdrew in sadness from public affairs, my home received and soothed me; but I cannot now take refuge from domestic grief in public life, to find relief in what it offers. And so I stay away from home and Forum alike, for neither public nor private life can any longer comfort the distress which each occasions me.

All the more then do I look forward to your return and desire to see you as soon as possible. No abstract reflection can bring me greater comfort than our fellowship in daily life and talk. However, from what I hear, I hope your arrival is imminent. One reason among many why I am anxious to see you as soon as may be is that I should like us to ponder together how we should best pass through this present time, all of which must be accommodated to the wishes of a single individual. He is a man of sense and generosity, and I think I have cause to believe him no enemy of mine and a very good friend of yours. Even so, what line we are to take needs careful consideration. I am not thinking of any positive action, but of retirement by his leave and favour.

Goodbye.

SERVIUS SULPICIUS RUFUS TO CICERO

Athens, 31 May 45

From Servius to Cicero cordial greetings.

I know that my news will not be of the most agreeable[438] to you and other friends. But chance and nature are our masters. Stand the matter how it may, I feel it my duty to inform you.

On 23 May I took ship from Epidaurus to Piraeus, where I met my colleague M. Marcellus, and spent the day there to be with him. I took leave of him the following day, intending to travel from Athens to Boeotia and conclude what remained of my assizes. He proposed, as he told me, to sail round Cape Malea towards Italy. Two days later I was about to set out from Athens, when about three o'clock in the morning a friend of his, P. Postumius, arrived to tell me that my colleague[439] M. Marcellus had been attacked with a dagger by P. Magius Cilo, a friend of his, after dinner, and had received two wounds, one in the stomach and one in the head behind the ear. He hoped, however, that there was a chance of life. Magius had later committed suicide, and he himself had been sent to me by Marcellus to tell me what had occurred and ask me to send him doctors. Accordingly, I collected some doctors and set out straight away for Piraeus as day broke. I was not far away, when a boy of Acidinus' met me on the road with a note which stated that Marcellus had breathed his last shortly before dawn. So a very eminent man has been tragically murdered by a villain. He was spared by the respect of his enemies only to meet his death at the hand of a friend.

None the less I proceeded to his tent. I found two freedmen and a handful of slaves. They said the rest had fled in a panic, because their master had been killed in front of his tent. I had to bring him back to the city in the litter in which I myself had travelled, using my own bearers; and there I saw to his funeral, on as handsome a scale as the resources of Athens could provide. I could not induce the townspeople to grant him burial within the city precincts; they pleaded a religious bar, and it is a fact that they had never given such permission in the past. The next best thing they did

---

438. An odd meiosis; but Sulpicius' writing is not of the most sensitive.
439. As Consul in 51.

allow, to bury him in a public hall, whichever I wished. So I chose a spot in the most celebrated hall in the world, the Academy. There we cremated him, and I later saw to it that the people of Athens should arrange for the erection of a monument to him in marble on the spot. So I have done all that in me lay for my colleague and kinsman, in life and in death.

Goodbye.

Dispatched 31 May, Athens.

105
CICERO TO ATTICUS

Tusculum, 18 (?) June 45

Little wonder you are shocked by the news about Marcellus and see new causes for alarm! Who could have feared anything so unprecedented, so apparently outside the course of nature? Clearly we are safe from nothing. But you make a historical slip, you of all people, when you speak of me as the last surviving Consular.[440] What do you call Servius? Not of course that this is of any importance, especially to me, to whom the dead seem no worse off than the living. What are we after all, or what can we be, at home or abroad? If it had not occurred to me to write these books of mine, such as they are, I should not know what to do with myself.

For Dolabella[441] I think I must do as you say and find some general subject with a political flavour. I certainly must do something – he wants it badly.

If Brutus[442] takes any step, be sure to let me know. I think he ought not to lose any time, especially if he has made up his mind. He will extinguish or damp down all the tittle-tattle, some of which has reached even my ears. But he will be the best judge, especially if he talks to you about it.

My intention is to leave on the 21st. There is nothing for me to do here – nor there[443] either for that matter, nor anywhere else; but still there is a little there. I am expecting Spinther today – Brutus has sent me word.

440. Atticus must have referred to those Consulars who took part with Pompey in the war.
441. He had asked Cicero to dedicate a book to him.
442. Brutus was about to divorce his wife in order to marry Cato's daughter Porcia.
443. In Arpinum.

He writes exculpating Caesar in the matter of Marcellus' death. Even if he had been killed by stealth, no suspicion would have fallen upon Caesar. As it is, since the facts about Magius are unquestioned, does not his fit of madness account for the whole tragedy? I really don't know what he means, so please explain – though the only doubt in my mind is what caused Magius himself to take leave of his senses. I actually went surety for him. And no doubt that was it – he was ruined. I expect he asked Marcellus to do something for him and got a rather firm answer, as was Marcellus' way.

106

CICERO TO ATTICUS

Arpinum, 28 June 45

You see the virtue of propinquity. Well, let us secure a property in the suburbs. When I was at Tusculum it was as though we talked to one another, letters passed to and fro so rapidly. But it will soon be so again. Meanwhile I have taken your hint and finished off some neat little volumes[444] addressed to Varro. None the less I am awaiting your answer to my questions: (*a*) how you gathered that he coveted a dedication from me, when he himself, extremely prolific as he is, has never taken the initiative, and (*b*) whom you gathered him to be jealous of; if it's not Brutus, much less can it be Hortensius or the speakers on the Republic. The point above all which I should really be glad if you would make clear to me is whether you hold to your opinion that I should address my work to him or whether you see no need. But we shall discuss this together.

444. Cicero's *Academic Questions*. He was much exercised about the proposed dedication to Varro.

VATINIUS TO CICERO

Narona, 11 July 45

From Vatinius, Imperator, to his friend Cicero greetings.

I trust you are well, as I am and my army.

Do you still keep up your practice of standing by old clients? If so, here comes one of them by the name of P. Vatinius, who wants an advocate to take his case! Surely you won't turn your back now I stand well in the world after taking me on when it was touch and go. As for me, whom should I choose and turn to but my old defender, who taught me how to win? When I think what a combination of powerful persons you disregarded to save my life, I can hardly doubt your readiness to smash and squash a set of petty backbiters with their spiteful tittle-tattle, when it's a question of an honour.[445]

Well then, if you love me as you usually do, let me put myself wholly in your hands. Look upon this load, such as it is, as yours to shoulder, a task you ought to perform for the sake of my standing. You know that somehow or other my career is apt to find tongues to carp at it – truly no fault of mine, but what difference does that make if the thing happens just the same, fated as it were? If anyone *does* show a disposition to stand in my light, may I ask you to defend me in my absence with no less than your usual generosity? I am appending the text of my dispatch to the Senate on my military operations for your perusal.

They tell me that a runaway slave[446] of yours, a reader, is with the Vardaei. You gave me no commission about him, but I have none the less issued instructions in advance that he be searched for by land and sea, and no doubt I shall find him for you, unless he has made off into Dalmatia – though even there I shall winkle him out sooner or later. Don't forget me.

Goodbye.

11 July, from camp at Narona.

---

445. A Supplication for Vatinius' military successes in Illyricum.
446. His name was Dionysius; see *Letters to Friends* 255 and Letter 108.

VATINIUS TO CICERO

Narona, late December 45 or January 44

From Vatinius to his friend Cicero greetings.

I trust you are well, as I am and my army.

So far I cannot fish anything out about your man Dionysius, especially as the Dalmatian cold, which drove me out from there, has frozen me up here too. But I shall not give up till sooner or later I winkle him out. But you are a hard taskmaster! You write me what reads like a very earnest intercession on behalf of Catilius. Get along with you, and our friend Sex. Servilius too! Upon my word, I think a lot of him, as you do. But is this the kind of client and case you people take on – a monster of savagery, who has murdered and kidnapped and ruined all those freeborn men and matrons and Roman citizens, and laid whole districts waste? This ape, this worthless ruffian, bore arms against me, and I took him prisoner of war. But really, my dear Cicero, what can I do? Upon my word, I am anxious to obey your every command. My own right to inflict condign punishment upon him as my captive, which I was going to exercise, I forgo in deference to your request. But what am I to say to those who demand redress by process of law for the plunder of their property, the seizure of their ships, the slaughter of brothers, children, and parents? Upon my word, I could not face it out, not if I had the impudence of Appius, whose shoes I wear.[447] Well then, I shall spare no pains to meet your wishes, as I know them. He is defended by Q. Volusius, a pupil of yours[448] – perhaps that circumstance may rout the other side. There lies the best hope. You will defend me in Rome, if need arises.

---

447. Literally 'into whose place I was elected'. Vatinius had succeeded to the vacancy in the College of Augurs left by Ap. Pulcher's death in 48.

448. He may have taken lessons in declamation from Cicero, like Hirtius and Dolabella.

109

CICERO TO MINUCIUS BASILUS

Date uncertain[449]

From Cicero to Basilus greetings.

Congratulations. I am delighted on my own account. Be sure of my affection and active concern for your interests. I hope I have *your* affection, and want to hear what you are doing and what is going on.

110

CICERO TO ATTICUS

Puteoli (?), 19 December 45

Strange that so onerous a guest should leave a memory not disagreeable! It was really very pleasant. But when he arrived at Philippus' place on the evening of 18 December, the house was so thronged by the soldiers that there was hardly a spare room for Caesar himself to dine in. Two thousand men, no less! I was a good deal perturbed about what would happen next day, but Cassius Barba came to the rescue and posted sentries. Camp was pitched in the open and a guard placed on the house. On the 19th Caesar stayed with Philippus until 1 o'clock admitting nobody – at accounts, I believe, with Balbus. Then he took a walk on the shore. Towards two he ent to his bath. That was when he heard about Mamurra;[450] his face did not change. After anointing he took his place at dinner. He was following a course of emetics, and so both ate and drank with uninhibited enjoyment. It was really a fine, well-appointed meal, and not only that but

cooked and garnished well,
good talking too – in fact a pleasant meal.[451]

449. There are serious objections to the common view that this evidently hasty note refers to Caesar's assassination.

450. Perhaps his death.

451. From Lucilius.

His entourage moreover were lavishly entertained in three other dining-rooms. The humbler freedmen and slaves had all they wanted – the smarter ones I entertained in style. In a word, I showed I knew how to live. But my guest was not the kind of person to whom one says 'Do come again when you are next in the neighbourhood.' Once is enough. We talked of nothing serious, but a good deal on literary matters. All in all, he was pleased and enjoyed himself. He said he would spend a day at Puteoli and another at Baiae.

There you are – a visit, or should I call it a billeting, which as I said was troublesome to me but not disagreeable. I shall stay here for a short while, then to Tusculum.

When he was passing Dolabella's house, and nowhere else, the whole armed escort rode to right and left of him.[452] This comes from Nicias.

III
CICERO TO ATTICUS

Tusculum, end of December 45

He[453] came to see me, 'right down in the mouth'. I greeted him with ' "You there, why so pensive?" '[454] 'Need you ask,' was the answer, 'considering that I have a journey in front of me, and a journey to war,[455] a dishonourable journey too as well as a dangerous one?' 'What's the compulsion?' I inquired. 'Debt,' he answered, 'and yet I haven't so much as my travelling expenses.' At that I borrowed some of your eloquence – I held my tongue. He went on: 'What distresses me most is my uncle.'[456] 'How so?' 'Because he's annoyed with me.' 'Why do you let him be annoyed? I prefer to say "let" rather than "make".' 'I shan't any more,' he answered. 'I shall do away with the reason.' 'Admirable,' said I. 'But if you don't mind my asking, I should be interested to know what the reason is.' 'It's because I

452. Apparently by way of compliment, unless it was for Caesar's protection; but Dolabella seems to have been much in Caesar's favour.

453. Quintus junior.

454. This and the previous question are in Greek, probably cited from Menander.

455. Caesar's projected Parthian campaign. It was dishonourable for Quintus because he was escaping from his creditors.

456. Atticus.

couldn't make up my mind whom to marry. My mother was displeased with me, and so consequently was he. Now I don't care what I do to put things right. I'll do what they want.' 'Good luck then,' said I, 'and congratulations on your decision. But when is it to be?' 'The time makes no odds to me,' said he, 'now that I accept the thing itself.' 'Well,' I said, 'I should do it before I left if I were you. That way you will please your father too.' 'I shall take your advice,' he replied. Thus ended our dialogue.

Now attention please! You know my birthday is on 3 January. I shall expect you accordingly.

I had just finished, when up comes a message from Lepidus, begging me to come over. I suppose he wants Augurs to consecrate the temple. I must go – anything for a quiet life. So I shall be seeing you.

112

D. BRUTUS TO M. BRUTUS AND CASSIUS

Rome, c. 22 (?) March 44[457]

From D. Brutus to his friend Brutus and to Cassius greetings.

Let me tell you how we stand. Yesterday evening Hirtius was at my house. He made Antony's disposition clear – as bad and treacherous as can be. Antony says he is unable to give me my province,[458] and that he thinks none of us is safe in Rome with the soldiers and populace in their present agitated state of mind. I expect you observe the falsehood of both contentions, the truth being, as Hirtius made evident, that he is afraid lest, if our position were enhanced even to a moderate extent, these people would have no further part to play in public affairs.

Finding myself in so difficult a predicament, I thought it best to ask for a Free Commission[459] for myself and the rest of our friends, so as to get a fair excuse for going away. Hirtius promised to get this agreed to, but I have no confidence that he will, in view of the general insolence and

457. At least half-a-dozen dates have been assigned to this letter, of which Cicero no doubt received a copy from the recipients. I accept the view that it was written soon after the disturbances which followed Caesar's funeral on 20 March.
458. Cisalpine Gaul according to Caesar's assignment.
459. See Glossary of Terms under 'Legate'.

vilification of us. And even if they give us what we ask, I think it won't be long before we are branded as public enemies or placed under interdict.

You may ask what I advise. I think we must give way to fortune, leave Italy, go to live in Rhodes or anywhere under the sun. If things go better, we shall return to Rome. If moderately, we shall live in exile. If the worst happens, we shall take any and every means to help ourselves. Perhaps one of you will wonder at this point why we should wait till the last moment instead of setting something on foot now. Because we have nowhere to base ourselves, except for Sex. Pompeius[460] and Caecilius Bassus – I imagine their hands will be strengthened when this news about Caesar gets through. It will be time enough for us to join them when we know what their power amounts to. I shall give any undertaking you and Cassius wish on your behalf. Hirtius demands that I do this.

Please let me have your reply as soon as possible. I don't doubt that Hirtius will inform me on these points before ten o'clock. Let me know where we can meet, where you wish me to come.

After Hirtius' latest talk I have thought it right to demand that we be allowed to stay in Rome with a public bodyguard. I don't suppose they will agree – we shall be putting them in a very invidious light. However, I think I ought not to refrain from demanding anything that I consider fair.[461]

113

CICERO TO ATTICUS

Matius' house near Rome, 7 April 44

I have broken my journey at the house of the person[462] of whom we were talking this morning. Utterly deplorable! According to him our problems are insoluble: 'for if a man of Caesar's genius could find no way out, who will find one now?' In short he said Rome was finished – I am inclined to agree, but *he* said it with relish – and declared that the Gauls will be up

---

460. Pompey's younger son, still fighting in Spain.
461. This paragraph is probably not, as generally supposed, a postscript added after Hirtius' return, since it does not say what answer Hirtius brought back.
462. C. Matius.

within three weeks. He told me that since the Ides of March[463] he has talked to nobody except Lepidus. In sum, his opinion is that it cannot all just pass quietly off. Wise Oppius! He regrets Caesar no less, but says nothing which any honest man could take amiss. But enough of this.

Now pray don't grudge the effort of writing any news – and I am expecting many items – including whether the report about Sextus[464] can be taken as established, but especially about our friend Brutus. With reference to him my present host tells me that Caesar used to say 'It's a great question *what* he wants; but whatever he wants, he wants it with a will.' This had struck him when Brutus spoke for Deiotarus at Nicaea; he had been impressed by the force and boldness of Brutus' speech. Matius also told me (I may as well put things down as they occur to me) that recently, when I called on Caesar at Sestius' behest and was sitting waiting to be summoned, Caesar remarked 'I must be a most unpopular man. There's M. Cicero sitting waiting and can't get to see me at his own convenience. He is the most easy-going of mankind, but I don't doubt he detests me.' This and much else of the same sort. But to return to my point – whatever crops up, great or small never mind, let me know. There shall be no intermission on *my* side.

II4
CICERO TO ATTICUS

Puteoli, 22 April 44

Atticus, I fear the Ides of March have brought us nothing except joy and a satisfaction for our hatred and grief. The things I hear from Rome! And the things I see here! ' 'Twas a fine deed, but half done!'[465] You know how warm a feeling I have for the Sicilians and what an honour I consider it to have them as my clients. Caesar was generous to them and I was not sorry that he should be – though the Latin franchise[466] was intolerable,

463. i.e., Caesar's assassination.
464. See n. 460.
465. Greek, perhaps quoted from a play.
466. A lower form of citizenship, apparently granted to Sicily, or to some Sicilian communities, by Caesar.

but let that pass. Well, here is Antony posting up (in return for a massive bribe) a law allegedly carried by the Dictator in the Assembly under which the Sicilians become Roman citizens, a thing never mentioned in his lifetime! Then there is Deiotarus' case. Isn't it much the same? No doubt he deserves any kingdom we can give him, but not through Fulvia.[467] There are any number of such things. However it brings me back to this: surely we shall gain our point at least in part in so well-known, well-attested and just a cause as that of Buthrotum. The greater the number of such operations the more confident we can be.

Octavius is with me here – most respectful and friendly. His followers call him Caesar, but Philippus does not, so neither do I. My judgement is that he cannot be a good citizen. There are too many around him. They threaten death to our friends and call the present state of things intolerable. What do you think they will say when the boy comes to Rome, where our liberators cannot go safe? They have won eternal glory, and happiness too in the consciousness of what they did; but for us, if I am not mistaken, there is only humiliation ahead. So I long to be away 'Where nevermore of Pelops' line . . .',[468] as the poet says. Nor do I greatly care for these Designates[469] of ours, who furthermore have made me give lessons in oratory, so that I am not allowed to rest even here at the waters. But this comes of my too easy-going nature. Time was when that sort of thing was more or less necessary, but now, stand things as they may, it's not the same.

What a long time it is since I had anything to write to you about! Still I go on writing, not to give you pleasure with my letters but to evoke yours. Tell me any other news you have and at all events something about Brutus, no matter what. I have put this together on the 22nd at dinner with Vestorius, a practical mathematician however ignorant of dialectics.[470]

467. Wife of Antony, previously married to P. Clodius, then to Curio.
468. From an unknown Latin play: 'Where I may never hear the name or deeds or fame of the sons of Pelops.'
469. Hirtius and Pansa, appointed Consuls for 43 by Caesar.
470. Vestorius, the plain businessman (see n. 223), was good at figures; and mathematics was a recognized branch of culture.

CICERO TO TREBATIUS

Rome 44 (?)

From Cicero to Trebatius greetings.

You made game of me yesterday over our cups for saying that it was a moot point whether an heir can properly take action for theft in respect of a theft previously committed.[471] So when I got home, though late and well in tipple, I noted the relevant section[472] and send you a transcript. You will find that the view which, according to you, has never been held by anybody was in fact held by Sex. Aelius, Manius Manilius, and M. Brutus.[473] However, for my part I agree with Scaevola and Testa.

116

CICERO TO ATTICUS

Puteoli, 11 May 44

On the 11th, a short while after I had dispatched a letter to you by Cassius' courier, my courier arrived bringing (astonishing phenomenon!) no letter from you. But I soon guessed that you were at Lanuvium. Eros was in a hurry to get a letter of Dolabella's through to me, not about my affair (he had not had mine when he wrote), but in reply to the one of which I sent you a copy – not by any means a bad reply either.

Just after I had sent Cassius' courier on his way, Balbus called. Heavens above, how easily one could see his fear of peace! – and you know how cagey he is. Still he told me of Antony's plans – that he is going the rounds of the veterans to get them to stand by Caesar's measures and take an oath to that effect, instructing them all to keep their arms ready and have them inspected monthly by the colonial magistrates. Balbus also complained

471. i.e. in the interval between the testator's death and the heir's taking possession. A theft committed during the testator's lifetime *was* actionable.
472. No doubt in Scaevola the Pontifex's great treatise on civil law.
473. Three eminent second-century jurists.

about his own unpopularity, and the whole tenor of his talk argued friendship for Antony. In short I don't trust him a yard.

There is no doubt in my mind that we are moving towards war. That affair was handled with the courage of men and the policy of children. Anyone could see that an heir to the throne was left behind. The folly of it! 'Strange *this* to fear and *that* to set at naught!'[474] Why even now there is a good deal that might be called incongruous. Think of Pontius' house near Naples occupied by the Tyrannicide's mother![475] I ought to re-read the 'Cato the Elder'[476] which I dedicated to you. Old age is making me more cantankerous, everything irritates me. But I have had my time. Let the young men worry. Please go on looking after my private affairs.

I wrote or rather dictated this over dessert at Vestorius'. Tomorrow I propose to dine with Hirtius, Hirtius the Gastronome (?).[477] That is how I am planning to bring him over to the optimates. *Enfantillage!* That lot are scared of peace, every man of them. So I had best find wings for my boots, for anything is better than soldiering.

Please give Attica my best love. I am waiting to hear about Octavian's speech and any other news, especially whether Dolabella is jingling his pockets – or has he declared a Cancellation in my particular case?

117

CICERO TO ATTICUS

Sinuessa, 18 May 44

I dispatched a letter to you yesterday as I was leaving Puteoli and then turned in at my place near Cumae. There I found Pilia in good health. Indeed I saw her soon afterwards at Cumae, where she had gone to attend a funeral at which I too put in an appearance. Our good friend Cn. Lucceius was burying his mother. So I stayed the night at my place near Sinuessa and am scribbling this letter early the following morning before I leave for Arpinum.

---

474. From an unknown Latin play.
475. Servilia. Pontius must have been a Pompeian.
476. Cicero's essay *On Old Age*.
477. The meaning of Hirtius' (Greek) nickname is doubtful.

I have no news either to tell or to inquire of you, unless perhaps you think the following of interest. Brutus has sent me his speech delivered to the meeting on the Capitol,[478] asking me to correct it candidly before publication. The speech is a most elegant composition, the wording and the turn of the sentences could not be bettered. But if I had been handling the material I should have put more fire into it, considering the nature of the theme and the role of the speaker. Accordingly I felt unable to offer improvements. Given his chosen style[479] and his judgement of what is the best style in oratory, our good Brutus has in this speech attained it with perfect elegance. But I have aimed at something different, whether rightly or wrongly. However I should like you to read the speech, if you have not already done so, and let me know your own opinion. I fear though that you may be led astray by your surname and judge too Attically. But you have only to call to mind Demosthenes' thunderbolts to realize that a speaker can be both impeccably Attic and profoundly impressive. But we shall talk of this together. Here and now I did not want Metrodorus to go to you without a letter or with an empty one.

118
CICERO TO ATTICUS

Antium (?), c. 7 June 44

I arrived at Antium before midday. Brutus was glad to see me. Then before a large company, including Servilia, Tertulla, and Porcia,[480] he asked me what I thought he ought to do. Favonius too was present. I gave the advice I had prepared on the way, to accept the Asiatic corn commission. I said his safety was all that concerned us now; it was the bulwark of the Republic itself. I was fairly launched on this theme when Cassius walked in. I repeated what I had already said, whereupon Cassius, looking most valorous I assure you, the picture of a warrior, announced that he had no intention of going to Sicily. 'Should I have taken an insult as though it had been a favour?' 'What do you mean to do then?' I inquired. He replied that

478. On the day after Caesar's murder.
479. See Glossary of Terms (ATTIC(ISM)).
480. The three ladies were respectively Brutus' mother, half-sister (wife of Cassius), and wife.

he would go to Greece. 'How about you, Brutus?' said I. 'To Rome,' he answered, 'if you agree.' 'But I don't agree at all. You won't be safe there.' 'Well, supposing I could be safe, would you approve?' 'Of course, and what is more I should be against your leaving for a province either now or after your Praetorship. But I cannot advise you to risk your life in Rome.' I went on to state reasons, which no doubt occur to you, why he would not be safe.

A deal of talk followed, in which they complained, Cassius especially, about the opportunities that had been let slip, and Decimus came in for severe criticism. To that I said it was no use crying over spilt milk, but I agreed all the same. And when I began to give my views on what should have been done (nothing original, only what everyone is saying all the time), not however touching on the point that someone else[481] ought to have been dealt with, only that they should have summoned the Senate, urged the popular enthusiasm to action with greater vigour, assumed leadership of the whole commonwealth, your lady friend[482] exclaimed 'Well, upon my word! I never heard the like!' I held my tongue. Anyway it looked to me as though Cassius would go (Servilia undertook to get the corn commission removed from the decree), and our friend Brutus was soon persuaded to drop his empty talk about wanting to be in Rome. He therefore decided that the games should be held in his absence under his name. It looked to me as though he wanted to go to Asia direct from Antium.

In short, nothing in my visit gave me any satisfaction except the consciousness of having made it. It would not have been right to let him leave Italy without seeing me. Apart from this obligation of affection and duty I could only say to myself 'Prophet, what signifies your journey now?'[483] I found the ship going to pieces, or rather its scattered fragments. No plan, no thought, no method. Hence, though I had no doubts even before, I am now all the more determined to fly from here, and as soon as I possibly can, 'where nevermore of Pelops' line I'll hear the deeds or fame'.[484]

And look here! In case you don't know, Dolabella appointed me to his staff on the 3rd. I was informed of this yesterday evening. You too did not like the idea of a votive commission. It would really have been absurd for

481. i.e., Antony.
482. Servilia.
483. From a Greek play.
484. See n. 468.

me to pay vows after the overthrow of the Republic which I supposedly made for its safety. Besides free commissions[485] have a time limit under the lex Julia, or so I believe, and it is not easy to add to that type of commission a licence to come and go as one pleases. This additional advantage I now have. Also it's agreeable to have the privilege to use as one pleases for five years – though why should I be thinking of five years? I have the feeling that the sands are running out. But *absit omen*.

119
CICERO TO ATTICUS

Astura (?), 12 June 44 (?)

This district, let me tell you, is charming; at any rate it's secluded and free from observers if one wants to do some writing. And yet, somehow or other, 'home's best'; so my feet are carrying me back to Tusculum. After all I think one would soon get tired of the picture scenery of this scrap of wooded coast. What is more, I am afraid of rain, if my *Prognostics*[486] are to be trusted, for the frogs are speechifying. Would you please let me know where and what day I can see Brutus?

120
CICERO TO ATTICUS

Vibo, 25 July 44[487]

So far (I have now reached Sicca's place at Vibo) my voyage has been comfortable rather than strenuous, by oar in large part. No sign of the seasonable northerly gales. We were in luck to cross both the two bays we had to cross (of Paestum and of Vibo) with sheets level. So I arrived at

485. Including those in discharge of vow. See Glossary of Terms (LEGATE).
486. Cicero's version of a Greek poem on weather-signs.
487. *En route* for Greece.

Sicca's a week after leaving Pompeii, having stopped for one day at Velia, where I had a very pleasant time at our friend Talna's house. My reception, particularly as he was away, could not have been more handsome. So to Sicca's on the 24th. Here of course it is like being in my own home, so I am swallowing up the next day as well. But when I reach Regium I suppose I shall there have to consider, 'pondering a lengthy voyage',[488] whether to make for Patrae by cargo boat or for Tarentine Leucopetra and thence Corcyra by rowing-boats; and if by freighter, whether direct from the Straits or from Syracuse. I shall write to you on the subject from Regium.

But upon my soul, my dear Atticus, I often say to myself 'what signifies your journey?'[489] Why am I not with you? Why am I not gazing at those pearls of Italy, my little houses in the country? But it's enough and more than enough that I am not with you. What am I running away from? Danger? At present, unless I am mistaken, there is none. It is just the danger period to which you counsel me to return. You say that my going abroad is enthusiastically approved, but on the understanding that I get back before the Kalends of January, which I shall certainly make every effort to do. I would rather be frightened at home than secure in your Athens. However, watch the way things tend in Rome and write to me, or else, as I should much prefer, bring your news in person. So much for that.

I hope you will not mind if I ask your help in a matter in which I know you feel a deeper concern than I do myself. For heaven's sake clear off my debts, pay the lot. I have left behind a fine lot of balances due; but some care will be needed to see that my co-heirs are paid for the Cluvius property on the Kalends of August. You will judge how to proceed with Publilius. He ought not to press since we are not standing on our legal rights. None the less I certainly want him too to be satisfied. Terentia, I need hardly say, likewise – even *before* the settlement day if you can manage it. In fact, if, as I hope, you are leaving shortly for Epirus, let me ask you to arrange in advance for full clearance of my secured debts and to set all to rights and leave a clean slate. But enough of this – I am afraid you may think it overmuch.

Now I have to own up to a piece of carelessness. I sent the book *On Glory* to you and in it a preface which is in Book III of the *Academics*. This happened because I have a volume of prefaces from which I am in the habit of selecting when I have put a work in hand. And so back at Tusculum

488. From *Odyssey*, III, 169.
489. See n. 483.

I pushed this preface into the book which I have sent to you, forgetting that I had used it up already. But in sending the *Academics* on shipboard I noticed my mistake. So I scribbled out a new preface straight away, and send it herewith. Please cut the other off and glue this one on. Give my love to Pilia and my heart's darling Attica.

121
CICERO TO TREBATIUS

Regium, 28 July 44

From Cicero to Trebatius greetings.

This will show how highly I regard you – as indeed I ought, for your affection is no less warm than my own; but anyhow, that request of yours to which to your face I said something a little like no, and at any rate did not say yes – in your absence I could not let it go unanswered. As soon as my boat left Velia, I set to work on writing up Aristotle's *Topics*.[490] The town itself, in which you are so well-loved a figure, reminded me of you. I am sending the book to you from Regium, written in as clear a style as the material admits.[491] If you find it in places hard to follow, you must remember that no technical subject can be acquired by reading, without an interpreter and a certain amount of practice. You will not have far to go for an illustration – can your Civil Law be learned from books? There are any number of them, but they need a teacher and experience. However, if you read and re-read carefully, you will understand everything correctly by your own efforts. But only practice will make the 'topics' present themselves to your mind automatically when a question is proposed. I shall keep you hard at it, if I get back safely and find all safe with you.

28 July, Regium.

490. In fact Cicero's *Topics* (on the sources of proof, *topoi*) is not based on Aristotle's work of the same name, which he had perhaps never seen. He seems to have used Antiochus of Ascalon, who claimed to be following Aristotle.
491. A somewhat defensive qualification. The *Topics* is the most difficult of Cicero's works, the examples being taken from Roman law in compliment to Trebatius.

M. CICERO JUNIOR TO TIRO

Athens, August (?) 44

From Cicero junior[492] to his beloved Tiro greetings.

I was eagerly expecting couriers every day, and at last they have come, forty-five days after leaving home. I was delighted by their arrival. My kindest and dearest father's letter gave me great pleasure, and then your own most agreeable letter put the finishing touch to my happiness. I am no longer sorry to have made a break in our correspondence, rather the contrary, since as a result of my letters falling silent I am repaid by this example of your good nature. I am truly delighted that you have accepted my excuses without question.

I don't doubt that you are pleased with the reports you are hearing of me, dearest Tiro, and that they are such as you wished to hear. I shall make sure and work hard to see that this tiny new image of mine goes on getting bigger and bigger[493] as the days go by. So you can carry out your promise to be my publicity agent with every confidence. Young men make mistakes, and mine have brought me so much unhappiness and torment that I hate to think of what I did, or even hear it mentioned. Very well do I know that you shared my worry and unhappiness, as well you might, for you wanted all to go right for me not for my sake only but for your own too, because I have always wanted you to have a part in any good things that come my way. Well, since I gave you unhappiness then, I shall make sure to give you twice as much happiness now.

I can tell you that Cratippus and I are very close, more like father and son than teacher and pupil. I enjoy hearing him lecture, and quite delight in his own pleasant company. I spend all day with him and often part of the night, for I beg him into dining with me as frequently as possible. Now that he has got into the habit, he often drops in on us at dinner unawares, and then he puts off the grave philosopher and jokes with us in the most genial way. So you must try to meet him as soon as possible – he is such a pleasant, excellent man.

492. Now a student in Athens.
493. Literally 'is doubled more and more', a phrase of which Cicero senior would hardly have approved.

As for Bruttius,[494] what can I say? I never let him out of my sight. He lives simply and strictly, and he is the best of company too. Fun goes hand in hand with literary study and daily disputation. I have rented a lodging for him near mine, and as he is a poor man, I help him as best I can out of my own meagre funds. Also I have started regular declamation in Greek with Cassius,[495] and I want to practise in Latin with Bruttius. Some people whom Cratippus brought over from Mytilene, scholars whom he entirely approves of, are my friends and daily associates. I see a lot of Epicrates too (a leading man in Athenian society), and Leonides, and people of that sort. So as to myself – *voilà*!

As for what you say about Gorgias,[496] he *was* useful to me in declamation practice, but I have put obedience to my father's directions above all other considerations. He had written telling me *sans phrase* to get rid of Gorgias at once. I thought I had better not boggle over it – if I made too much fuss, he might think it suspicious. Also it came to my mind that I should be taking a lot upon myself in judging my father's judgement. All the same, I am very grateful for your concern and advice.

I quite accept your excuse about shortage of time. I know how busy you generally are. I'm really delighted to hear that you have bought a property, and hope it turns out a successful investment. Don't be surprised at my congratulations coming at this stage in my letter – that was about the point where *you* put the news of your purchase. Well, you are a landed proprietor! You must shed your town-bred ways – you are now a Roman squire! How amusing to picture the delightful sight of you now! I imagine you buying farm tackle, talking to the bailiff, hoarding pips at dessert in your jacket pockets! But seriously, I am as sorry as you that I was not there to lend you a hand. However, dear Tiro, I *shall* help you, provided luck helps me, especially as I know you have bought the place to share with us.

Thank you for attending to my commissions. But do please get a clerk sent out to me, preferably a Greek. I waste a lot of time copying out my notes.

Take care of your health first and foremost, so that we can be students together. I commend Anterus[497] to you.

494. Nothing more known, but no doubt an Italian.
495. Another unknown professor of rhetoric.
496. Later a noted rhetorician in Rome, he is said by Plutarch ('Life of Cicero', 24) to have led M. Cicero junior into bad ways and to have received an angry letter (in Greek) from his father.
497. Presumably the slave who carried the letter. The form *Anterum* here seems to come from a hybrid form 'Anterus' (instead of 'Anterōs') which is also found in inscriptions.

CICERO TO CASSIUS

Rome, early October 44

From Cicero to Cassius greetings.

Your friend[498] gets crazier every day. To begin with he has inscribed the statue[499] which he set up on the Rostra 'To Father and Benefactor' – so that you are now set down, not only as assassins, but as parricides to boot! I say 'you', but ought rather to say 'we', for the madman declares that I was the promoter of your noble enterprise. If only I had been! He would not be giving us any trouble then. But all that is your responsibility, and now that it is past and gone, I only wish I had some advice to offer you. But I cannot even think what to do myself. What can be done against violence except by violence?

Their whole plan is to avenge Caesar's death. On 2 October Antony was brought before a public meeting by Cannutius. He came off ignominiously indeed, but still he spoke of the country's saviours in terms appropriate to her betrayers. Of myself he declared unequivocally that everything you and your friends did and Cannutius is doing was on my advice. As a specimen of their behaviour in general, take the fact that they have deprived your Legate[500] of his travelling allowance. What do you suppose they infer by that? Presumably that the money was being conveyed to a public enemy.

It is a lamentable picture. We could not tolerate a master, so we are in bondage to our fellow-slave. However, hope still remains in your valour (though for me it is a case of wishing rather than of hoping). But where are your forces? For the rest I prefer you to consult your own conscience rather than listen to words of mine.

Goodbye.

498. Antony.
499. Of Caesar.
500. Cassius had been appointed governor of Cyrene. The names of his Legates are unknown.

MATIUS TO CICERO

Rome, October (?) 44

Matius to Cicero greetings.

Your letter[501] gave me great pleasure, because it told me that you think of me as I had expected and desired. Although I was not in any doubt on this score, the high importance I attach to your good opinion made me anxious that it should remain unimpaired. My conscience assured me that I had not been guilty of any act which could give offence to any honest man. I was therefore all the less disposed to believe that a man of your great and many-sided attainments would let himself be persuaded of anything hastily, especially in view of my ready and never-failing good-will towards yourself. Now that I know this is as I hoped, I will make some reply to the charges which you, as befitted the singular kindness of your heart and the friendly relations between us, have often rebutted on my behalf.

I am well aware of the criticisms which people have levelled at me since Caesar's death. They make it a point against me that I bear the death of a friend hard and am indignant that the man I loved has been destroyed. They say that country should come before friendship – as though they have already proved that his death was to the public advantage. But I shall not make debating points. I acknowledge that I have not yet arrived at that philosophical level. It was not Caesar I followed in the civil conflict, but a friend whom I did not desert, even though I did not like what he was doing. I never approved of civil war or indeed of the origin of the conflict, which I did my very utmost to get nipped in the bud. And so, when my friend emerged triumphant, I was not caught by the lure of office or money, prizes of which others, whose influence with Caesar was less than my own, took immoderate advantage. My estate was actually reduced by a law of Caesar's,[502] thanks to which many who rejoice at his death are still inside the community. For mercy to our defeated fellow-countrymen I struggled as for my own life.

501. *Letters to Friends*, 348. It concerns a complaint by Matius to their common friend Trebatius about alleged unfriendly remarks made by Cicero to third parties.
502. On debt.

Well then, can I, who desired every man's preservation, help feeling indignant at the slaughter of the man who granted it – all the more when the very persons[503] who brought him unpopularity were responsible for his destruction? 'Very well,' say they, 'you shall be punished for daring to disapprove of our action.' What unheard-of arrogance! Some may glory in the deed, while others may not even grieve with impunity! Even slaves have always had liberty to feel hope or fear or joy or sorrow of their own impulse, not someone else's. That freedom the 'authors of our liberty', as these persons like to describe themselves, are trying to snatch from us by intimidation. But they are wasting their breath. No threats of danger shall ever make me false to obligation and good feeling. I never thought an honourable death a thing to shun, indeed I should often have welcomed it.

Why are they angry with me for praying that they may be sorry for what they have done? I want every man's heart to be sore for Caesar's death. But I shall be told that as a citizen I ought to wish the good of the commonwealth. Unless my past life and hopes for the future prove that I so desire without words of mine, then I do not ask anyone to accept it because I say so. Therefore I earnestly request you to consider facts rather than words, and, if you perceive that it is to my advantage that things go as they should, to believe that I cannot have any part or lot with rascals.[504] Is it likely that in my declining years I should reverse the record of my youth (*then* I might have been pardoned for going astray) and undo the fabric of my life? Nor shall I give any offence, except that I grieve for the tragic fate of a great man to whom I was intimately bound. But if I were differently disposed, I should never deny what I was doing, and risk being thought a rascal for my misconduct and a cowardly hypocrite for trying to conceal it.

Well, but I superintended the Games for Caesar's Victory given by his young heir. That was a matter of private service, which has nothing to do with the state of the commonwealth. It was, however, an office which I owed to the memory and distinction of a dear friend even after his death, and one which I could not deny to the request of a most promising young man, thoroughly worthy of the name he bears. Also I have often called on Consul Antony to pay my respects; and you will find that those who think *me* a poor patriot are continually flocking to his house to make their

503. Such as D. Brutus, who had 'taken immoderate advantage' of their position as leading Caesarians.

504. i.e. subversive elements (*improbi*). Matius is here asserting his loyalty to established order.

petitions or carry off his favours. The presumption of it! Caesar never put any obstacles in the way of my associating with whom I pleased, even persons whom he himself did not like. And shall the people who have robbed me of my friend try to stop me with their carping tongues from liking whom I choose?

However, I don't doubt that the moderation of my career will be a strong enough defence against the false reports in time to come; and I am equally confident that even those who do not love me because of my loyalty to Caesar would rather have friends like me than like themselves. If my prayers are granted, I shall spend the remainder of my days quietly in Rhodes; but if some chance interferes with my plan, I shall live in Rome as one whose desire will ever be that things go as they should.

I am most grateful to our friend Trebatius for revealing the straight-forward and amicable nature of your sentiments towards me, thus adding to the reasons why I ought to pay respect and attention to one whom I have always been glad to regard as a friend.

I bid you goodbye and hope to have your affection.

125
CICERO TO ATTICUS

Puteoli, 4 November 44

Two letters from Octavian in one day! Now wants me to return to Rome at once, says he wants to work through the Senate. I replied that the Senate could not meet before the Kalends of January, which I believe is the case. He adds 'with your advice'. In short, he presses and I play for time. I don't trust his age and I don't know what he's after. I don't want to do anything without your friend Pansa. I'm nervous of Antony's power and don't want to leave the coast. But I'm afraid of some star performance during my absence. Varro doesn't think much of the boy's plan, I take a different view. He has a strong force at his back and *can* have Brutus.[505] And he's going to work quite openly, forming companies at Capua and paying out bounties. War is evidently coming any minute now. Let me

505. Decimus.

have an answer to all this. I am surprised that my courier left Rome on the Kalends without a letter from you.

126
CICERO TO D. BRUTUS

Rome, mid December 44

From M. Cicero to D. Brutus, Imperator, Consul-Elect, greetings.

Lupus asked myself, Libo, and your cousin Servius[506] to meet him at my house. I think you will have heard the view I expressed from M. Seius, who was present at our colloquy. Other matters you will be able to learn from Graeceius, although he left just after Seius.

The main point, which I want you thoroughly to grasp and remember in the future, is that in safeguarding the liberty and welfare of the Roman People you must not wait to be authorized by a Senate which is not yet free. If you did, you would be condemning your own act, for you did not liberate the commonwealth by any public authority – a fact which makes the exploit all the greater and more glorious. You would also be implying that the young man, or rather boy, Caesar had acted inconsiderately in taking upon himself so weighty a public cause at his private initiative. Further, you would be implying that the soldiers, country folk but brave men and loyal citizens, had taken leave of their senses – that is to say firstly, the veterans,[507] your own comrades in arms, and secondly the Martian and Fourth Legions, which branded their Consul as a public enemy and rallied to the defence of the commonwealth. The will of the Senate should be accepted in lieu of authority when its authority is trammelled by fear. Lastly, you are already committed, for you have twice taken the cause upon yourself – first on the Ides of March, and again recently when you raised a new army and forces. Therefore you should be ready for every contingency. Your attitude must be, not that you will do nothing except on orders, but that you will take such action as will earn the highest praise and admiration from us all.

506. The younger Ser. Sulpicius Rufus.

507. Settled in Caesar's Campanian colonies. They had rallied to Octavian early in November and were later joined by two of the four 'Macedonian' legions, the Martian and Fourth.

CICERO TO PAPIRIUS PAETUS

Rome, January 43

Cicero to Paetus greetings.

I should assist your friend Rufus,[508] about whom you now write to me for the second time, to the best of my ability, even if he had done me an injury, seeing how concerned you are on his behalf. But understanding and concluding as I do both from your letters and from one he has sent me himself that he has been greatly exercised about my safety, I cannot but be his friend, not only because of your recommendation (which carries the greatest weight with me, as is right and proper) but from my personal inclination and judgement. For I want you to know, my dear Paetus, that my suspicions and diligent precautions all started with your letter, which was followed by letters to like effect from many other correspondents. Plots were laid against me both at Aquinum and at Fabrateria of which something evidently came to your ears. They[509] put all their energies into catching me unawares, as though they had a presentiment of what a thorn in their flesh I was to become. Unsuspecting as I was, I might have laid myself open but for your admonition. Therefore this friend of yours needs no recommendation to me. I only hope the Fortune of the commonwealth may be such as to enable him to discover that gratitude is a strong point with me. So much for that.

I am sorry to hear that you have given up dining out. You have deprived yourself of a great deal of amusement and pleasure. Furthermore (you will not mind my being candid), I am afraid you will unlearn what little you used to know, and forget how to give little dinner-parties. For if you made such small progress in the art when you had models to imitate, what am I to expect of you now? When I laid the facts before Spurinna and explained to him your former mode of life, he pronounced a grave danger to the supreme interests of the state unless you resume your old habits when

508. Otherwise unknown.

509. Partisans of Mark Antony. We hear something of plots against Cicero's person by L. Antonius in the summer of 44; cf. *Letters to Atticus* 385, 390. *Phil.* XII.20.

Favonius[510] starts to blow; at the present time of year he said he thought it might be borne, if *you* could not bear the cold.

And really, my dear Paetus, all joking apart I advise you, as something which I regard as relevant to happiness, to spend time in honest, pleasant, and friendly company. Nothing becomes life better, or is more in harmony with its happy living. I am not thinking of physical pleasure, but of community of life and habit and of mental recreation, of which familiar conversation is the most effective agent; and conversation is at its most agreeable at dinner-parties. In this respect our countrymen are wiser than the Greeks. They use words meaning literally 'co-drinkings' or 'co-dinings',[511] but we say 'co-livings',[512] because at dinner-parties more than anywhere else life is lived in company. You see how I try to bring you back to dinners by philosophizing!

Take care of your health – which you will most easily compass by constantly dining abroad.

But do not suppose, if you love me, that because I write rather flippantly I have put aside my concern for the commonwealth. You may be sure, my dear Paetus, that my days and nights are passed in one sole care and occupation – the safety and freedom of my countrymen. I lose no opportunity of admonition or action or precaution. Finally it is my feeling that, if I must lay down my life in my present care and direction of public affairs, I shall consider myself very fortunate in my destiny.

Once again, goodbye.

128

CICERO TO CASSIUS

Rome, early February 43

From Cicero to Cassius greetings.

I dare say it is the winter weather that has so far prevented us getting any certain news of you – your doings and, above all, your whereabouts.

---

510. The west wind, harbinger of spring.
511. 'Symposia', 'syndeipna'.
512. *convivia*.

But everybody is saying (I imagine because they would like it to be so) that you are in Syria at the head of a force. This report gains the readier credence because it has a ring of probability. Our friend Brutus has won golden opinions. His achievements have been no less important than unexpected, so that, welcome as they are intrinsically, they are enhanced by their rapidity. If you hold the areas we think you do, the national cause has massive forces at its back. From the shores of Greece down to Egypt we shall have a rampart of commands and armies in thoroughly patriotic hands.

And yet, if I am in error, the position is that the decision of the whole war depends entirely on D. Brutus. If, as we hope, he breaks out of Mutina, it seems unlikely that there will be any further fighting. In fact the forces besieging him are now small, because Antony is holding Bononia with a large garrison. Our friend Hirtius is at Claterna, Caesar at Forum Cornelium, both with a strong army; and Pansa has got together a large force in Rome, raised by levy throughout Italy. The winter has so far prevented action. Hirtius seems determined to leave nothing to chance, as he intimates in frequent letters to me. Except for Bononia, Regium Lepidi, and Parma, all Gaul is in our hands, enthusiastically loyal to the state. Even your clients[513] beyond the Po are marvellously attached to the cause. The Senate is thoroughly resolute, except for the Consulars, of whom only L. Caesar is staunch and straight. With Servius Sulpicius' death we have lost a tower of strength. The rest are without energy or without principle. Some are jealous of the credit of those whose statesmanship they see gaining approval. But the unanimity of the People of Rome and of all Italy is quite remarkable.

That is about all I wanted you to know. I pray now that from those lands of the sunrise the light of your valour may shine.

Goodbye.

---

513. Why the Transpadanes are called clients of Cassius is unknown. They were indebted to Caesar the Dictator for Roman citizenship.

CICERO TO PLANCUS

Rome, 11 April 43

From Cicero to Plancus.

I must heartily rejoice for our country's sake that you have brought such large resources to her defence and aid at an almost desperate hour. And yet, as truly as I hope to embrace you victorious in a restored commonwealth, a great part of my happiness is in your prestige, which I know is already of the highest and will so remain. I assure you that no dispatch ever read in the Senate was more favourably received than yours,[514] an effect due not only to the peculiar importance of your public services but also to the impressiveness of the words and sentiments. It was all no novelty to me, who knew you and remembered the promises you made in your letters to me and had been thoroughly apprised of your intentions by our friend Furnius; but the Senate felt that their expectations had been surpassed – not that they ever doubted your goodwill, but they were not altogether clear as to how much you could do or how far you wished to go.

Accordingly, when M. Varisidius gave me your letter on the morning of 7 April and I read it, I was transported with delight; and as I was escorted from my house by a large throng of loyal patriots, I lost no time in making all of them sharers in my pleasure. Meanwhile our friend Munatius[515] called on me as usual, so I showed him your letter – he knew nothing about it beforehand, because Varisidius had come to me first, on your instructions as he said. A little later the same Munatius gave me the letter you had sent him together with your official dispatch for me to read. We decided to lay the dispatch immediately before Cornutus, the City Praetor, who in the absence of the Consuls is discharging consular functions according to traditional practice. The Senate was convoked at once and met in large numbers, attracted by the report of your dispatch and their eagerness to hear it. After the dispatch had been read out, a religious scruple arose: Cornutus was apprised by the Keepers of the Chickens of an inadvertence in his taking of the auspices, and their representations

514. *Letters to Friends* 371.
515. Who this T. Munatius (cf. end of letter) was and how related to Plancus is unknown.

were confirmed by our College.[516] Business was therefore deferred till the following day, on which I had a great struggle with Servilius so that you should get your due. By personal influence he managed to get his motion taken first, but a large majority of the Senate left him and voted against it. My motion, which was taken second, was gaining widespread assent, when P. Titius at Servilius' request interposed his veto. The matter was adjourned to the day following. Servilius arrived ready for the fray, 'wrath with Jove himself',[517] in whose temple the meeting was taking place. How I tamed him and how vigorously I put down Titius with his veto I prefer you to learn from other correspondents. One thing, though, you may learn from me: the Senate could not have been more responsible, resolute, and disposed to hear your praises than it was on that occasion; and the community at large is no less well disposed towards you than the Senate. Marvellous indeed is the unanimity with which the entire Roman People, and every type and order therein, has rallied to the cause of freedom.

Continue then in your present course, and hand down your name to eternity. Despite all these prizes that have only the semblance of glory, deriving from meaningless badges of distinction; hold them for brief, unreal, perishable things. True dignity lies in virtue; and virtue is most conspicuously displayed in eminent services to the state. Such you have a splendid opportunity to render. You have grasped it; do not let it slip. Make your country's debt to you no less than yours to her. You shall find me prompt not only to support but to amplify your standing. That I consider I owe both to the commonwealth, which is dearer to me than my life, and to our friendship. Let me add that in my recent endeavours for your credit I have had great pleasure in perceiving more clearly what I already knew well – the sound sense and loyalty of T. Munatius, shown in his truly remarkable goodwill and devotion to yourself.

11 April.

---

516. The Augurs.
517. Proverbial for violent anger or truculence.

GALBA TO CICERO[518]

Camp at Mutina, 15 April 43

Galba to Cicero greetings.

On 14 April, that being the day Pansa was to have joined Hirtius' camp (I was with him, having gone 100 miles to meet him and expedite his arrival), Antony led out two legions, the Second and Thirty-Fifth, and two praetorian cohorts,[519] one his own and the other Silanus', together with part of his reservists. In this strength he advanced to meet us, thinking that we had only four legions of recruits. But the previous night Hirtius had sent us the Martian Legion, which used to be under my command, and the two praetorian cohorts for our better security on the march to his camp.

When Antony's cavalry came into sight, there was no holding the Martian Legion and the praetorian cohorts. We started to follow them willy-nilly, since we had not been able to hold them back. Antony kept his forces at Forum Gallorum, wanting to conceal the fact that he had the legions; he only showed his cavalry and light-armed. When Pansa saw the legion advancing contrary to his intention, he ordered two legions of recruits to follow him. Having traversed a narrow route through marsh and woodland, we drew up a battle-line of twelve cohorts; the two legions had not yet come up. Suddenly Antony led his forces out of the village, drew them up and immediately engaged. Both sides at first fought as fiercely as men could fight. But the right wing, where I was placed with eight cohorts of the Martian Legion, threw back Antony's Thirty-Fifth at the first charge, and advanced more than half a mile from its original position in the line. The cavalry then tried to surround our wing, so I started to retire, setting our light-armed against the Moorish horse to stop them attacking our men in the rear. Meanwhile I found myself in the thick of the Antonians, with Antony some distance behind me. All at once I rode at a gallop towards a legion of recruits which was on its way up from our camp, throwing my shield over my shoulders. The Antonians chased me,

---

518. An eye-witness account of the battle of Forum Gallorum. On 27 April Antony suffered a second defeat (in which, however, the Consul Hirtius was killed) and was forced to raise the siege of Mutina.

519. The name given to a special unit forming the general's bodyguard.

while our men were about to hurl their javelins. In this predicament some providence came to my rescue – I was quickly recognized by our men.

On the Aemilian Way itself, where Caesar's praetorian cohort was stationed, there was a long struggle. The left wing, which was weaker, consisting of two cohorts of the Martian Legion and one praetorian cohort, began to give ground, because they were being surrounded by cavalry, which is Antony's strongest arm. When all our ranks had withdrawn, I started to retreat to the camp, the last to do so. Having won the battle, as he considered, Antony thought he could take the camp, but when he arrived he lost a number of men there and achieved nothing.

Having heard what had happened, Hirtius with twenty veteran cohorts met Antony on his way back to his camp and completely destroyed or routed his forces, on the very ground of the previous engagement near Forum Gallorum. Antony withdrew with his horse to his camp at Mutina about 10 o'clock at night. Hirtius then returned to the camp from which Pansa[520] had marched out and where he had left two legions, which had been assaulted by Antony. So Antony has lost the greater part of his veteran troops; but this result was achieved at the cost of some losses in the praetorian cohorts and the Martian Legion. Two eagles and sixty standards of Antony's have been brought in. It is a victory.

16 April, from camp.

131
CICERO TO M. BRUTUS

Rome, c. 21 April 43

From Cicero to Brutus greetings.

Our affairs seem in better shape. I am sure your correspondents have informed you of what has occurred. The Consuls have proved such as I have often described them to you. As for the boy Caesar, his natural worth and manliness is extraordinary. I only pray that I may succeed in guiding and holding him in the fullness of honours and favour as easily as I have

520. Pansa had been taken to Bononia (Bologna), fatally wounded. Galba had evidently not heard of this.

done hitherto. That will be more difficult, it is true, but still I do not despair. The young man is persuaded (chiefly through me) that our survival is his work; and certain it is that if he had not turned Antony back from Rome, all would have been lost.

Three or four days before this splendid victory the whole city fell into a panic, and poured out with wives and children to join you; but on 20 April they recovered and would now like you to come over here instead. That day I reaped the richest of rewards for my many days of labour and nights of wakefulness – if there is any reward in true, genuine glory. The whole population of Rome thronged to my house and escorted me up to the Capitol, then set me on the Rostra amid tumultuous applause. I am not a vain man, I do not need to be; but the unison of all classes in thanks and congratulations does move me, for to be popular in serving the people's welfare is a fine thing. But I would rather you heard all this from others.

Please keep me very particularly informed about your doings and plans, and take care that your generosity does not look like laxity. It is the feeling of the Senate and People of Rome that no public enemies ever deserved the harshest penalties more than those Romans who have taken up arms against their country in this war. In all my speeches I punish and harry them with the approval of all honest men. Your view on the matter is for you to determine. Mine is that the three brothers are in one and the same boat.

132

M. BRUTUS TO CICERO

Dyrrachium, c. 7 May 43

From Brutus to Cicero greetings.

How delighted I am to learn of the successes of our friend Brutus and the Consuls it is easier for you to imagine than for me to write. I applaud and rejoice at all of it, but especially the fact that Brutus' break-out not only brought safety to himself but also made a major contribution to the victory.

You tell me that the three Antonii are in one and the same boat, and that my view is for me to determine. My only conclusion is that the Senate or the People of Rome must pass judgement on those citizens who have not died fighting. You will say that my calling men hostile to the state 'citizens' is an impropriety in itself. On the contrary, it is quite proper. What the Senate has not yet decreed, nor the People ordered, I do not take it upon myself to prejudge, I do not make myself the arbiter. This much I maintain: in dealing with a person[521] whose life circumstances did not oblige me to take I have neither despoiled him cruelly nor indulged him laxly, and I have kept him in my power for the duration of the war.

In my judgement it is much more honourable and from a public stand-point advantageous to refrain from bearing hard on the unfortunate than to make endless concessions to the powerful which may whet their appetite and arrogance. In which regard, my excellent and gallant friend, whom I love so well and so deservedly both on my own account and on that of the commonwealth, you seem to me to be trusting your hopes too fondly. The moment somebody behaves well you seem to set no bounds to your favours and concessions, as though a mind corrupted by largesse could not possibly be swayed to bad courses. Your heart is too good to take offence at a warning, especially where the common welfare is at stake. But you will do as you think best. I too, when you have informed me * * *.[522]

133
PLANCUS TO CICERO

Camp on the Isara, 13 (?) May 43

From Plancus to Cicero.

I should be ashamed to chop and change in my letters, were it not that these things depend on the fickleness of another person. I did everything in my power to combine with Lepidus for the defence of the common-wealth, so that I could oppose the desperados on terms which would leave you at home less cause for anxiety. I pledged myself to all he asked and made other promises voluntarily. The day before yesterday I wrote to you

521. C. Antonius.
522. The rest of the letter is lost.

that I was confident of finding Lepidus amenable and of conducting the war in concert with him. I relied on letters in his handwriting and on the assurance given in person by Laterensis, who was with me at the time, begging me to make up my quarrel with Lepidus and to trust him. It is now no longer possible to augur well of him. But at least I have taken, and shall continue to take, good care that the supreme interests of the state are not betrayed by my credulity.

After constructing in one day a bridge over the river Isara, I led my army across in all haste, as the importance of the emergency demanded, since Lepidus himself had requested me in writing to make all speed to go to him – only to be met by his orderly with a letter enjoining me not to come. He wrote that he could settle the business himself, and asked me in the meanwhile to wait on the Isara. I will tell you the rash plan I formed. I decided to go none the less, supposing that Lepidus did not want to share the glory. I reckoned that without in any way detracting from this paltry personage's credit I could be at hand somewhere in the vicinity, so as to come rapidly to the rescue if anything untoward should occur.

That is how in my innocence I gauged the situation. But Laterensis, who is a man of complete integrity, now sends me a letter in his own hand utterly despairing of himself, the army, and Lepidus' good faith, and complaining that he has been left in the lurch. He warns me in plain terms to beware of treachery, says that he himself has kept faith, and urges me not to fail the commonwealth. I am sending a copy of his letter to Titius.[523] All the autograph originals (both those which I believed and those which I considered untrustworthy) I shall give to Cispius Laevus, who has been privy to all these transactions, for him to take to Rome.

There is a further item. When Lepidus was addressing his soldiers, who are disloyal by inclination and have been further corrupted by their officers such as Canidius, Rufrenus, and others whose names you will know when the time comes, these honest patriots roared out that they wanted peace, that they would fight nobody now that two excellent Consuls had been killed and so many Romans lost to the fatherland, branded wholesale moreover as public enemies and their goods confiscated. Lepidus neither punished this outburst nor remedied the mischief.

For me to go this way and expose my thoroughly loyal army with its auxiliaries and the Gaulish chiefs and the whole province to two combined armies, would clearly be the height of folly and temerity. If I was overwhelmed and had sacrificed the state along with myself, I could expect no

523. Probably Plancus' brother-in-law L. Titius, not the Tribune P. Titius.

pity, much less honour, for such a death. Therefore I intend to go back, and shall not let these desperate men be presented with the possibility of such advantages.

I shall take care to keep my army in suitable locations, to protect my province even if Lepidus' army defects, and to preserve the whole position uncompromised until you send armies to my support and defend the commonwealth here as successfully as you have done in Italy. On behalf of you all I am ready, no man has ever been more so, either to fight it out if I get a fair opportunity, or to stand a siege if it prove necessary, or to die if chance so fall. Therefore I urge you, my dear Cicero, to do your utmost to get an army across the Alps here as soon as possible, and to make haste before the enemy's strength gros further and our men become unsettled. If speed is used in this operation, the state will remain in possession of its victory and the criminals will be destroyed.

Take care of your health and remember me kindly.

134
LEPIDUS TO THE MAGISTRATES, SENATE, AND PEOPLE

Pons Argenteus, 30 May 43

M. Lepidus, twice Imperator, Pontifex Maximus, to the Praetors, Tribunes of the Plebs, Senate, and People and Plebs of Rome greetings.

I trust you and your children are well, as I am and my army.

I call Gods and men to witness, Fathers Conscript, how my heart and mind have ever been disposed towards the commonwealth, how in my eyes nothing has taken precedence of the general welfare and freedom. Of this I should shortly have given you proof, had not fortune wrested my decision out of my hands. My entire army, faithful to its inveterate tendency to conserve Roman lives and the general peace, has mutinied; and, truth to tell, has compelled me to champion the preservation in life and estate of so vast a number of Roman citizens.

Herein, Fathers Conscript, I beg and implore you to put private quarrels aside and to consult the supreme interests of the state. Do not treat the compassion shown by myself and my army in a conflict between fellow-countrymen as a crime. If you take account of the welfare and dignity of all, you will better consult your own interests and those of the state.

Dispatched 30 May from Pons Argenteus.

135
PLANCUS TO CICERO

Cularo, 6 June 43

From Plancus to Cicero.

Never, my dear Cicero, shall I regret the grave risks I am taking for my country's sake, provided that I am free of the reproach of rashness if anything happens to me. I should confess to a mistake due to imprudence if I had ever in my heart trusted Lepidus. After all, credulity is an error rather than a sin, and one which slides into an honourable mind with peculiar ease. But it was not through any such tendency that I was almost hoodwinked, for I knew Lepidus only too well. The truth is that sensitivity to criticism, a most dangerous proclivity in military operations, impelled me to take this chance. I was afraid that, if I stayed where I was, some detractor might think I was too obstinately holding a grudge against Lepidus, and even that my inertia was responsible for the enlargement of the conflict.

Accordingly, I led my forces almost within sight of Lepidus and Antony, and took up a position at a distance of forty miles from which I could either make a rapid approach or a successful retreat. Further, I chose a position with a river to my front which would take time to cross, hard by the Vocontii, through whose territory I could count on a free and trustworthy passage. Lepidus made strenuous efforts to lure me on, but finally giving up hope of success he joined forces with Antony on 29 May, and they advanced against me on the same day. This intelligence reached me when they were twenty miles away. I took good care, under providence, to retreat rapidly, but without letting my departure look in any way like a flight, so that not a soldier nor a trooper nor an item of baggage was lost or intercepted by those red-hot rebels. So on 4 June I recrossed the Isara with my entire force and broke the bridge which I had constructed, so as to give people time to readjust while I myself effect a junction with my colleague. I am expecting him three days after the dispatch of this letter.

I shall always acknowledge the good faith and conspicuously patriotic spirit of our friend Laterensis. But his over-tenderness towards Lepidus undeniably made him less alert to perceive the dangers in which we stood. When he saw that he had been the victim of a deception, he tried to turn against himself the weapon which he might with greater justice have used to destroy Lepidus, but he was interrupted in the act. He is still alive, and is said to be likely to live. However, I have no certain information on the latter score.[524]

The traitors are deeply chagrined at my escape from their clutches. They came at me with the same fury that stirred them against their country, angry besides on several recent counts arising from these transactions: namely, that I have continually taken Lepidus to task and urged him to stamp out the war, that I censured the talks that were going on, that I refused to allow envoys sent to me under safe conduct from Lepidus into my sight, that I arrested C. Catius Vestinus, Military Tribune, carrying a letter to me from Antony, and treated him as an enemy. It gives me some satisfaction to think that at any rate their disappointment will annoy them in proportion to the viciousness with which they attacked me.

For your part, my dear Cicero, continue as hitherto to furnish us here in the front line with vigilant and energetic support. Let Caesar come with the very dependable force under his command, or, if he is personally prevented for some reason, let his army be sent. He is himself perilously[525] involved. All the elements that were ever likely to appear in the camp of the desperados to fight against their country have now joined forces. Why should we not use every means we possess to save Rome? As for me, if you at home do not fail me, I need hardly say that I shall do my patriotic duty to the very uttermost.

Of yourself, my dear Cicero, I do assure you I grow fonder daily; and every day your good offices sharpen my anxiety not to forfeit one jot of your affection or esteem. I pray that I may be able in person to add by my devoted services to the pleasure you take in your benefactions.

6 June, from Cularo, on the border of the Allobrogian territory.

---

524. He died.

525. This can hardly refer to plots by Antony against Octavian's life. Plancus is merely pointing out incidentally that Octavian had a personal interest in doing everything possible to achieve victory.

CICERO TO CASSIUS

Rome, c. 9 June 43

From Cicero to Cassius greetings.

I expect you have learned from the gazette, which I am sure is sent to you regularly, of the criminal behaviour of your relative Lepidus, his egregious faithlessness and fickleness. After the war had been finished, as we thought, we find ourselves waging it afresh, and pin all our hopes on D. Brutus and Plancus, or, if you will have the truth, on you and M. Brutus – not only for immediate refuge, should some reverse unfortunately occur, but for the assurance of freedom in perpetuity.

Satisfactory reports concerning Dolabella are reaching us here, but without reliable authority. You are in grand repute, let me tell you, both on present estimate and in expectation of things to come. Set that thought before you, and strive on to the heights! There is nothing that the People of Rome does not judge you capable of achieving and maintaining.

Goodbye.

CICERO TO M. BRUTUS

Rome, July 43

From Cicero to Brutus greetings.

Messalla is with you. However carefully I write, I cannot hope to explain the current proceedings and situation more precisely in a letter than he will expound them with his excellent and comprehensive knowledge, and his ability to present you with all the facts in lucid and well-chosen terms. For I do assure you, Brutus (not that there is any need for me to tell you what you already know, but I cannot pass over such all-round excellence in silence) – I assure you that in uprightness, resolution, concern, and patriotic zeal the like of Messalla does not exist. In him the gift of eloquence, which he possesses in a quite astonishing degree, hardly seems worth commending. And yet his good sense is specially conspicuous in that very sphere, for he has trained himself in the strictest school of oratory with serious judgement and a great deal of technical skill. He is so industrious and indefatigably studious that his pre-eminent natural ability seems a secondary qualification.

But my affection carries me too far. It is not the purpose of this letter to praise Messalla, especially to you, my friend, who know his worth as well as I and who know those very pursuits which I am eulogizing better than I do. My one consolation in the distress I feel at parting with him is that he is going to join you as my *alter ego*, is doing his duty, and seeking no mean laurels. But enough of this.

Now I come rather belatedly to a letter of yours in which, while paying me a number of compliments, you find one fault, namely that I am excessive and, so to speak, prodigal in voting honours. This you criticize; someone else perhaps might tax me with undue harshness in the infliction of punishments – or perhaps you would charge me with both. If so, I am anxious that you should be thoroughly acquainted with my judgement on either point. I will not just quote the saying of Solon, one of the Seven Wise Men and the only one to write a code of law. He said that a state depends on two things, reward and punishment. There is, of course, a due limit in both, as in all other things, a sort of balance in each of the two categories. But it is not my purpose to discuss so wide a theme here. I do, however, think it appropriate to reveal the principle which I have followed in the proposals I have made to the Senate during this war.

You will not have forgotten, Brutus, that after Caesar's death and your memorable Ides of March I said that you and your associates had left one thing undone and that a mighty storm was brewing over the common-wealth. You had driven away a great plague, wiped a great blot from the honour of the Roman people, and won immortal glory for yourselves; but the apparatus of monarchy descended to Lepidus and Antony, one more of a weathercock, the other more of a blackguard, both afraid of peace and hostile to domestic tranquillity. We had no force to pit against their passionate desire for a political upheaval. The community had risen unanimously in defence of freedom, but we appeared too bold, and you and your friends may perhaps have shown greater wisdom in leaving the city you had liberated and in asking nothing of Italy when she proffered you her enthusiastic support. And so, seeing that Rome was in the hands of traitors, that neither you nor Cassius could live there in safety, and that the city was crushed by Antony's armed force, I thought that I too had better go elsewhere. A community crushed by ruffians, with all hope of rendering help cut off, is a hideous spectacle. But my spirit, anchored as ever upon the love of country, could not endure separation from her perils. Halfway to Greece, when the Etesians should have been blowing, the South Wind carried me back to Italy, as though dissuading me from my plan. I saw you at Velia, and was deeply distressed. For you were retiring, Brutus – retiring, since our friends the Stoics say that the Wise Man never flees. On returning to Rome I immediately set myself in opposition to Antony's wickedness and folly. Having stirred him up against me, I embarked upon a policy to free the commonwealth – a truly Brutine policy, since such aspirations run in your family.

The sequel is long and not to be recounted here, since it is about myself. All I will say is that this young man Caesar, thanks to whom (if we choose to admit the truth) we are still alive, drew his inspiration from my counsels. I have given him no honours, Brutus, but what were due and necessary. When we first began to call freedom back, before even D. Brutus' superlative valour had visibly come into action, our only protection was this lad, who had thrust Antony away from our necks. What honour ought we *not* to have voted him? However I at that time paid him a verbal tribute, and that in moderation, and voted him military authority. That no doubt seemed an honour at his age, but it was necessary since he had an army; for what is an army without military authority? Philippus voted him a statue, Servius the right to stand for office in advance of the legal age, a privilege which was later extended by Servilius. Nothing seemed too much at the time.

But somehow or other it is easier to find goodwill in the hour of danger than gratitude in victory. There came that most joyful day of D. Brutus' liberation, which happened also to be Brutus' birthday. I proposed that Brutus' birthday should be entered in the Calendar beside that day, following the precedent of our ancestors who paid that compliment to a woman, Larentia,[526] at whose altar in Velabrum you Pontiffs offer sacrifice. In trying to confer that on Brutus I wished the Calendar to contain a permanent record of a most welcome victory. That day I realized that gratitude has somewhat fewer votes in the Senate than spite. During these same days I showered honours (if you like to put it that way) on the dead, Hirtius and Pansa, even Aquila. Who shall blame me, unless he forgets

526. Acca Larentia, a figure of early Roman legend. Various stories are told about her. Velabrum was a street on the Aventine Hill.

the bygone danger once the fear is laid aside? Besides the grateful memory of benefit I had another reason, one of advantage to posterity: I wanted memorials of the public hatred for those bloodthirsty rebels to stand for all time. I suspect that another proposal of mine is less to your liking – your friends, excellent persons but lacking political experience, did not like it either – namely that Caesar be granted leave to enter Rome in ovation. For my part (but perhaps I am mistaken, though it is not my way to be particularly pleased with my own performances), I do not think I have made a better proposal in the course of this war. Why that is so I had better not reveal, or I might seem more far-sighted than grateful. I have said too much as it is; so let us pass on.

I voted honours to D. Brutus and to L. Plancus. It is a noble mind that is attracted by glory; but the Senate has shown good sense in using every means, provided it be honourable, to draw this man and that to the aid of the state. But there is Lepidus. Oh yes, we are blamed there – we set up a statue for him in the Rostra and then pulled it down. We tried to bring him back from treason by honouring him, but our wisdom was defeated by the folly of a thoroughly irresponsible individual. Not but what the setting up of Lepidus' statue did less harm than the pulling down did good.

That's enough about honours. Let me now say a little about punishment. Your letters have often let me understand that you would like to earn praise by your clemency towards those you have defeated in war. For my part, I look upon anything that comes from you as wise. But to waive the punishment of crime (for that is what is called 'pardoning'), even if it is tolerable in other contexts, I consider to be fatal in this war. Of all the civil wars in our commonwealth that I remember there has not been one in which the prospect of some form of constitution did not exist whichever side won. In this war I should not like to be positive about what constitution we shall have if we win, but there will certainly be none ever again if we lose. Accordingly I proposed stern measures against Antony and against Lepidus too, not so much for vengeance's sake as to deter the criminals among us by terror from attacking our country in the present and to leave an object-lesson for the future, so that none shall be minded to imitate such madness. To be sure this proposal was no more mine than everybody's. One feature seems cruel, the extension of the penalty to innocent children. But that is an ancient rule, found in all communities. Even Themistocles' children lived in poverty. If the same penalty applies to citizens judicially condemned, how could we take a more lenient line with public enemies? And what complaint can anyone have of me who must needs admit that he would have treated me more harshly had he won?

There you have the rationale of my proposals so far as this category of honours and punishments is concerned. Of my speeches and votes on other matters I think you have heard.

But all this is not particularly crucial; what *is* extremely crucial, Brutus, is that you come back to Italy with your army as soon as possible. You are most eagerly awaited. As soon as you touch Italian soil there will be a universal rally to your side. If we turn out to have won the day, as won it we had most gloriously if Lepidus had not had a craving to destroy everything, including himself and his family, we need your prestige to establish some sort of civic settlement. Whereas if a contest is still to come, our best hope lies in your prestige and the strength of your army. But for heaven's sake hurry! You know how much depends on timing and on speed.

I expect you will hear from your mother and sister about the pains I am taking on behalf of your sister's children. In this I am taking more account of your wishes, which mean a great deal to me, than of my own consistency, as some people see it. But I want to be and seem consistent in nothing more than in my affection for you.

APPENDIX I

UNTIL Julius Caesar reformed the calendar the Roman year consisted of 355 days divided into twelve months, all of which bore the Latin forms of their present names except Quintilis (= July) and Sextilis (= August). Each month had 29 days, except February with 28 and March, May, July, and October with 31. The first, fifth and thirteenth days of each month were called the Kalends (*Kalendae*), Nones (*Nonae*), and Ides (*Idus*) respectively, except that in March, May, July, and October the Nones fell on the seventh and the Ides on the fifteenth. I have kept these names in translation.

The calendar was adjusted by means of 'intercalation'. At the discretion of the College of Pontiffs, usually every other year, an 'intercalary' month of 23 or 22 days was inserted after 24 or 23 February. But in the years immediately before the Civil War the College neglected this procedure, so that by 46 the calendar was well over two months in advance of the sun. Julius Caesar rectified the situation by inserting two 'intercalary' months totalling 67 days between November and December of that year in addition to the traditional one in February. He also gave the months their present numbers of days, thus almost obviating the need for future intercalations, though in 1582 a further discrepancy had to be met by the institution of a Leap-Year.

(ii) *Roman Money*

The normal unit of reckoning was the sesterce (HS), though the denarius, equal to 4 sesterces, was the silver coin most generally in use. Sometimes sums are expressed in Athenian currency. The drachma was about equal to the denarius, the mina (100 drachmae) to HS400, and the talent (60 minae) to HS2,400. The Asiatic cistophorus was worth about 4 drachmae.

(iii) Roman Names

A Roman bore the name of his clan (*gens*), the *nomen* or *nomen gentilicium*, usually ending in -*ius*, preceded by a personal name (*praenomen*) and often followed by a *cognomen*, which might distinguish different families in the same *gens*: e.g. Marcus Tullius Cicero. The *nomen* was always, and the *cognomen* usually, hereditary. Sometimes, as when a family split into branches, an additional *cognomen* was taken: e.g., Publius Licinius Crassus Dives. Other additional *cognomina* were honorific, sometimes taken from a conquered country as Africanus or Numidicus, or adoptive (see below). Women generally had only the one clan-name (e.g., Tullia), which they retained after marriage.

Only a few personal names were in use and they are generally abbreviated as follows: A. = Aulus; Ap(p). = Appius; C. = Gaius; Cn. = Gnaeus; D. = Decimus; L. = Lucius; M. = Marcus; M'. = Manius; N. = Numerius; P. = Publius; Q. = Quintus; Ser. = Servius; Sex. = Sextus; Sp. = Spurius; T. = Titus; Ti. = Tiberius (I omit one or two which do not occur in our text). The use of a *praenomen* by itself in address or reference is generally a sign of close intimacy, whether real or affected, but in the case of a rare or distinctive praenomen, as Appius and Servius, this is not so.

The practice of adoption, of males at any rate, was very common in Rome. According to traditional practice the adopted son took his new father's full name and added his old *nomen gentilicium* with the adjectival termination -*ianus* instead of -*ius*: e.g., C. Octavius adopted by C. Julius Caesar, became C. Julius Caesar Octavianus. But in Cicero's time the practice had become variable. Sometimes the original name remained in use.

A slave had only one name, and since many slaves came from the East, this was often Greek. If freed, he took his master's *praenomen* and *nomen*, adding his slave-name as a *cognomen*: e.g., Tiro, when freed by M. Tullius Cicero, became M. Tullius Tiro. Occasionally the *praenomen* might be somebody else's. Atticus' slave Dionysius became M. Pomponius Dionysius in compliment to Cicero (instead of Titus).

Much the same applied to Greek or other provincials on gaining Roman citizenship. Such a man retained his former name as a *cognomen* and acquired the *praenomen* and *nomen* of the person to whom he owed the grant: e.g., the philosopher Cratippus became M. Tullius Cratippus after Cicero had got Caesar to give him the citizenship.

APPENDIX II

Consuls, 68–43 B.C.

68 L. Caecilius Metellus
   Q. Marcius Rex

67 C. Calpurnius Piso
   M'. Acilius Glabrio

66 M'. Aemilius Lepidus
   L. Vulcatius Tullus

65 L. Aurelius Cotta
   L. Manlius Torquatus

64 L. Julius Caesar
   C. Marcius Figulus

63 M. Tullius Cicero
   C. Antonius

62 D. Junius Silanus
   L. Licinius Murena

61 M. Pupius Piso Frugi
   M. Valerius Messalla Niger

60 Q. Caecilius Metellus Celer
   L. Afranius

59 C. Julius Caesar
   M. Calpurnius Bibulus

58 L. Calpurnius Piso Caesoninus
   A. Gabinius

57 P. Cornelius Lentulus Spinther
   Q. Caecilius Metellus Nepos

56 Cn. Cornelius Lentulus
      Marcellinus
   L. Marcius Philippus

55 Cn. Pompeius Magnus
   M. Licinius Crassus

54 L. Domitius Ahenobarbus
   Ap. Claudius Pulcher

53 Cn. Domitius Calvinus
   M. Valerius Messalla

52 Cn. Pompeius Magnus
   (Sole Consul)
   . . . .
   Q. Caecilius Metellus Pius
      Scipio

51 Ser. Sulpicius Rufus
   M. Claudius Marcellus

50 L. Aemilius Paulus
   C. Claudius Marcellus

49 C. Claudius Marcellus
   L. Cornelius Lentulus Crus

48 C. Julius Caesar
   P. Servilius Isauricus

47 Q. Fufius Calenus
    P. Vatinius

46 C. Julius Caesar
    M. Aemilius Lepidus

45 C. Julius Caesar (Sole Consul)

    . . . .
    Q. Fabius Maximus (suffect)
    C. Trebonius (suffect)
    C. Caninius Rebilus (suffect)

44 C. Julius Caesar
    M. Antonius

    . . . .
    P. Cornelius Dolabella (suffect)

43 C. Vibius Pansa Caetronianus
    A. Hirtius

GLOSSARY
OF PERSONS

A number of unimportant names are omitted. 'Nobles' are marked with an asterisk.

ACASTUS: Slave of Cicero's.

ACIDINUS: See MANLIUS.

*M'. AEMILIUS Lepidus: Consul in 66. Seems to have died in Italy during the Civil War.

*M. AEMILIUS Lepidus: Consul in 46 and one of Caesar's leading followers. After Caesar's death succeeded him as Chief Pontiff and became governor of Narbonese Gaul and Hither Spain in 44–43. Joined Antony and became Triumvir, Consul again in 42, and governor of Africa in 40–36. Forced by Octavian to retire from public life.

*M. AEMILIUS Scaurus: (1) Consul in 115 and Leader of the Senate. *(2) His son, Praetor in 56. As candidate for the Consulship in 54 was successfully defended by Cicero on a charge of extortion in his province (Sardinia), but found guilty in a second trial for bribery (Cicero still defending) and disappeared into exile.

AESOPUS: See CLODIUS.

L. AFRANIUS (nicknamed 'Aulus' son'): Lieutenant of Pompey, who 'bought' him the Consulship of 60. Later governed Further Spain as Pompey's Legate and fought on his side in the Civil War. Perished in Africa after Caesar's victory in 46.

AFRICANUS: See CORNELIUS Scipio.

AGESILAUS: King of Sparta c. 401–360.

ALEXANDER: Of Macedon, world-conqueror.

ALEXIS: Favourite slave or freedman of Atticus.

C. AMAFINIUS: Probably the first writer on Epicureanism in Latin, usually thought to have 'flourished' early in the first century.

T. AMPIUS Balbus: Praetor in 59 and governor of Asia the following year, then transferred to Cilicia. Henchman of Pompey and friend of Cicero, who probably obtained permission for him to return to Italy in 46.

C. ANICIUS: Senator and friend of Cicero.

T. ANNIUS Milo: As Tribune in 57 stoutly championed Cicero's recall and raised armed bands against Clodius. Candidate for the Consulship in 53, was condemned after Clodius' murder in January 52 and retired to Massilia. In 48 returned to Italy to take part in Caelius Rufus' rising and was killed.

ANTERORUS: Name of one or more slaves in the Cicero family.

ANTIOCHUS: Of Ascalon, contemporary Greek philosopher. Succeeded Philo as head of the Academy.

*C. ANTONIUS: (1) Caesar's colleague in the Consulship of 63, having previously been expelled from the Senate for rapacity and insolvency. Governor of Macedonia in 62–60. Condemned after his return to Rome, went into exile but lived to become Censor (!) in 42. Mark Antony was his nephew. *(2) Brother of Mark Antony. A Caesarian officer in the Civil War, became Praetor in 44. Captured in 42 by Brutus in Greece and later executed.

*L. ANTONIUS: Youngest brother of Mark Antony. Quaestor in 50 to Q. Minucius Thermus in Asia, Tribune in 44, and Consul in 41, when he and Antony's wife Fulvia started an unsuccessful war against Octavian in Italy. His life was spared but probably ended soon afterwards.

M. ANTONIUS: (1) Grandfather of Mark Antony, Consul in 99, and a celebrated orator. *(2) Mark Antony. Caesar's Quaestor in 52 and one of his principal lieutenants in the Civil War. Tribune in 49. Consul with Caesar in 44 and would-be successor to his power, he eventually formed the Triumvirate of 43 along with Octavian and Lepidus. Later quarrelled with Octavian and committed suicide after defeat at Actium (31).

APELLES: The most famous painter of antiquity (late fourth-century).

APPIUS: See CLAUDIUS.

M. APULEIUS: One of Gabinius' would-be prosecutors in 54, Augur and Quaestor in 45, Consul in 20.

AQUILA: See PONTIUS.

C. AQUILIUS Gallus: Praetor in 66 and an eminent jurist.

ARCHIAS: See LICINIUS.

ARCHILOCHUS: Seventh-century poet, famous for the virulence of his lampoons.

ARIOBARZANES III: Succeeded his murdered father as King of Cappadocia in 52. Killed by Cassius' orders in 42.

ARISTARCHUS: Homeric critic and keeper of the Alexandrian library in the earlier second century.

ARISTIPPUS: Of Cyrene. Pupil of Socrates and author of a hedonistic system of philosophy.

ARISTOTLE: The great fourth-century philosopher and polymath.

ARISTUS: Brother of Antiochus of Ascalon, whom he succeeded as head of the Academy.

C. ARRIUS: Cicero's neighbour at Formiae.

Q. ARRIUS: Henchman of M. Crassus. He seems to have been exiled in 52 and dead by 46.

ARTAVASDES: King of Armenia. Dethroned by Antony in 34 and subsequently executed.

C. ASINIUS Pollio: Born about 76, Praetor in 45, Consul in 40. Soldier, orator, tragic dramatist, and historian. Governor of Further Spain at the time of Caesar's death, he joined Antony in 43 and remained his supporter, but lived on under Augustus until A.D. 5.

ATHENODORUS: Son of Sandon. A Stoic philosopher, tutor to the future Emperor Augustus.

ATTICA: See CAECILIA.

Aulus' son: See AFRANIUS.

*AURELIA Orestilla: Wife of Catiline, 'in whom no respectable person ever found anything to praise except her good looks' (Sallust).

P. AUTRONIUS Paetus: Elected Consul in 66 but deprived of office by a conviction for bribery. Condemned in 62 for complicity with Catiline, he went into exile in Greece.

C. AVIANIUS Evander: Freedman of Aemilius Avianianus and distinguished sculptor.

BALBUS: See CORNELIUS.

BASILUS: See MINUCIUS.

BASSUS: See CAECILIUS.

BIBULUS: See CALPURNIUS.

BRUTUS: See JUNIUS.

CAECILIA Attica: Atticus' daughter, born probably in 51.

Q. CAECILIUS: Atticus' maternal uncle, a Roman Knight. Died in 58 leaving Atticus his heir.

Q. CAECILIUS Bassus: Former Pompeian who raised a mutiny in 46 against Caesar's governor of Syria and took command of his troops.

C. CAECILIUS Cornutus: (1) Tribune in 61 and Praetor in 57, when he supported Cicero's recall. (2) Perhaps son of the foregoing, City Praetor in 43. Committed suicide when Octavian seized Rome.

*Q. CAECILIUS Metellus Celer: As Praetor in 63 cooperated with Cicero against Catiline. Governor of Cisalpine Gaul in 62, Consul in 60. Died in 59. His wife was the notorious Clodia ('Ox-Eyes').

*Q. CAECILIUS Metellus Nepos: Younger brother of Celer. Served with Pompey in the East. As Tribune in 62 agitated against Cicero and was suspended from office. Consul in 57 and then governor of Hither Spain. Celer and Nepos were P. Clodius' half-brothers.

*Q. CAECILIUS Metellus Numidicus: Consul in 109. In 100 he went into voluntary exile rather than swear an oath to uphold legislation by the demagogue Saturninus, and was brought back the following year.

*Q. CAECILIUS Metellus Pius Scipio: A Scipio Nasica adopted by a Metellus (Numidicus' son), 'vaunting an unmatched pedigree, yet ignorant as well as unworthy of his ancestors, corrupt and debauched in the way of his life' (R. Syme). Became Pompey's father-in-law and colleague in the Consulship of 52. After Pompey's death led the Republican forces in Africa and committed suicide after Thapsus.

M. CAELIUS Rufus: Born c. 88. Placed by his father under Cicero's patronage and successfully defended by him on a criminal charge in 56. Tribune in 52, Curule Aedile in 50. One of the leading speakers of his time. Previously an opponent of Caesar, he changed sides just before the outbreak of the Civil War and was made Praetor in 48. As such started an agitation in favour of debtors ending in an attempted rising against Caesar in which he and his partner Milo lost their lives.

CAEPIO: See M. JUNIUS Brutus.

CAESAR: See JULIUS.

M. CALIDIUS: Distinguished orator. As Praetor in 57 supported Cicero's recall. A Caesarian in the Civil War, he died as governor of Cisalpine Gaul in 47.

CALLISTHENES: Latter-fourth-century historian.

*L. CALPURNIUS Bestia: (1) Tribune in 62 and enemy of Cicero. *(2) Friend of Cicero, defended by him in 56.

*L. CALPURNIUS Bibulus: Son of the following. Joined his step-father

Brutus in 43 but after Philippi served Antony, dying as governor of Syria in 32.

*M. CALPURNIUS Bibulus: As Consul in 59 opposed Caesar's legislation, shutting himself in his house and 'watching the skies'. Governor of Syria in 51–50. Died of overstrain while commanding Pompey's fleet in 48. Married Cato's daughter Porcia, later wife of Brutus.

*C. CALPURNIUS Piso: Consul in 67, then governor of Transalpine and Cisalpine Gaul. Defended by Cicero on a charge brought in this connection in 63.

*L. CALPURNIUS Piso Caesoninus: Consul in 58, when he took a line unfriendly to Cicero. Hence a bitter attack (extant) in 55. As Censor in 50 tried to moderate his colleague Appius Pulcher's harsh measures. Neutral in the Civil War (Caesar was his son-in-law), he opposed Antony in 44 but in 43 tried to promote an understanding.

*C. CALPURNIUS Piso Frugi: Tullia's first husband. Quaestor in 58, he died before Cicero's return from exile.

CALVINUS: See DOMITIUS.

C. CAMILLUS: An expert on business law, friend of Atticus and Cicero.

P. CANIDIUS Crassus: Consul-Suffect in 40. Commanded Antony's land forces at Actium and was executed by Octavian.

L. CANINIUS Gallus: Friend of Cicero, who defended him in 55. As Tribune in 56 he worked for Pompey's appointment to replace Ptolemy the Piper on his throne. Died in 44.

Ti. CANNUTIUS: As Tribune in 43 bitterly hostile to Antony. Escaped proscription, but was later executed by Octavian.

CARBO: See PAPIRIUS.

CASSIUS Barba: Caesarian officer, later supporter of Antony.

*C. CASSIUS Longinus: As Quaestor took charge of Syria after Crassus' death at Carrhae in 53. Gained a success against invading Parthians in 51. As Tribune in 49 joined Pompey. Pardoned and favoured by Caesar, he became Praetor in 44 and one of the leading conspirators against Caesar's life. Subsequently organized forces against the Triumvirs in the East and perished with Brutus at Philippi in 42. Married to Brutus' half-sister, Junia Tertulla.

*L. CASSIUS Longinus: Brother of the above but a Caesarian, Tribune in 44.

*Q. CASSIUS Longinus: Cousin of the foregoing. Formerly a favourite with Pompey, as Tribune in 49 he supported Caesar. His misgovernment of Hither Spain (49–47) provoked mutiny and his attempted assassination. Recalled by Caesar, he died at sea.

CATILINE: See SERGIUS.

CATIUS: Native of Cisalpine Gaul and author of a treatise or treatises on Epicureanism.

CATO: See PORCIUS.

CATULUS: See LUTATIUS.

CELER: See CAECILIUS Metellus and PILIUS.

CICERO: See TULLIUS.

L. CINCIUS: Man of business and confidential agent of Atticus.

CINEAS: Minister of King Pyrrhus and author (or rather epitomizer) of a work on strategy.

CINNA: See CORNELIUS.

L.(?) CISPIUS Laevus: Officer (not necessarily Legate) of Plancus in 43.

*C. CLAUDIUS Marcellus: (1) Praetor in 80. *(2) Son of the foregoing. As Consul in 50 in opposition to Caesar, but neutral in the Civil War. Married Caesar's great-niece Octavia. *(3) Cousin of the foregoing and Consul in 49. A naval commander under Pompey in 48, he seems to have died before Pharsalia.

*M. CLAUDIUS Marcellus: Brother of Gaius (no. 3), Consul in 51. A steady though not fanatical opponent of Caesar, he joined Pompey in the war but retired to Mytilene after Pharsalia. Publicly pardoned by Caesar in 46 (hence Cicero's extant speech of gratitude), he was murdered by a friend on his way home.

*Ti. CLAUDIUS Nero: One of Tullia's suitors in 50, he served and held office under Caesar. Praetor in 42, died after various vicissitudes about 35. His wife Livia married Octavian; his son became Octavian's (Augustus') successor, the Emperor Tiberius.

*Ap. CLAUDIUS Pulcher: As Praetor in 57 at enmity with Cicero but later reconciled. Consul in 54, he became Cicero's predecessor as governor of Cilicia. Censor in 50. Supported Pompey in the Civil War, but died before Pharsalia. One of his daughters married Pompey's elder son, another M. Brutus.

*CLODIA (CLAUDIA, 'Ox-Eyes'): Sister to P. Claudius Pulcher (CLODIUS, below) and wife of Metellus Celer; probably the 'Lesbia' to whom Catullus wrote his love-poems. Perhaps owner of a suburban property which Cicero wanted to buy in 45. The Clodia mentioned in Letters to Atticus 172 (IX.6).3 may have been her sister.

L. CLODIUS: 'Prefect of Engineers' to Ap. Pulcher in 51.

CLODIUS Aesopus: Great tragic actor, well known to Cicero personally. His son (mentioned also by Horace) was a notorious reprobate.

*P. CLODIUS Pulcher: Younger brother of Appius and Gaius. As Tribune in 58 drove Cicero into exile and remained his arch-enemy. From then until his death in an affray with Milo in 52 he was a power in politics through his popularity with the Roman mob and organized street-rowdyism. Often called Publius or Pulchellus ('Little Beauty', 'Pretty-boy') in Cicero's letters.

M. CLUVIUS: Wealthy banker of Puteoli from whom Cicero inherited an estate there.

*C. COELIUS Caldus: Quaestor to Cicero in 50 and left by him in charge of Cilicia.

L. CORNELIUS Balbus: (1) Native of Gades (Cadiz), received Roman citizenship in 72 through L. Cornelius Lentulus Crus. Attached himself to Caesar, becoming his confidential agent and financial adviser, and later to Octavian. Appointed Consul-Suffect in 40, not having held (at least until Caesar's death) any previous magistracy. Present at Atticus' death-bed in 32. (2) Nephew of the foregoing. In Caesar's entourage during the Civil War, he became Quaestor in 44, serving under Pollio in Spain. Rose to Consular rank under Augustus and triumphed in 19.

*L. CORNELIUS Cinna: Consul in 87. Expelled from Rome he reestablished himself by military force and after Marius' death remained at the head of affairs until his own death in 84.

*P. CORNELIUS Dolabella (after adoption Cn. Cornelius Lentulus Dolabella?): Defended by Cicero on two capital charges, he married Tullia in 50, but was divorced in 46. A favoured follower of Caesar (despite demagogic activities as Tribune in 47), whom he succeeded as Consul in 44. After some wavering joined Antony and left for his province of Syria late in the year. On the way killed C. Trebonius, governor of Asia and one of Caesar's assassins. Soon afterwards committed suicide to avoid capture by Cassius.

*L. CORNELIUS Lentulus Crus: Praetor in 58 (friendly to Cicero), Consul in 49. After Pharsalia fled to Egypt, where he was murdered in prison.

*Cn. CORNELIUS Lentulus Marcellinus: Consul in 56. Not heard of thereafter.

*L. CORNELIUS Lentulus Niger: Flamen of Mars. Died in 55.

P. CORNELIUS Lentulus Spinther: (1) As Consul in 57 took a leading part in Cicero's restoration. Governor of Cilicia 56–54. Supported Pompey in the Civil War. Taken prisoner by Caesar at Corfinium and released, he joined Pompey in Greece. Put to death in Africa in 46, perhaps by Caesar's orders. The name Spinther, derived from an actor who resembled him, is used by Cicero only for his son.(2) Son of the foregoing. Falsely claimed to have taken part in Caesar's murder. Went to Asia in 43 as Quaesto to Trebonius, after whose death he was active in support of Brutus and Cassius. Probably put to death after Philippi.

*P. CORNELIUS Scipio Aemilianus Africanus: Destroyer of Carthage in 146 and leading Roman statesman, idealized by Cicero, who gave him the chief role in his dialogue *On the Republic.*

*Faustus CORNELIUS Sulla: Son of the Dictator, Served with distinction in the East under Pompey, whose daughter he married. Active Republican in the Civil War, killed in Africa.

*P. CORNELIUS Sulla: (1) Nephew of the Dictator. Elected to the Consul-ship in 66 along with P. Autronius and deprived of office for the same reason, he retired to Naples. Defended in 62 by Cicero in an extant speech on a charge of complicity in Catiline's plot. Prominent after Caesar's victory, he enriched himself by buying confiscated property. Died in 46. *(2) Son of the foregoing. It was probably he rather than his father who held military commands in the Civil War, including that of Caesar's right at Pharsalia.

*L. CORNELIUS Sulla Felix: The Dictator. Held supreme power in Rome from 82 till his abdication in 79. Died in 78.

Q. CORNIFICIUS: (1) Praetor in 67 or 66 and a fellow-candidate with Cicero for the Consulship of 63. (2) Son of the above. Quaestor in 48, he served Caesar in and after the Civil War. Governor of Africa 44–42, until defeated and killed by the neighbouring governor, T. Sextius. A notable orator and poet, friend and correspondent of Cicero.

CORNUTUS: See CAECILUS.

CRASSIPES: See FURIUS.

CRASSUS: See LICINIUS.

CRATIPPUS: Eminent philosopher of the Peripatetic (Aristotelian) school, mentor of young M. Cicero at Athens, Cicero obtained him Roman citizenship from Caesar.

CULLEO: See TERENTIUS.

CURIO: See SCRIBONIUS.

M'. CURIUS: Roman businessman resident at Patrae, a close friend of Atticus and later of Cicero.

M. Curtius: Recommended by Cicero to Caesar for a military Tribunate in 54.

Curtius Nicias: A noted scholar. In 45–44 closely attached to Dolabella, who perhaps introduced him to Cicero. Sometimes identified with a despot of Cos, his native island, during Antony's régime.

Cytheris: See Volumnia.

*Damasippus: Well-known art expert who, as we learn from Horace, went bankrupt and turned Stoic philosopher. Probably son of the Crassus Junianus of Letter 36.

Darius III: King of Persia, conquered by Alexander.

Decimus: See Junius.

Deiotarus: Tetrarch of part of Galatia, made king by Pompey, whom he supported in the Civil War. Caesar let him keep his throne and acquitted him on a charge of attempted assassination (Cicero's defence is extant). Died about 40 in extreme old age. His son and namesake, also given the royal title by the Senate, probably pre-deceased him.

Demosthenes: Great fourth-century Athenian orator and patriot.

Dicaearchus: Pupil of Aristotle and like him a polymath, author of works on philosophy, history, literature, etc.

Diodotus: Stoic philosopher and Cicero's teacher. Lived in Cicero's house for many years and died leaving him his money.

Dionysius: (1) Fourth-century despot of Syracuse. (2) His son and successor. (3) Freedman and librarian of Cicero, pilfered his books and ran away. (4) See Attius, Pomponius.

Dolabella: See Cornelius.

*L. Domitius Ahenobarbus: Cato's brother-in-law and bitter opponent of Caesar. Captured at Corfinium in 49 and released, he stood siege in Massilia but fled before the town fell to Caesar's forces. Commanded Pompey's left at Pharsalia and was killed in flight.

*Cn. Domitius Calvinus: Consul in 53. Probably condemned for bribery and restored from exile by Caesar. Held high commands in the war, and a second Consulship and Triumph after Caesar's death.

Drusus: See Livius.

Q. Ennius: Third- and second-century Latin poet.

Epaminondas: Theban soldier and statesman, killed in the battle of Mantinea (362).

EPICURUS: Fourth-century philosopher.

ERATOSTHENES: Third-century savant, head of the Alexandrian library and founder of scientific geography.

EROS: Slave (perhaps of Philotimus) or freedman who looked after Cicero's finances in 45–44.

EURIPIDES: Athenian writer of tragedy.

M. FABIUS Gallus: Usually but wrongly called Fadius. Friend of Cicero, author, Epicurean, connoisseur of art.

T. FADIUS: Cicero's Quaestor in 63, Tribune in 57 (supported Cicero's recall), probably Praetor in a later year. Condemned for bribery in 52.

FAUSTUS: See CORNELIUS Sulla.

M. FAVONIUS: Follower of Cato. Fled from Pharsalia with Pompey. Later pardoned by Caesar, but proscribed in 43 and put to death at Philippi.

L. FLAVIUS: As Tribune in 60 acted in Pompey's interest. Praetor in 58. The Caesarian officer of Letters to Atticus 190 (X.1).2 may or may not be the same.

FUFIDIUS: The Fufidii were a prominent family in Arpinum.

Q. FUFIUS Calenus: Tribune in 61, Praetor in 59. Served under Caesar in Gaul and the Civil War. Governor of Greece in 48, Consul in 47. After Caesar's death supported Antony in Rome. Disliked by Cicero, who had known and respected his father.

*FULVIA: Wife of P. Crassus, Curio, and Antony.

*FURIUS Crassipes: Married Tullia about 55, soon afterwards divorced. Quaestor in Bithynia, perhaps in 54.

C. FURNIUS: Friend of Cicero, Tribune in 50. A Caesarian, he served as Munatius Plancus' Legate in 43 and later supported Mark Antony and his brother Lucius. Pardoned and dignified by Octavian, he lived to see his son Consul in 17.

A. GABINIUS: Military lieutenant and political supporter of Pompey. As Consul in 58 backed Clodius against Cicero. As governor of Syria restored Ptolemy the Piper to his throne in 55. Went into exile in 54 after conviction on charges of extortion. Reappears as Caesar's Legate in 48. Died in 47.

GALBA: See SULPICIUS.

GELLIUS Poplicola: Brother of L. Gellius Poplicola, Consul in 72, and a follower of Clodius.

GNAEUS: See POMPEIUS.

GRAECEIUS: Friend of Cassius and D. Brutus.

HERODOTUS: Fifth-century historian.

HIPPARCHUS: Second-century astronomer and geographer.

HIRRUS: See LUCILIUS.

A. HIRTIUS: Caesarian officer, Praetor in 46 and Consul in 43 until his death at Mutina. Man of letters and gourmet. Nine or more books of his correspondence with Cicero were extant in antiquity.

*Q. HORTENSIUS Hortalus: (1) Consul in 69 and before Cicero Rome's leading forensic orator. A devoted friend of Atticus, his relations with Cicero varied. Died in 50. *(2) Son of the foregoing and on bad terms with him. Joined Caesar in the Civil War, who made him Praetor and governor of Macedonia. Joined Brutus in 43. Put to death after Philippi by Antony in reprisal for the execution of his brother Gaius.

ISOCRATES: Fourth-century Athenian rhetorician.

*C. JULIUS Caesar: The Dictator.

*L. JULIUS Caesar: (1) Distant relative of the above. Consul in 64 and Legate in Gaul, he stood neutral in the Civil War. Proscribed in 43, he was saved by his sister, Antony's mother Julia. *(2) Son of the above. After acting as messenger in abortive peace negotiations early in the Civil War he joined Pompey. Killed after Thapsus, perhaps at Caesar's orders.

*C. JULIUS Caesar Octavianus: Caesar's great-nephew and adopted son. Later Triumvir and Emperor Augustus.

*JUNIA: Half-sister of Brutus and wife of Lepidus.

*JUNIA Tertia (or Tertulla): Sister of the above and wife of C. Cassius. Her funeral in A.D. 22 is described by Tacitus.

L. JUNIUS Brutus: Rome's first Consul, who drove out the last king, Tarquin the Proud.

*M. JUNIUS Brutus: Sometimes called (Q. Servilius) Caepio (Brutus) after adoption by his uncle Q. Servilius Caepio. Leader of the conspiracy to assassinate Caesar; committed suicide after Philippi.

*D. JUNIUS Brutus Albinus: Not closely related to the above. Served under Caesar in Gaul and the Civil War, governor of Transalpine Gaul in 48–46. Regarded by Caesar with special favour and named as Consul for 42 along with L. Plancus, he became a leading conspirator against his life. Later besieged by Antony at Mutina in his province of

Cisalpine Gaul, after Antony's defeat and escape he too crossed the Alps to join Plancus. When the latter went over to Antony he fled, but was killed by a Celtic chieftain on Antony's orders.

*D. JUNIUS Silanus: Consul in 62. Married Brutus' mother Servilia by whom he had three daughters (see JUNIA).

*M. JUNIUS Silanus: Officer of Lepidus in 43, who (probably) sent him to Antony at Mutina but later disavowed him. Consul in 25.

*M. JUVENTIUS Laterensis: Praetor in 51. As Lepidus' Legate, killed himself when his chief joined Antony.

T. LABIENUS: Tribune in 63. Caesar's principal lieutenant in Gaul, but deserted him at the outbreak of the Civil War and fought against him to the end. Killed at Munda.

*C. LAELIUS Sapiens: Consul in 140 and life-long friend of the younger Scipio Africanus.

LAÏS: Famous Corinthian courtesan.

LATERENSIS: See JUVENTIUS.

LENTULUS: See CORNELIUS.

LEONIDES: Athenian, apparently of high position, who kept an eye on M. Cicero junior in 45–44.

LEPIDUS: See AEMILIUS.

LEPTA: See PACONIUS.

LIBO: See SCRIBONIUS.

A. LICINIUS Archias: Poet, author of some surviving epigrams. Cicero successfully defended his title to Roman citizenship in an extant speech (62).

*M. LICINIUS Crassus: (1) Consul in 70 and 55. Joined Pompey and Caesar in 60 to form the so-called First Triumvirate. Left for Syria late in 55. Defeated and killed at Carrhae in 53 leading an invasion of Parthia.

*P. LICINIUS Crassus: Son of the 'Triumvir'. Much attached to Cicero in his early days, he served brilliantly under Caesar in Gaul. Went out to Syria with his father and was killed at Carrhae. In the *Brutus* Cicero seems to blame him for the disaster.

*L. LICINIUS LUCULLUS: Lieutenant of Sulla and Consul in 74. In 73–66 waged a brilliant series of campaigns against King Mithridates of Pontus, ending ingloriously through disaffection in his army. After supersession by Pompey returned to Rome to live in ease and luxury until his death in 56

*M. LICINIUS Lucullus: See TERENTIUS.

A. LIGURIUS: Caesarian officer and friend of Cicero's.

*M. LIVIUS Drusus Claudianus: Father of Augustus' wife Livia, originally a Claudius Pulcher. Successfully defended by Cicero in 54. Praetor or President of Court in 50. Owner of suburban estate coveted by Cicero in 45. Killed himself in his tent at Philippi.

M. LOLLIUS Palicanus: Tribune in 71. Mob orator and agitator against the post-Sullan régime.

Cn. LUCCEIUS: Member of a locally aristocratic family of Cumae, friend of Cicero and Brutus.

L. LUCCEIUS (son of Quintus): Praetor in 67 and unsuccessful candidate for the Consulship in 60. On amicable terms with Cicero, he remained one of Pompey's most intimate friends until Pharsalia. Pardoned by Caesar, he may have died in the proscriptions of 43. Cicero admired his historical work, which was perhaps never published.

C. LUCILIUS: Roman satirist late in the second century.

C. LUCILIUS Hirrus: Great-nephew (probably) of the above and cousin to Pompey. Tribune in 53, he annoyed Cicero by standing against him for the Augurate. Defeated in 51 in his candidature for the Aedileship. Followed Pompey in the Civil War but survived to lend Caesar 6,000 fish for his triumphal banquet in 45 and flee proscription in 43–42. A great land-owner and in Cicero's opinion an egregious ass.

T. LUCRETIUS Carus: One of Rome's greatest poets. His work *On the Nature of Things* is an exposition of Epicurus' physical philosophy.

LUCULLUS: See LICINIUS.

LUPUS: (1) Friend of D. Brutus. (2) See RUTILIUS.

*Q. LUTATIUS Catulus: (1) Colleague of Marius as Consul in 102, killed by his orders in 87. *(2) Son of the foregoing. Consul in 78 and leading conservative figure until his death in 61 or 60.

LYSIPPUS: Fourth-century sculptor.

LYSO: Friend and host of Cicero at Patrae.

P. MAGIUS Cilo: Friend and murderer of M. Marcellus.

MAMURRA: 'Prefect of Engineers' to Caesar and a *nouveau riche*. Savagely lampooned by Catullus.

*MANLIUS Acidinus: Student at Athens in 45, perhaps identical with Horace's friend Torquatus.

*A. MANLIUS Torquatus: Praetor perhaps in 70 and friend of Cicero, who tried through Dolabella to get Caesar's permission for him, as an ex-

Pompeian living in Athens, to return to Italy. After Caesar's death an active republican, he was befriended by his old friend Atticus after Philippi.

MARCELLINUS: See CORNELIUS Lentulus.

MARCELLUS: See CLAUDIUS.

*L. MARCIUS Philippus: (1) Consul in 91. Censor under Cinna's régime, but joined Sulla when he returned to Italy. *(2) Son of the foregoing. Consul in 56. Husband of Caesar's niece and Cato's father-in-law, he took no part in the Civil War. Counselled caution to his stepson Octavian in 44. A moderating influence in the struggle between the Senate and Antony.

C. MARIUS: Of Arpinum. Great general, seven times Consul, destroyer of invading northern tribes. Driven into exile by Sulla in 88, returned to Rome by force in 87 and killed off numbers of opponents before his own death early the following year.

M. MARIUS: Friend, correspondent, and perhaps relative of Cicero, resident near Pompeii.

C. MATIUS: Old friend of Cicero's, closely attached to Caesar, whom he accompanied in Gaul without official rank. Cicero calls him by nicknames referring to his baldness.

C. MEMMIUS (son of Lucius): First husband of Sulla's daughter Fausta, who was a ward of L. Lucullus, hence perhaps an enemy of the two Luculli. An erratic political career ended in exile after conviction for bribery in 52. Noted orator and poet, generally supposed to be the friend to whom Lucretius dedicated his poem *On the Nature of Things*.

L. MESCINIUS Rufus: Cicero's Quaestor in Cilicia. Seems to have joined Pompey in the Civil War bt was allowed to return to Italy in 46.

MESSALLA: See VALERIUS.

C. MESSIUS: Pro-Ciceronian Tribune in 57 and adherent of Pompey; but in 46 Legate to Caesar in Africa.

METELLUS: See CAECILIUS.

METRODORUS: A doctor, probably a freedman of Cicero's.

MILO: See ANNIUS.

L. MINUCIUS Basilus: Legate of Caesar in Gaul and the Civil War and Praetor in 45, joined the conspiracy in 44. Murdered by his slaves the following year. A friend of Cicero.

*Q. MINUCIUS Thermus: Governor of Asia in 51–50. A Pompeian in the Civil War and proscribed in 43, he escaped to join Sex. Pompeius and then Antony.

*Q. MUCIUS Scaevola: *Pontifex Maximus. Consul in 95. A great jurist and a model governor of Asia, well known to Cicero until his murder by the Marians in 82.

L. MUNATIUS Plancus: Family friend of Cicero. Served under Caesar in Gaul and the Civil War. City Prefect during Caesar's absence in 46–45. As governor of Transalpine Gaul (except the Narbonensis), he finally joined Antony in 43. Consul in 42. Changed sides again before Actium and became Censor in 22.

T. MUNATIUS Plancus Bursa: Brother of the above. Tribune in 52 and follower of Clodius, he was successfully prosecuted by Cicero as a ringleader in the riots following Clodius' death. In exile joined Caesar, who brought him back in 49. Later an active supporter of Antony.

Cn. NAEVIUS: Early Roman epic and dramatic poet.

NASICA: See CAECILIUS Metellus Pius Scipio.

NEPOS: See CAECILIUS Metellus.

NICIAS: See CURTIUS.

Servius OCELLA: Subject of a Roman scandal in 50.

OCTAVIANUS or OCTAVIUS: See JULIUS.

C. OPPIUS: Roman Knight, friend and agent of Caesar, usually mentioned in conjunction with Cornelius Balbus and like him a friend of Atticus and Cicero.

ORESTILLA: See AURELIA.

Q. PACONIUS(?) Lepta: Cicero's 'Prefect of Engineers' in Cilicia.

PAETUS: See PAPIRIUS.

PALICANUS: See LOLLIUS.

PANSA: See VIBIUS.

C. PAPIRIUS Carbo, Consul in 120. Suspected of murdering Scipio Aemilianus in 129.

L. PAPIRIUS Paetus: Wealthy resident of Naples and an old friend of Cicero.

Q.(?) PATISCUS: Apparently a Roman businessman in Asia, then a Caesarian officer, in 43 a Republican Proquaestor taking part in naval operations in the East (if these are identical).

PATRO: Successor of Phaedrus as head of the Epicurean school at Athens, old friend and protégé of Atticus and Cicero.

PHAEDRUS: Patro's predecessor as head of the Epicurean school. Cicero as a boy heard him lecture in Rome.

PHARNACES: Son of Mithridates the Great of Pontus and King of Bosporus. Recovered his father's kingdom in 48 and defeated Caesar's lieutenant, Domitius Calvinus. Caesar 'came, saw, and conquered' him the following year.

PHILIP (PUS): King of Macedonia, father of Alexander the Great.

PHILIPPUS: See MARCIUS.

PHILO: Of Larissa. Antiochus' predecessor as head of the Academic school of philosophy.

PHILOGENES: Freedman of Atticus, employed in financial transactions with Cicero.

PHILOTIMUS: Freedman of Terentia, up till 50 much employed by Cicero in financial business.

PILIA: Atticus' wife, married in 56. May have died in 44.

Q. PILIUS Celer: Relative, probably brother, of the above. Supported Caesar in the Civil War and brought letters from M. Brutus and C. Antonius to the Senate in 43. Cicero thought well of him as a speaker.

PISO: See CALPURNIUS and PUPIUS.

PLATO: Fourth-century Athenian philosopher, founder of the Academy.

POLLIO: See ASINIUS.

POLYBIUS: Second-century historian.

POLYDAMAS: Senior Trojan in the *Iliad*.

*Cn. POMPEIUS Magnus: (1) Pompey the Great. *(2) Elder son of the fore-going, killed in Spain after the battle of Munda.

*Sex. POMPEIUS Magnus: Younger son of Pompey the Great. After Caesar's death revived the war in Spain, then came to terms with Lepidus. Eventually gained control of Sicily and was a thorn in Octavian's flesh until defeated in 36. Fled to the East and after further adventures was captured and executed by an officer of Antony's.

*Q. POMPEIUS Rufus: Sulla's grandson, but an associate of P. Clodius, condemned for his part as Tribune in 52 in the riots following Clodius' murder. His prosecutor was Caelius Rufus, who later befriended him when he was living in poverty in Bauli.

POMPONIA: Sister of Atticus, married to Q. Cicero from about 70 until their divorce in 45 or 44.

T. POMPONIUS Atticus (Q. Caecilius Pomponianus Atticus): Cicero's friend and correspondent.

M. POMPONIUS Dionysius: Learned freedman of Atticus and tutor to the young Ciceros. Cicero charged him with ingratitude in 49.

C. POMPTINUS: Praetor in 63, then governor of Narbonese Gaul, where he crushed a tribal revolt. Finally granted a Triumph in 54. Legate to Cicero in Cilicia.

PONTIUS Aquila: Tribune in 45 and assassin of Caesar. Legate to D. Brutus in 43. Killed at Mutina.

*PORCIA: (1) Cato's sister, wife of L. Domitius Ahenobarbus. Died in 45. (2) Cato's daughter, married first to M. Bibulus, then to M. Brutus. Died, allegedly by suicide, in 43.

*C. PORCIUS Cato: As Tribune in 56 at first opposed, then supported Pompey (perhaps leagued with Crassus). Tried and acquitted in 54.

*M. PORCIUS Cato: (1) 'Of Utica'. Leader of conservative opposition to the 'First Triumvirate'. Later made common cause with Pompey against Caesar, and after Pompey's death became the life and soul of continuing resistance. Committed suicide at Utica after the republican defeat in 46. Family connections included Servilia (half-sister), her son Brutus, M. Bibulus, L. Domitius, and Hortensius. *(2) Son of the foregoing, who left Cicero and Atticus as his guardians. Killed at Philippi.

PROTOGENES: Fourth-century painter.

PTOLEMY XII: Called 'The Piper', King of Egypt. Driven out by his subjects in 58, restored by Gabinius in 55, died in 51.

PUBLILIA: Cicero's ward and second wife, married towards the end of 46, divorced a few months later.

PUBLILIUS: Relative, probably brother, of the above.

PUBLIUS, PULCHELLUS, PULCHER: See CLODIUS.

*M. PUPIUS Piso Frugi: Friend of Cicero's youth, to whom he gave a role in his De Finibus. After his Consulship in 61 (severely criticized by Cicero) he disappears.

PYRRHUS: King of Epirus. Campaigned against Rome in 281–275. Wrote a treatise on tactics.

*T.(?) RUFRENUS: Officer in Lepidus' army in 43. Apparently Tribune the following year.

*P. RUTILIUS Lupus: Tribune and supporter of Pompey in 56. Praetor in 49. Served under Pompey in Greece in 48.

Cn. SALLUSTIUS: Friend of Cicero and Atticus.

SCAURUS: See AEMILIUS.

SCIPIO: See CAECILIUS and CORNELIUS.

*C. SCRIBONIUS Curio: (1) Consul in 76, notable general and orator. Died in 53. *(2) His son, Cicero's friend and correspondent. After some variations appeared as Tribune in 50 in the role of a fervent optimate, but suddenly went over to Caesar, allegedly for a vast bribe. Led expedition to Africa in 49, where he was defeated and killed.

M. SEIUS: Roman Knight and man of business, supporter of Caesar. Mentioned by Varro and Pliny the Elder as a noted producer of poultry, etc.

Q. SELICIUS: Friend of Lentulus Spinther, perhaps identical with a wealthy money-lender mentioned in letters to Atticus.

SERAPIO: (1) Author of a work on mathematical geography, after Eratosthenes and perhaps before Hipparchus. (2) Owner (?) of a ship in 49.

*L. SERGIUS Catilina: Cicero's rival for the Consulship in 64. Plotted a *coup d'état* in 63, Killed in battle the following year.

*SERVILIA: Mother of M. Brutus, half-sister of Cato, allegedly mistress of Caesar, and close friend of Atticus.

*P. SERVILIUS Isauricus: Earlier an associate of Cato and married to his niece, he joined Caesar in the Civil War and became Consul in 48. Governor of Asia 46–44. Moderate opponent of Antony after Caesar's death, but later reconciled. Consul again in 41.

SERVIUS: See SULPICIUS.

P. SESTIUS: Quaestor in Macedonia in 62. As tribune in 57 took a leading part in promoting Cicero's recall. Defended on charges in this connection by Cicero in 56 (speech extant). Later Praetor and Cicero's successor as governor of Cilicia in 49. Went over to Caesar after Pharsalia. Supported Cicero in 43, but kept his life and status in the thirties. A notoriously wearisome speaker.

SEXTUS: See POMPEIUS.

SICCA: Friend of Cicero's, often mentioned in letters to Atticus and Terentia, perhaps a fellow-Arpinate and Cicero's 'Prefect of Engineers' in 63.

P. SILIUS: Governor of Bithynia in 51–50 and owner of a property which Cicero wished to buy in 45.

SOCRATES: Plato's teacher and principal speaker in his dialogues.

SOLON: Sixth-century Athenian statesman and law-giver.

SOPHOCLES: fifth-century Athenian tragic dramatist.

SPURINNA: Haruspex (diviner from entrails). Warned Caesar that his life was in danger before his assassination.

STATIUS: Slave, then freedman, of Q. Cicero.

SULLA: See CORNELIUS.

*Ser. SULPICIUS Galba: Legate to C. Pomptinus, then to Caesar in Gaul. Praetor in 54. Supported Caesar in the Civil War and joined the conspiracy in 44. Fought under Pansa at the battle of Forum Gallorum. Probably killed in 43.

*Ser. SULPICIUS Rufus: (1) Friend and contemporary of Cicero's and one of the most famous of Roman jurists. Consul in 51, he worked to avoid the coming clash with Caesar, but in 49 after initial wavering joined Pompey (the common view that he remained neutral is mistaken). After Pharsalia he retired to Samos, but was appointed governor of Achaia by Caesar in 46. Died in 43 on a mission to Antony. *(2) His son. Joined Caesar's army at Brundisium in March 49, but further part in the war is unknown. After Caesar's death a republican and probably a victim of the Proscriptions.

TERENTIA: Cicero's wife from about 80 to 46.

Q. TERENTIUS Culleo: Tribune in 58 and friend of Pompey.

P. TERENTIUS Hispo: Friend of Cicero, worked for a tax-farming company (or companies) in Asia and Bithynia.

M. TERENTIUS Varro: Of Reate, the most learned and prolific author of his time. Born in 116. After a distinguished military and political career under Pompey's aegis, he gave up the republican cause after Pharsalia and became head of Caesar's new library. Narrowly escaping proscription in 43 he lived till 27 in tireless literary activity. Of his vast and varied output only a small part, and perhaps the least interesting, survives apart from fragments.

*M. TERENTIUS Varro Lucullus: Brother by birth of L. Lucullus and an almost equally distinguished soldier. Consul in 73. Triumphed for victories in the Balkans. Died not long after Lucius.

*A. TERENTIUS Varro Murena: Friend of Cicero and Ap. Pulcher.

TERTIA, TERITULLA: See JUNIA.

TESTA: See TREBATIUS.

THEMISTOCLES: Athenian leader in the Persian War of 481–479. Later exiled and took refuge with the King of Persia.

THEOPHRASTUS: Pupil of Aristotle and prolific writer on philosophy, politics, and natural science.

THEOPOMPUS: Of Chios. Fourth-century historian noted for censoriousness.

THERMUS: See MINUCIUS.

THRASYBULUS: Athenian statesman, who overthrew the oligarchy in 403.

THYILLUS: poet, three of whose epigrams survive in the Greek Anthology.

TIMAEUS: Fourth- and third-century historian.

TIMOLEON: Democratic leader in Sicily in the fourth century.

TIRO: See TULLIUS.

P. TITIUS: Tribune in 43 and proposer of the law establishing the Triumvirate. Died in office.

TORQUATUS: See MANLIUS.

C. TREBATIUS Testa: Of Velia. Friend and correspondent of Cicero, about twenty years his junior, recommended by him to Caesar in 54. Supported Caesar in the Civil War and lived to a ripe old age. Cicero's *Topica* is dedicated to him. Eminent jurist.

C. TREBONIUS: Tribune in 55, put through a law extending Caesar's term of command. Legate to Caesar in Gallic and Civil Wars and Praetor in 48. Governor of Further Spain 47–46. Consul-Suffect 45. Joined the conspiracy in 44. Brutally murdered by Dolabella shortly after his arrival in Asia as governor. Friend and correspondent of Cicero.

TRIARIUS: See VALERIUS.

*TULLIA: Cicero's daughter. Died February 45.

L. TULLIUS: Legate to Cicero in Cilicia.

M. TULLIUS Cicero: (1) The orator. *(2) His son.

Q. TULLIUS Cicero: (1) Brother of the orator. (2) His son, Cicero's and Atticus' nephew.

M. TULLIUS Tiro: Slave of Cicero, manumitted in 53, a confidential secretary and literary assistant. After Cicero's death devoted himself to propagating his work and memory.

TYRANNIO: Of Amisus, originally called Theophrastus. Settled in Rome about 68 and became rich and well known as a scholar and teacher. Wrote on grammatical and literary subjects. The geographer Strabo was his pupil.

Paula (Polla) VALERIA: Of the Triarius family. Married D. Brutus in 50.

*M. VALERIUS Messalla Corvinus: Son of the following. At Athens with young M. Cicero in 45. Distinguished orator and one of the great figures of the Augustan period.

*M. VALERIUS Messalla Niger: As Consul in 61 took an optimate line, but later a supporter of Pompey. Censor in 55–54, apparently died shortly before the Civil War.

*M. VALERIUS Messalla Rufus: Brother-in-law to Sulla and Hortensius' nephew, friend of Atticus and Cicero. Consul in 53, later condemned for electoral malpractice and rehabilitated by Caesar. After Caesar's death lived in scholarly retirement to an advanced age. Wrote on augury.

C. VALERIUS Triarius: Apparently fell on the Pompeian side at Pharsalia. Cicero gave him a role in the *De Finibus*.

P. VALERIUS Triarius: Brother of the above.

VARRO: See TERENTIUS.

P. VATINIUS: Tribune in 59, carried through legislation on Caesar's behalf. Praetor in 55, Consul in 47, governor of Illyricum, triumphed in 42. Cicero attacked him in an extant speech, but in 54 became reconciled under pressure and defended him in court. From then on they remained on good terms.

C. VESTORIUS: Businessman of Puteoli, friendly with Atticus and Cicero (who was apt to make fun of his lack of culture).

L. VETTIUS: Roman Knight from Picenum, who turned informer against his Catilinarian associates in 63–62 and was prosecuted and imprisoned for making false charges against Caesar. Revealed or fabricated a plot against Pompey's life in 59. Died mysteriously in prison.

C. VIBIUS Pansa Caetronianus: Son of one of Sulla's victims, served under Caesar in Gaul. Tribune in 51. Governed Bithynia and Cisalpine Gaul under Caesar. Consul in 43, died of wounds received in the battle of Forum Gallorum.

L. VIBULLIUS Rufus: Henchman of Pompey and his 'Prefect of Engineers' in 49.

VOLUMNIA Cytheris: Freedwoman; a well-known actress. Mistress of Mark Antony and allegedly the Lycoris to whom Virgil's friend Cornelius Gallus wrote love poems.

P. VOLUMNIUS Eutrapelus: Roman Knight and celebrated wit. After Caesar's death an adherent of Antony, probably his 'Prefect of Engineers' in 43–42.

Q. VOLUSIUS: On Cicero's staff in Cilicia.

L. VULCATIUS (or VOLCACIUS) Tullus: Consul in 66. In and after the Civil War his political moderation seems to have turned into subservience to Caesar.

XENO: (1) Friend and agent of Atticus in Athens. (2) Of Apollonia, commended by Atticus to Cicero in 51.

XENOCRATES: Pupil of Plato and third head of the Academy.

XENOPHON: Fifth- and fourth-century Athenian historian.

GLOSSARY
OF PLACES

SOME names are omitted as generally familiar or explained in the notes. Italics are used for modern equivalents.

ACHAIA: Southern Greece.

AEGINA: Island on the Saronic Gulf, south-west of Athens.

AEMILIAN WAY: Roman road running north-west from Ariminum through Mutina.

AETOLIA: District of Greece, north-west of the Gulf of Corinth.

ALABANDA: Town in Caria.

ALBA: Alba Longa north-east of Rome (Mt Albanus = *Monte Cavi*).

ALLOBROGES: Chief tribe of Narbonese Gaul.

ALSIUM (*Palo*): Town on the coast of Etruria.

AMANUS: Mountain range separating Cilicia from Syria.

ANAGNIA (*Anagni*): Town about 25 miles west of Arpinum.

ANTILIBANUS: Range of mountains in Syria.

ANTIOCH: Capital of Syria, about 40 miles west of modern Aleppo.

ANTIUM (*Anzio*): Coast town south of Rome, where Cicero owned a house.

APAMEA: Town in Phrygia.

APPIA: Town in Phrygia.

APPIAN WAY: The great road linking Rome with Brundisium.

APULIA: District in south-eastern Italy.

AQUINUM (*Aquino*): Town just south of Arpinum.

ARCANUM: Village between Aquinum and Arpinum.

ARGENTEUS, PONS (= 'Silverbridge'): Bridge over the river Argens in Narbonese Gaul.

ARGILETUM: District of Rome.

ARPINUM (*Arpino*): Cicero's home town in central Italy.

ASIA: (1) The continent. (2) The Roman province, comprising the western part of Asia Minor.

ASTURA: Small island (joined to the mainland) off the coast south of Antium, where Cicero had a villa.

AVENTINE: One of the Seven Hills of Rome, south of the Palatine.

BAIAE: Famous resort on the Bay of Naples, near Cumae.

BITHYNIA: Region in north-western Asia Minor; as a Roman province (Bithynia and Pontus) stretching much further east.

BOEOTIA: Greek territory north of Attica.

BONONIA: *Bologna*.

BRUNDISIUM (*Brindisi*): Adriatic port in the heel of Italy.

BUTHROTUM: Town on the coast of Epirus opposite Corfù. Atticus had an estate near by.

CAIETA (*Gaeta*): Port of Formiae.

CALES (*Calvi*): Town in northern Campania.

CAMPANIA: District south of Latium.

CANUSIUM: Apulian town between Arpi and Brundisium.

CAPENA, PORTA: Entrance to Rome from the Appian Way.

CAPITOL: Highest of the Roman Hills, overlooking the Forum.

CAPPADOCIA: Kingdom in east-central Asia Minor.

CAPUA: Chief town of Campania.

CARIA: Region in south-western Asia Minor.

CARINAE: District of Rome north of the Colosseum.

CERMALUS: North-western part of the Palatine Hill, towards the Tiber.

CILICIA: (1) Coastal strip in south-eastern Asia Minor. (2) Roman province comprising the whole southern coast, much of the interior, and the island of Cyprus.

CISALPINE GAUL: 'Gaul this side of the Alps', i.e., northern Italy between the Alps and the Apennines.

CLATERNA (*Quaderna*): Town in Cisalpine Gaul, on the Aemilian Way between Bononia and Forum Cornelii.

CORCYRA (*Corfù*): Island off the coast of Epirus.

CORDUBA: *Cordoba*, in southern Spain.

CORFINIUM: Chief town of the Paeligni, east of Lake Fucino.

CULARO: *Grenoble*.

CUMAE (*Cuma*): Coastal town a few miles west of Naples. Cicero had a villa in its territory.

CYBISTRA: Town in the south-western corner of Cappadocia.

CYZICUS: Town on the Asiatic coast of the Propontis (*Sea of Marmora*).

DYRRACHIUM (*Durazzo*): Town on the western coast of the Roman province of Macedonia.

ELEUSIS: Town in Attica where the Mysteries were celebrated.

EPHESUS: On the western coast of Asia Minor, chief town of the province of Asia.

EPIDAURUS: Town on the eastern coast of the Peloponnese opposite Piraeus.

EPIRUS: District of north-western Greece opposite Corfù.

ETRURIA: *Tuscany*.

FABRATERIA (VETUS and NOVA): Towns in Latium.

FLAMINIUS, CIRCUS: In the Campus Martius.

FORMIAE (*Formia*): Town on the coast of Latium close to the Campanian border. Cicero had a villa near by.

FORUM CORNELIUM (or CORNELII): Town about 20 miles down the Aemilian Way east from Bononia.

FORUM GALLORUM: Village between Mutina and Bononia.

FRUSINO (*Frosinone*): Latian town a few miles north-west of Fabrateria Nova.

HERCULANEUM: Town near Pompeii.

ICONIUM (*Konya*): Town in Lycaonia.

ILLYRICUM: Region bordering the Adriatic from Epirus to the Gulf of Trieste.

ISARA (*Isère*): River, tributary of the Rhône.

ISSUS: Cilician town on gulf of the same name in the south-eastern corner of the province.

LANUVIUM: Latian town just off the Appian Way about 20 miles from Rome.

LAODICEA: (1) Town in the south-west of Phrygia. (2) Town in Syria on the coast south of Antioch.

LATERIUM: Village between Arpinum and Anagnia where Q. Cicero had a property.

LATIUM: Territory to the south and east of Rome.

LAVERNIUM: Place in the neighbourhood of Formiae.

LESBOS: Large island in the northern Aegean.

LEUCAS: Town on the island of the same name between Actium and Alyzia.

LEUCOPETRA (*Tarentine*): Headland in the heel of Italy (*Capo S. Maria di Leuca*).

LUCA (*Lucca*): Town in north-western Etruria.

LUCERIA (*Lucera*): Town in Apulia.

MAGNESIA BY MT SIPYLUS: Town north-east of Smyrna.

MALEA (*Malia*): Headland at the south-eastern end of the Peloponnese.

MANTINEA: Town in Arcadia, scene of famous battle between Spartans and Thebans.

MEGARA: Town on the Isthmus of Corinth.

MINTURNAE: Town a few miles south-east of Formiae.

MISENUM: Headland bounding the Bay of Naples to the north.

MUTINA: *Modena.*

MYTILENE: Principal town of Lesbos.

NARBONESE GAUL: Old Roman province in southern France.

NARONA: Roman colony in Dalmatia.

NERVII: Tribe of north-eastern Gaul (Belgium).

NICAEA: Town in Bithynia.

NUMANTIA: Town in north-east Spain, captured by the Romans after a long struggle.

NYSA: Town in Caria.

OLBIA (*Terranova*): Town in Sardinia.

OSTIA (*Ostia*): Port of Rome.

PALATINE: Large hill south of the Forum, where according to tradition Rome began. A number of prominent people had houses on it, including Cicero.

PAMPHYLIA: Region on the south coast of Asia Minor between Lycia and Cilicia.

PANHORMUS: *Palermo.*

PARMA: (*Parma*): Town in northern Italy.

PATRAE (*Patras*): Town on the northern coast of the Peloponnese.

PHILOMELIUM: Town in south-east Phrygia.

PHRYGIA: Region in the middle of western Asia Minor.

PICENUM: Territory bordering the Adriatic south of Ancona.

PINDENISSUM: Town of the 'Free Cilicians' in the Amanus mountains.

PIRAEUS: Port of Athens.

PISAE: *Pisa*.

POMPEII: Town on the Bay of Naples where Cicero had a villa.

PONS ARGENTEUS: See ARGENTEUS.

PONTUS: Region in north-eastern Asia Minor.

PORTA CAPENA: See CAPENA.

PUTEOLI (*Pozzuoli*): Town east of Naples on the Bay. Cicero inherited an estate there in 45.

RAVENNA (*Ravenna*): Coastal town in north-east Italy.

REGIUM (*Reggio*): Town at the toe of Italy.

REGIUM (LEPIDI, *Reggio Emilia*): Town on the Aemilian Way west of Mutina.

SAMOS: Aegean island close to Ephesus.

SELEUCIA: City close to the right bank of the Tigris, near the site of ancient Babylon.

SICYON: Greek town west of Corinth.

SIDE or SIDA: Harbour town in Pamphylia.

SIGEUM: Town at the entrance of the Hellespont near ancient Troy.

SINUESSA (*Mondragone*): Town on the coast south of Formiae.

STABIAE: Town on the Bay of Cumae a few miles south of Pompeii.

SYNNADA: Town in Phrygia.

TARENTUM (*Taranto*): Town on the south coast of Italy.

TARSUS: Chief town of Cilicia proper.

TAURUS: Mountain range in south-eastern Asia Minor.

TENEDOS: Island south of the Hellespont.

THESSALONICA: *Salonika*.

THYRREUM: Inland town east of Leucas.

TIBUR (*Tivoli*): Town in Latium 18 miles east of Rome.

TRALLES: Town in Caria.

TRES TABERNAE (= 'Three Cottages'): Station on the Appian Way between Lanuvium and Forum Appii.

TUSCULUM: Latian town near modern Frascati. Cicero spent much time at his villa near by.

VARDAEI: Illyrian tribe.

VELABRUM: District of Rome south of the Capitol.

VELIA: Town in south-western Italy south of Paestum. Also an area on the Palatine.

VENUSIA (*Venosa*): Town in western Apulia on the Appian Way.

VIBO (*Bivona*): Town on the western coast of modern Calabria.

VOCONTII: People of Narbonese Gaul between the Rhône and the Alps.

GLOSSARY
OF TERMS

ACADEMY (*Academia*): A hall (*gymnasium*) and park at Athens sacred to the hero Academus, in which Plato established his philosophical school. Hence Plato's school or system of philosophy, which went through various phases after his time. Cicero gave the name 'Academy' to a hall which he built on his estate at Tusculum.

AEDILE (*aedilis*): Third in rank of the regular Roman magistracies. Four at this time were elected annually, two Curule and two Plebeian. They were responsible for city administration and the holding of certain public Games. The chief magistrates in some municipalities were also so called.

ASSEMBLY: I sometimes so translate *populus* or *comitia*, as describing the Roman people convened for electoral or legislative purposes. There were several different sorts varying with the convening magistrate and the business to be done.

ATTIC(ISM): One use of the word was in connection with Roman oratory. In Cicero's time a movement principally represented by Calvus and M. Brutus favoured an austere style like that of the Athenian Lysias.

AUGUR: The priestly College of Augurs were official diviners interpreting signs (mostly from the flight and cries of wild birds or the behaviour of the Sacred Chickens) before major acts of public (and sometimes private) business. The College, like that of Pontiffs, was in practice almost a preserve of the nobility, so that for a 'new man' like Cicero membership was a coveted social distinction.

AUSPICES (*auspicia*): Divination from birds or other signs was officially necessary as a preliminary to major acts by magistrates, who were said to 'have auspices', i.e., the power of taking them.

BONA DEA: See GOOD GODDESS.

BOY (*puer*): Male slaves of any age were so called, as in later times.

CAMPANIAN LAND (DOMAIN – *ager Campanus*): Fertile land in Campania, originally confiscated by Rome in 211 and leased to small tenants. Caesar as Consul passed a bill (the Campanian Law) to distribute it among Pompey's veterans and the Roman poor.

CAMPUS (MARTIUS): The plain adjoining the Tiber on which assemblies of the Centuries were held, often for elections.

CENSOR: Two magistrates usually elected every five years for a tenure of eighteen months. They revised the roll of citizens, with property assessments, also the rolls of Knights and Senators, removing those deemed guilty of misconduct. They further supervised public contracts, including the lease of revenues to the tax-farmers, and issued decrees as guardians of public morals.

CENTURIES, ASSEMBLY OF (*comitia centuriata*): Form of assembly in which voting took place by 'Centuries', i.e., groups unequally composed so as to give preponderance to birth and wealth. It elected Consuls and Praetors, and voted on legislation proposed by them. The first Century to vote (*centuria praerogativa*) traditionally had a determining effect on the rest.

CENTURION: See LEGION.

COHORT: See LEGION.

COMITIAL DAYS: Days in the Roman calendar on which the popular assemblies (*comitia*) could legally be held. The Senate was normally not allowed to meet on these days.

COMITIUM: An area north of the Forum where assemblies were held.

COMMISSION, FREE or VOTIVE: See LEGATE.

CONSUL: Highest of the annual Roman magistrates. Two were elected, usually in July, to take office on the following 1 January.

CONSULAR: An ex-Consul. The Consulars made up a corps of elder statesmen to whom the Senate would normally look for leadership.

CURIATE LAW (*lex curiata*): A law passed by the Curies (*curiae*), the oldest form of Roman assembly. In Cicero's time it survived only in form, each of the thirty Curies being represented by a lictor, but still had certain legislative functions, notably the passage of laws to confirm the executive authority (*imperium*) of individual magistrates; but the precise nature of these laws is much in doubt.

CURULE CHAIR (*sella curulis*): Ivory chair, or rather stool, of state used by regular 'curule' magistrates, i.e., Consuls, Praetors, and Curule Aediles, and certain others.

DICTATOR: A supreme magistrate with quasi-regal powers appointed to deal with emergencies under the early Republic; his second-in-command, the Master of the Horse, was appointed by himself. The office was revived to legitimize the autocratic régimes of Sulla and of Julius Caesar.

EDICT: A public announcement or manifesto issued by a magistrate.

EPICUREANISM: A materialistic school of philosophy named after its founder Epicurus, much in vogue among the Roman intelligentsia in Cicero's time.

EQUESTRIAN ORDER: See KNIGHTS.

ETESIAN WINDS (*etesiae*): Northerly winds which blew every year during the Dog-days.

FASCES: Bundles of rods carried by lictors in front of magistrates as a symbol of authority. Those of victorious generals were wreathed in laurel.

FORUM: The chief square of Rome, centre of civic life.

FREEDMAN (*libertus*): A 'manumitted' slave.

GAMES (*ludi*): Gladiatorial and other shows, some recurring annually and supervised by magistrates, others put on for an occasion by private individuals. Of the former the Roman Games (*ludi Romani*) were held from 5 to 19 September, the Games of Apollo (*ludi Apollinares*) from 5 to 13 July. 'Greek Games' seem to have consisted of performances of Greek plays in the original language.

GOOD GODDESS (*Bona Dea*): A goddess whose worship was confined to women. Her yearly festival was held in the house of a Consul or Praetor and supervised by his wife.

GOWN (*toga*): Formal civilian dress of a Roman citizen. The gown of boys and curule magistrates (*toga praetexta*) had a purple hem. At fifteen or sixteen at his father's discretion a boy was given his White (or 'Manly') Gown (*toga pura, toga virilis*).

GREEK GAMES: See GAMES.

GREEKS: In Cicero's time the word was loosely used to include the more or less hellenized inhabitants of Western Asia and Egypt as well as those of Greece proper and the old Greek settlements elsewhere.

HONEST MEN: So I translate Cicero's *boni* ('good men', *les gens de bien*), a semi-political term for people of substance and respectability, supporters of the established order. Their opposites he calls *improbi* ('rascals').

IMPERATOR: Commander of a Roman army. But at this period the title was conferred on Generals by their soldiers after a victory and retained until they relinquished their *imperium*.

IMPERIUM: Literally 'command'; the executive authority appertaining to higher magisterial and promagisterial office.

INTERREGNUM: If through death or otherwise the consular office stood vacant and no patrician magistrates holding *imperium* were in office, an Interrex was appointed from among the patrician members of the Senate to exercise consular functions for five days. He was then replaced by another Interrex, and so on until new Consuls could be elected.

KNIGHTS (*equites*): In effect non-Senators of free birth possessing property over a certain level. They were regarded as forming a class of their own (*ordo equestris*) with special privileges and insignia.

LECTURE HALL (*gymnasium*): The Greek gymnasium was originally a sports ground containing a *palaestra* (see below). But literature, philosophy, and music were also taught in them.

LEGATE (*legatus*): A provincial governor took several Legates, normally Senators, on his staff as deputies. Caesar in Gaul made them commanders of legions. The duties might, however, be purely nominal. The Senate could also appoint its members to 'free' or 'votive' (i.e., to discharge a vow) *legationes*, thus enabling them to travel abroad with official status. I sometimes translate with 'commission(er)'. The word can also be used for any kind of envoy.

LEGION: Roman army unit with full complement of 6,000 men divided into ten cohorts. Each legion was officered by six Military Tribunes. Each cohort had six Centurions, the highest in rank being called *primi pili* (Chief Centurion). The ensign of a Legion was an eagle, and each cohort had its standard (*signum*).

LEX CORNELIA (*de provinciis*): Law of Sulla regulating provincial administration.

LEX CURIATA: See above, CURIATE LAW.

LEX JULIA (*de provinciis*): Consular law of Caesar's on provincial administration.

LEX ROSCIA: A law of 67 assigning the first fourteen rows in the theatre to the Knights (the Senate sat below in the Orchestra).

LEX SCANTINIA: A law of uncertain date penalizing homosexual acts committed upon persons of free birth.

LICTOR: Official attendant of persons possessing magisterial authority (*imperium*), the number varying with the rank.

MANUMISSION: Process of freeing a slave. This could be done either formally or informally ('between friends'), but in the latter case the master could revoke it at will.

MILE (*mille passus*): The Roman mile was 1,618 yards.

MIME (*mimus*): Type of entertainment with dancing, music, and dialogue which became highly popular in the first century B.C. It was considered more sophisticated and risqué than the Atellan Farce, which it virtually superseded.

NOBILITY: Practically, a noble (*nobilis*) at this period meant a direct descendant of a Consul in the male line. In the early Republic the Roman community was divided into patricians and plebeians, the former holding a virtual monopoly of political power. But after the Consulship was thrown open to plebeians in the fourth century many plebeian families became 'noble', and the remaining patricians were distinguished chiefly by their ineligibility to hold both Consulships in one year and for the plebeian offices of Tribune and Plebeian Aedile.

NOMENCLATOR: A slave whose duty it was to remind his master of the names of clients and acquaintances whom he happened to meet.

OPTIMATES: Literally 'those belonging to the best' – the leading conservatives in the Senate and their supporters throughout the community. Sometimes the term is practically equivalent to the 'honest men' (*boni*), though more purely political in its implications.

OVATION: A lesser form of Triumph.

PALAESTRA: A space surrounded by colonnades, found in all *gymnasia*. Literally 'wrestling-school' (Greek).

PATRICIANS: See NOBILITY.

PAYMASTER-TRIBUNES (*tribuni aerarii*): At this time probably a class similar to the Knights but with a lower property qualification. Under the lex Aurelia of 70, juries were composed in equal numbers of Senators, Knights, and Paymaster-Tribunes.

PLEBEIANS: See NOBILITY.

PONTIFF (*pontifex*): These formed a priestly College in general charge of Roman religious institutions (including the Calendar), presided over by the Chief Pontiff (*pontifex maximus*), who was Julius Caesar from 63 until his death.

PRAETOR: Second in rank of the annual magistracies. Eight were elected at this period until Caesar increased the number to twenty. The City Praetor (*praetor urbanus*) was in charge of the administration of justice between Roman citizens, others presided over the standing criminal courts. After his year of office a Praetor normally went to govern a province as Propraetor or Proconsul.

PREFECT: Officer appointed by a magistrate (usually as provincial governor) for military or civil duties. These might be only nominal, the appointment merely conferring official status and privileges. The 'Prefect of Engineers' (*praefectus fabrum*) acted as adjutant to his chief – no longer any connection with engineers.

PROCONSUL (*pro consule*): 'Acting Consul', one who, not holding the office, exercised consular authority outside Rome by senatorial appointment. Similarly Propraetor (*pro praetore*) and Proquaestor (*pro quaestore*).

PROSCRIPTION (*proscriptio*): A procedure first employed by Sulla, then by the Triumvirs in 43. Lists of names were published, the persons thus 'proscribed' being declared outlaws and their goods confiscated. Their killers were rewarded, their protectors punished.

QUAESTOR: The first stage in the regular 'course of offices', election to which carried life-membership of the Senate. Since Sulla's time twenty were elected annually. The two City Quaestors (*quaestores urbani*) had charge of the Treasury and the Quaestors assigned to provincial governors (usually by lot) were largely concerned with finance.

ROSTRA: The speakers' platform in the comitium, so called from the beaks (*rostra*) of captured warships which decorated it.

SENATE: Governing body of the Roman Republic, numbering about 600 (increased to 900 by Caesar) and composed of magistrates and ex-magistrates.

STOICISM: Philosophical school, named from the portico (*stoa*) in which its founder, Zeno of Citium (*c.* 300), taught. Cato was its most prominent Roman adherent in Cicero's time.

SUMPTUARY LAW: A series of laws during the Republic attempted to impose restrictions on luxury spending, especially on food. One was enacted by Julius Caesar in 46.

SUPPLICATION (*supplicatio*): A thanksgiving ceremony decreed by the Senate in honour of a military success, the number of days varying according to the importance of the victory. It was generally regarded as a preliminary to a Triumph.

TABLETS (*codicilli*): Wooden tablets coated with wax and fastened together with thread, used for memoranda and short notes.

TAX-FARMERS (*publicani*): Roman taxes, as on grazing-land in the provinces or excise, were largely farmed out by the Censors to private companies who bid for the right of collection. The capitalists in Rome as well as their local agents were called *publicani*. In political terms *publicani* and Knights often amount to the same thing.

TREASURY (*aerarium*): The Roman state treasury was in the temple of Saturn in the Forum, managed by the City Quaestors with the assistance of Secretaries.

TRIBE (*tribus*): A division, mainly by locality, of the Roman citizen body. The number had risen over the centuries from three to thirty-five (four of them 'urban', the rest 'rustic'). Assemblies voting by tribes (*comitia tributa*) elected magistrates below Praetor and could pass legislation proposed by Tribunes.

TRIBUNE: (1) Of the Plebs. A board of ten, originally appointed to protect plebeians from patrician high-handedness. They had wide constitutional powers, the most important being that any one of them could veto any piece of public business, including laws and senatorial decrees. They could also initiate these. They took office on 10 December. (2) Military: See LEGION. (3) See PAYMASTER-TRIBUNES.

TRIUMPH: Victory celebration by a general on his return to Rome. Permission had to be granted by the Senate.

UNIFORM: Magistrates leaving to take command of armies wore the general's red cloak (*paludamentum*) and were said to set out *paludati*.

VALUATION (*aestimatio*): Process by which a debtor's property could be transferred to his creditor. Caesar made such transfers compulsory on terms favourable to the debtor.

MAPS

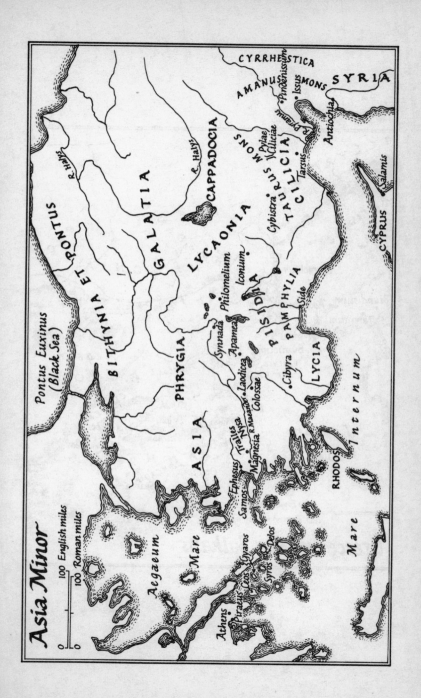

Asia Minor

100 English miles
100 Roman miles

Pontus Euxinus
(Black Sea)

CYRRHESTICA

SYRIA

AMANUS MONS

Pinarus

Issus

Antiochia

R. Pyramus

R. Halys

CAPPADOCIA

GALATIA

LYCAONIA

BITHYNIA ET PONTUS

Cybistra

TAURUS MONS

Pylae Ciliciae

CILICIA

Tarsus

CYPRUS

Salamis

Philomelium

Iconium

Synnada

Apamea

PISIDIA

PAMPHYLIA

Side

Laodicea

Colossae

R. Maeander

LYCIA

PHRYGIA

Cibyra

ASIA

Tralles

Nysa

Magnesia

Ephesus

Samos

RHODOS

Mare Internum

Mare

Aegaeum

Mare

Athens

Piraeus

Ceos

Cyaros

Syros

Delos

Mare

ILLYRICUM

Adriatic
Sea

THRACE

DARDANIA

MACEDONIA

Dyrrachium

Via Egnatia

CANDAVIA

Brundisium   Apollonia
Tarentum

CHAONIA

Pelia

Thessalonica

Hydrus
Buthrotum
Corcyra
CORCYRA

EPIRUS

Dodona

THESSALY

Aegean
Sea

Actium
Leucas

Pharsalus

AETOLIA

EUBOEA

Ionian
Sea

Delphi

BOEOTIA

Thebes

Patrae

Eleusis
Athens

Dyme

ACHAIA

Sicyon

Megara

Olympia

ARCADIA

Delos

Sparta

0 ━━━━━━ 100 English miles
0 ━━━━━━ 100 Roman miles

Greece and the Balkans

Italy and Sicily

PROVINCE OF CISALPINE GAUL

Via Aemilia

Mutina
Bononia

Luca
Pisae
Volaterrae

Pistoria
R. Arno
Faesulae

ETRURIA

Via Aurelia

Arretium

R. Tiber

Via Flaminia

Ameria

Ariminum
Pisaurum
Ancona

PICENIUM

ILLYRICUM

Adriatic Sea

Corfinium

Rome
Praeneste
Tasculum
Alba
Sora
Antium
Arpinum
Astura
Formiae

SAMNIUM

Luceria

Capua

Cumae
Baiae
Puteoli
Neapolis

CAMPANIA

Pompeii

Via Appia

CALABRIA

Brundisium

LUCANIA

Tarentum

Tyrrhenian Sea

BRUTTIUM

Mt Eryx
Lilybaeum

Messana
Rhegium

PROVINCE OF SICILY

Ionian Sea

Syracuse

English miles
0   50   100

50   100
Roman miles

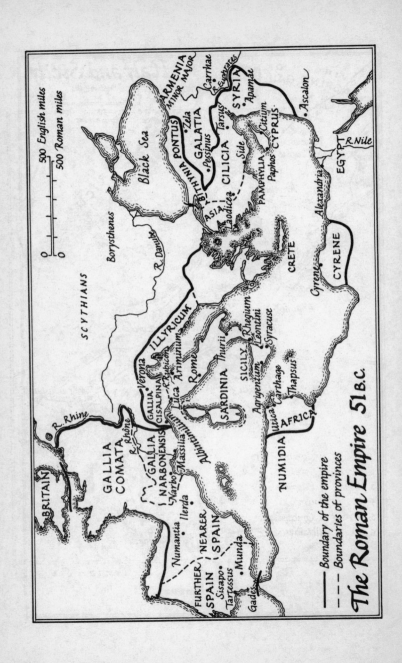

The Roman Empire 51 B.C.

Boundary of the empire
Boundaries of provinces

500 English miles
500 Roman miles

BRITAIN

SCYTHIANS

R. Rhine

R. Rhone

GALLIA COMATA

Rhone

GALLIA NARBONENSIS

Narbo

Massilia

Albintimilium

Numantia

Ilerda

FURTHER SPAIN

NEARER SPAIN

Sisapo

Munda

Tartessus

Gades

Borysthenes

R. Danube

Black Sea

Verona

GALLIA CISALPINA

R. Rubicon

Luca Ariminum

Rome

SARDINIA

Thurii

Rhegium

Leontini

SICILY

Agrigentum

Syracuse

Carthage

Utica

Thapsus

AFRICA

NUMIDIA

ARMENIA MINOR

ARMENIA MAJOR

R. Euphrates

Carrhae

Zela

PONTUS

BITHYNIA

GALATIA

Pessinus

ASIA

Laodicea

CILICIA

Tarsus

Side

PAMPHYLIA

Paphos

SYRIA

Apamea

Citium

CYPRUS

Ascalon

R. Nile

EGYPT

Alexandria

CYRENE

Cyrene

CRETE

ILLYRICUM

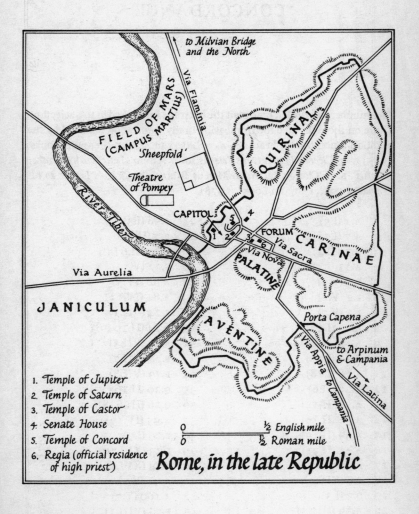

to Milvian Bridge
and the North

Via Flaminia

FIELD OF MARS
(CAMPUS MARTIUS)

'Sheepfold'

Theatre
of Pompey

River Tiber

QUIRINAL

CAPITOL

x 4

5
1
2

3 6

FORUM

CARINAE

Via Sacra

Via Nova

Via Aurelia

PALATINE

JANICULUM

AVENTINE

Porta Capena

Via Appia to Campania

to Arpinum
& Campania

Via Latina

1. Temple of Jupiter
2. Temple of Saturn
3. Temple of Castor
4. Senate House
5. Temple of Concord
6. Regia (official residence
   of high priest)

0   ½ English mile
0   ½ Roman mile

Rome, in the late Republic

CONCORDANCE

THE numbers on the left represent the letters as numbered in this selection. Those on the right give the numbering in my translation followed by the traditional notation in brackets. A. = *Letters to Atticus*, (Penguin Books, 1975) F. = '*Cicero's Letters to his Friends*', Q. = '*Cicero's Letters to his Brother Quintus*', B. = '*Cicero's Letters to Marcus Brutus*' (in *Cicero's Letters to his Friends*, 2 vols., Penguin Books, 1978).

1	A.1 (I.5)	24	F.56 (I.3)
2	A.7 (I.11)	25	Q.7 (II.3)
3	A.10 (I.1)	26	Q.10 (II.6 (5))
4	A.11 (I.2)	27	F.22 (V.12)
5	F.1 (V.1)	28	A.80 (IV.5)
6	F.2 (V.2)	29	A.81 (IV.12)
7	F.3 (V.7)	30	F.24 (VII.1)
8	A.13 (I.13)	31	Q.14 (II.10 (9))
9	A.14 (I.14)	32	F.26 (VII.5)
10	A.16 (I.16)	33	F.28 (VII.7)
11	A.18 (I.18)	34	F.29 (VII.8)
12	A.26 (II.6)	35	Q.20 (II.16 (15))
13	A.34 (II.14)	36	Q.26 (III.6 (8))
14	A.36 (II.16)	37	A.93 (IV.19)
15	A.39 (II.19)	38	F.20 (I.9)
16	A.41 (II.21)	39	F.43 (XVI.10)
17	A.47 (III.3)	40	F.44 (XVI.16)
18	F.6 (XIV.4)	41	A.94 (V.1)
19	Q.3 (I.3)	42	A.100 (V.7)
20	A.59 (III.13)	43	F.77 (VIII.1)
21	A.73 (IV.1)	44	A.103 (V.10)
22	A.75 (IV.3)	45	F.63 (XIII.1)
23	F.13 (I.2)	46	A.107 (V.14)

READ MORE IN PENGUIN

In every corner of the world, on every subject under the sun, Penguin represents quality and variety – the very best in publishing today.

For complete information about books available from Penguin – including Puffins, Penguin Classics and Arkana – and how to order them, write to us at the appropriate address below. Please note that for copyright reasons the selection of books varies from country to country.

In the United Kingdom: Please write to *Dept. JC, Penguin Books Ltd, FREEPOST, West Drayton, Middlesex UB7 OBR*

If you have any difficulty in obtaining a title, please send your order with the correct money, plus ten per cent for postage and packaging, to *PO Box No. 11, West Drayton, Middlesex UB7 OBR*

In the United States: Please write to *Penguin USA Inc., 375 Hudson Street, New York, NY 10014*

In Canada: Please write to *Penguin Books Canada Ltd, 10 Alcorn Avenue, Suite 300, Toronto, Ontario M4V 3B2*

In Australia: Please write to *Penguin Books Australia Ltd, 487 Maroondah Highway, Ringwood, Victoria 3134*

In New Zealand: Please write to *Penguin Books (NZ) Ltd,182–190 Wairau Road, Private Bag, Takapuna, Auckland 9*

In India: Please write to *Penguin Books India Pvt Ltd, 706 Eros Apartments, 56 Nehru Place, New Delhi 110 019*

In the Netherlands: Please write to *Penguin Books Netherlands B.V., Keizersgracht 231 NL–1016 DV Amsterdam*

In Germany: Please write to *Penguin Books Deutschland GmbH, Friedrichstrasse 10–12, W–6000 Frankfurt/Main 1*

In Spain: Please write to *Penguin Books S. A., C. San Bernardo 117–6° E–28015 Madrid*

In Italy: Please write to *Penguin Italia s.r.l., Via Felice Casati 20, 1–20124 Milano*

In France: Please write to *Penguin France S. A., 17 rue Lejeune, F–31000 Toulouse*

In Japan: Please write to *Penguin Books Japan, Ishikiribashi Building, 2–5–4, Suido, Bunkyo-ku, Tokyo 112*

In Greece: Please write to *Penguin Hellas Ltd, Dimocritou 3, GR–106 71 Athens*

In South Africa: Please write to *Longman Penguin Southern Africa (Pty) Ltd, Private Bag X08, Bertsham 2013*

READ MORE IN PENGUIN

A CHOICE OF CLASSICS

READ MORE IN PENGUIN

A CHOICE OF CLASSICS

Hesiod/Theognis	**Theogony** and **Works and Days/ Elegies**
Hippocrates	**Hippocratic Writings**
Homer	**The Iliad**
	The Odyssey
Horace	**Complete Odes and Epodes**
Horace/Persius	**Satires** and **Epistles**
Juvenal	**Sixteen Satires**
Livy	**The Early History of Rome**
	Rome and Italy
	Rome and the Mediterranean
	The War with Hannibal
Lucretius	**On the Nature of the Universe**
Marcus Aurelius	**Meditations**
Martial	**Epigrams**
Ovid	**The Erotic Poems**
	Heroides
	Metamorphoses
Pausanias	**Guide to Greece** (in two volumes)
Petronius/Seneca	**The Satyricon/The Apocolocyntosis**
Pindar	**The Odes**
Plato	**Early Socratic Dialogues**
	Gorgias
	The Last Days of Socrates (Euthyphro/ The Apology/Crito/Phaedo)
	The Laws
	Phaedrus and **Letters VII and VIII**
	Philebus
	Protagoras and **Meno**
	The Republic
	The Symposium
	Theaetetus
	Timaeus and **Critias**

READ MORE IN PENGUIN

A CHOICE OF CLASSICS

Plautus	**The Pot of Gold/The Prisoners/The Brothers Menaechmus/The Swaggering Soldier/Pseudolus**
	The Rope/Amphitryo/The Ghost/A Three-Dollar Day
Pliny	**The Letters of the Younger Pliny**
Pliny the Elder	**Natural History**
Plotinus	**The Enneads**
Plutarch	**The Age of Alexander** (Nine Greek Lives)
	The Fall of the Roman Republic (Six Lives)
	The Makers of Rome (Nine Lives)
	The Rise and Fall of Athens (Nine Greek Lives)
	Plutarch on Sparta
Polybius	**The Rise of the Roman Empire**
Procopius	**The Secret History**
Propertius	**The Poems**
Quintus Curtius Rufus	**The History of Alexander**
Sallust	**The Jugurthine War** and **The Conspiracy of Cataline**
Seneca	**Four Tragedies** and **Octavia**
	Letters from a Stoic
Sophocles	**Electra/Women of Trachis/Philoctetes/Ajax**
	The Theban Plays
Suetonius	**The Twelve Caesars**
Tacitus	**The Agricola** and **The Germania**
	The Annals of Imperial Rome
	The Histories
Terence	**The Comedies (The Girl from Andros/The Self-Tormentor/TheEunuch/Phormio/The Mother-in-Law/The Brothers)**
Thucydides	**The History of the Peloponnesian War**
Virgil	**The Aeneid**
	The Eclogues
	The Georgics
Xenophon	**Conversations of Socrates**
	A History of My Times
	The Persian Expedition